ALSO BY RONALD E. MÜLLER

GLOBAL REACH: The Power of the Multinational Corporations
(with Richard J. Barnet)

Revitalizing America

POLITICS FOR PROSPERITY

by RONALD E. MÜLLER

Simon and Schuster
New York

Published by Simon and Schuster
A Division of Gulf & Western Corporation
Simon & Schuster Building
Rockefeller Center
1230 Avenue of the Americas
New York, New York 10020
SIMON AND SCHUSTER and colophon are
trademarks of Simon & Schuster
Designed by Eliot Kimble/Irving Perkins Associates
Manufactured in the United States of America
1 2 3 4 5 6 7 8 9 10

Library of Congress Cataloging in Publication Data

Müller, Ronald E.
Revitalizing America

Includes bibliographical references and index.
1. United States—Economic policy—1971–
2. International economic relations. I. Title.
HC106.7.M83 337.73 79-28569
ISBN 0-671-24889-8

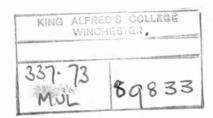

Author's Note:

Without the collaboration of my two closest associates, this book would be less than it is.

Michael Mosettig, a former NBC National News producer and UPI correspondent, collaborated with me on the writing, editing, and research on U.S. and European politics. He brought a dedication, pragmatism, and skepticism absolutely essential to the effort.

David Moore, now a senior economist with The Analytic Sciences Corporation, and I have been associates for many years. His brilliant intellectual collaboration and his direction of much of the research are what made the book's dimensions possible.

This book is as much theirs as mine.

Acknowledgments

THIS BOOK COULD NOT HAVE BEEN WRITTEN without the assistance of many people. I benefited greatly from the following in terms of research and administrative support, ideas, information, suggestions, or criticisms they gave me: Michael Aho, Helmut Arndt, Lloyd Atkinson, Drag Avramovitz, Frank Barros, Richard Brennen, Nicholas Bruck, Simon Alberto Consalvi, John Cox, Mauricio de Maria y Campos, Arthur Domike, Everett Ehrlich, Jose Epstein, Noel Epstein, John Kenneth Galbraith, Jacques Gansler, Louis Goodman, Sandy Grieves, Richard King, Hans Kroller, Michael Maccoby, Mahbul ul Haq, Johann Maramis, Dana Mooring, Dan Morgan, Joseph Napolitan, Knute Nordal, Peter Noterman, Drena Owens, Arnold Packer, John Portella, Charles Powers, Marianna Pratt, Victor Richardson, Achmed Rhazaoui, Christopher Roper, Michael Rowan, M. K. Samuels, Kalman Silvert, Eugene Stockwell, Paul Streeten, Terry Thometz, Brian Turner, Constantine Vaitsos, Rene Villarreal, Julie Watson, James Weaver, Frank Weil, Michael Weiss, Benny Widyono, Miguel Wionczek, and Al Wolfe.

My personal thanks also go to the many business, government, and labor officials, in the United States and abroad, who gave freely of their time in providing close-in information cited in sections of Parts II and III but wished to remain anonymous.

At an early stage, Jorge Bande's work on Latin America and Robin Hahnel's on comparative U.S.–European economic policy helped crystalize significant portions of the book.

The intellectual and research collaboration of William Castner, one of my closest associates throughout the project, has been indispensable.

Carl Brandt has given me encouragement from the beginning. Alice Mayhew provided the necessary push at important stages, and Carole Müller supplied the understanding and needed sense of humor for recovering from cyclical lows.

To the American voter and
other decision-makers of the 1980s,
searching to find stability where
there has been little

CONTENTS

Author's Foreword

THE DECISION to write this book was made on a speaker's podium in Geneva, Switzerland, in the fall of 1975. As the coauthor of the recently released *Global Reach: The Power of the Multinational Corporations,* I had been asked to address a conference on the "global interdependence" of nation-states—the then voguish term for the revolutionary economic changes underway since the end of World War II. In front of me, there was a large audience that included leaders and experts from business, government, labor, and the press from around the world. And in the minds of the audience, I suspected, was the belief that I would focus on the operations of the multinationals as the major unresolved problem of the world's economy.

In striking contrast to the mood of the previous spring, the mood of this audience was optimistic. In spite of predictions of imminent collapse which had heralded the new year, the United States and the rest of the world had just weathered the worst recession since the Great Depression of the 1930s. Now the general public—and the experts before me—believed that the "shock" of OPEC's quadrupling of oil prices had been absorbed. The world could resume the unprecedented increases in economic growth and prosperity which had been the business-as-usual track record of the prior two decades. And it *was* an impressive pace for the world economy, even if the majorities in industrial democracies had sprinted while those from the underdeveloped nations of the Third World had managed barely to crawl.

The audience was, to put it mildly, surprised by my prognosis that, by the start of 1980, and once more led by the U.S. economy, the world would again face a recession as severe as the one that had just passed. That surprise, no doubt, sprang as much from the prognosis as it did from its basis in the workings of politics and government policy, not of the planet's largest corporations.

If the audience was surprised, so was I. What surprised me was not the intense disagreement, particularly by Americans, but their unwillingness to deal with a simple observation: the problems that had led to the bust of 1974–75 had in no way been removed by that severe downturn. Contrary to conventional thinking, conservative and liberal, they were growing worse.

The plummeting of U.S. productivity rates, which statistics officially inaugurated in 1965, persisted. Third World debt, sanctified as a problem of monumental proportions by presidential commissions throughout the 1960s, continued to grow. Jittery financial, foreign exchange, and banking systems, as well as protracted inflation and unemployment, were even more visible than when they first surfaced in the late 1960s. These problems together had created others even more worrisome for the U.S. and the world economy: especially, a precipitous falloff in the building of the new factories and technologies upon which many of our own jobs and most of those of our children's generation would depend. That problem, like the others, was no further toward solution in 1975 than when it had first emerged at the start of the seventies. (They all remain unresolved at the start of the 1980s.)

When I answered questions after my speech, two familiar patterns were struck. First, concerning the major economic problems I had mentioned, experts on each agreed readily that the problems were indeed intensifying. Yet few had added up what these mounting problems spelled out for future stability and prosperity. A second and analogous reaction was a blind spot in seeing the links between economics and politics. While politics is not always the cause of national and international economic problems, the persistence and growing severity of so many major problems is a failure of management. And the economic management of nation-states is now inescapably the responsibility of politics and politicians.

At the time, it was perhaps understandable that politicians of the mid-1970s should convince themselves and their constituents that OPEC was the villain behind their economic suffering—even if most of the actual causes had been well in motion long before OPEC came on the scene. For after all, their intellectual advisors called the period an "anomaly" and attributed it largely to OPEC, and some of the more famous among the counselors went so far as to predict the quick disintegration of the oil nations' cartel and the return of the price of oil to its former levels. In this and the other ways, my audience on that uneventful and balmy fall day in Geneva more than fulfilled its role as a mirror of representative thinking around the globe.

Geneva was the culmination of a series of experiences that helped me to develop the theme of this book—the politics of economic management for rebuilding America in the eighties. Its scope is dictated by the most salient characteristic of the 1980s: "interdependence," in terms both of the new postwar links forged between the U.S. and the rest of the world as well as of the ever more intimate econopolitical links between industry, labor, finance, energy, taxes, and prices. The book is intended for voters, politicians, investors, and managers in government, business, and labor. They share the bonds of interdependence. They are decision makers who must consider a chain of issues that will confront them and America in the next decade, and they will not have the luxury of being able to spend a lifetime preoccupied with any one link. When a nation is at a critical juncture it is not permitted the luxury of handling its problems piecemeal. The politics of such moments must view the parts in context and form a national agenda from an interrelated set of policy measures.

For the skeptic on this last point, let history be a reminder. It teaches us that every forty years or so since the industrial revolution, society has undergone a major transformation, resulting from changing technology, values, and power relations. A watershed is then reached where the intensifying problems of inflation, unemployment, resource scarcity, and ruptured foreign relations converge to reveal the inadequacy of current policies and politics. The resulting crisis has always required a grasp of the "whole" picture for a decision to be made on the major political reforms and innovations needed for engineering new economic and foreign policy principles and programs. The 1930s marked America's last such watershed, and the 1980s are its current one.

This book's sample of principles and programs for rebuilding America in the eighties was developed from what at times appeared an almost infinite list of alternatives. In part, the selection was based on what my staff and I came to call the "acid test." If an idea was simply a blueprint or ivory tower abstraction, it was rejected. If it was actually in operation or being experimented with in a real life situation, it was studied both in the field as well as through the more conventional research techniques of interviewing and of reading the literature. The book is thus as much a product of actual work experiences as it is of scholarly research. It reflects many journeys into the heartlands of economics and politics in the U.S. and in Europe, Asia, Latin America, and Africa. Work with practitioners ranging from heads of state, ministers, and other politicians, to career managers in government, business, and labor has led me to reject, modify, and reinforce many of the original ideas for the book. I hope that its contents may prove one form of catalyst for thinking and doing in the 1980s.

Washington, D.C.
June 22, 1980

PART I

The Post-Market World

CHAPTER 1

Global Revolution

I

FROM THE TREASURY MINISTRIES OF WASHINGTON, Bonn, and Tokyo to the counting houses of London and the skyscrapers of New York, the men who manage nations and the fortunes of the industrial world survey their domains and ask, as if in unison, "What has gone wrong?"

A mere decade ago they presided over a new economic Jerusalem, conferring on their fellow citizens ever-expanding riches, unending economic growth, stable prices, and record levels of personal consumption. Then, just as the industrial world had begun to accept its prosperity as a permanent condition, the boom ended. What has followed since is a new economic condition, a mixture of persistent stagnation, intractable unemployment, uncontrollable inflation, and periodic recession. It is a condition so far lacking a cure but not a name—*stagflation*.

Stagflation is the most visible and festering symptom of a global economic revolution that was born and took root in the prosperity of the 1950s and 1960s. The dynamic of the revolution, like the dynamic of those decades, was the growth and spread of government in the economies of all nations and the rise of companies, banks, communications, and currencies that spilled over national boundaries and spread throughout the world.

The revolution produced a transformation from economies within nations operating more or less under the regulation of market conditions to a global economy operating increasingly in disregard of the marketplace and knowing no national bounds. In ever-tightening chains of interdependence, the revolution has produced a global economy that binds the industrial world to the burgeoning power of the "poor" in the Third World.

The global economy has become an economy of many links —links between nations, links between transnational enterprises, links between transnational banks and the unregulated trillion-dollar Eurocurrency system, links between resource producers and resource consumers. For two and a half decades, as the global economy flourished, these links appeared to be made of gold and, therefore, indestructible. Instead, the glitter proved to be of an alchemist's brew. And the global economy, only as strong as the weakest of the links, has become a vulnerable economy. It no longer responds to the old politics that governed and shielded national economies from instability in the first two and a half decades after World War II. Now it is wracked by massive adjustment crises in oil and energy, water and food, international trade and finance, and minerals and raw materials.

For politicians and their economic policy-makers, this transformation has meant a loss of control, a loss they are hesitant to acknowledge, much less remedy. As stagflation persists, economic management becomes the principal issue of American politics and foreign policy. But just as economics are increasingly intruding into politics, all kinds of noneconomic factors are impinging on the economic sphere. Former Commerce Secretary Peter Peterson coined the term *econopolitics* to describe the intermingling of both. Political motivations increasingly are governed by economic concerns.

Economic management is similarly becoming central to our foreign policy, where a new and dangerous "dualism" has emerged. The United States remains a military superpower with the nuclear potential to destroy sections of the globe. But it is no longer an economic superpower—rather, a first among equals, a situation brought about in part because its military power protected and its economic power fostered the postwar revival of Western Europe and Japan. In contrast to Britain, which lost its great power role because it could no longer afford it, the United States faces threats to its vital interests and credibility not only because of its inability to apply military power but also because its allies are pursuing separate economic and political interests in the world. This became painfully obvious in 1979–80, in the fragmented responses to the seizure of the U.S. embassy in Iran and to the Soviet invasion of Afghanistan. The jingoistic reaction is simply to call for more military power. But whatever the needs may be for military improvements, the more difficult problem is to forge a foreign policy strategy that synchronizes military and economic power.

For all the fears of nuclear confrontation and destruction, the most devastating weapon unleashed in the seventies has turned out to be economic. The October 1973 Middle East war—initially one of limited political and territorial objectives—became a global economic war. By embargoing oil, and with their dollar deposits becoming a dominant force in European money markets, the OPEC nations created economic and political trauma in the Western world. Economics became an entrenched part of warfare—crucial to big power diplomacy and the survival of nations, not merely incidental to it.

The global economic revolution will no longer allow world leaders to echo the words of the German general in World War I: "Don't bother me with economics. I am busy conducting a war." Even the most ordinary citizens came quickly to realize that their modern, comfortable, convenience-laden society was part of an interdependent world and, as a result, extraordinarily vulnerable.

October 1973 was a critical turning point. Just as October 1929 rang down the roaring twenties, October 1973 ended the unprecedented twenty-five-year period of constant postwar economic growth, expanding prosperity, and stable prices in the industrial world. The oil embargo and the quadrupling of oil prices did not in themselves bring the old era to an end, just as the stock market crash by itself did not end the boom time of the 1920s. Both were signals, later confirmed, that transformed economic structures were overtaking and disabling antiquated politics and policies. Both were preceded by less-visible early-warning signs: the boiling over of unregulated credit starting in the mid-twenties and, for the current critical juncture, the commencement of stagflation in 1970.

II

The transformations of the 1920s and of recent years were not the first that capitalist societies have undergone. Both capitalism's greatest defender, Joseph Schumpeter, and its most noted antagonist, Karl Marx, agreed on at least one point: the system is governed by "laws of motion," which, over time, drive it from one stage of development to another.

During each of the critical junctures between these stages, politics was marked by an initial regression to previously held conservative ideas about the management of the economy and foreign policy (not to mention fashion, music, and architecture) before new ideas were finally enshrined.

Internationally, each of these junctures was marked by a race among nations for dwindling supplies of natural resources, in the years prior to 1914 and again prior to 1941. Domestically, the transition between each of these stages was characterized by growing concentration in the private sector. Each was marked by a belated government response to the mounting changes. The first major antitrust legislation was passed in 1890, in response to the abuses growing out of the rise of national corporations and the country's first great wave of private-sector concentration. The Federal Reserve System was created in 1913 after credit and money had become integrated from coast to coast. The "New Deal" was a delayed response to the broad transformation underway since 1865, at its critical juncture of the Great Depression.

The current global revolution is yet another transformation, but there are crucial differences that make today's problems far more complex. First are the new and manifold links forged between the U.S. and the other economies of the world, seen best in the unprecedented global spread of multinational corporations and the Eurobanking creation of a vast pool of international money. This is a *systemic* phenomenon that challenges the sovereign power of nations to control both their production and their money. Second is the complex diffusion of global power following the era of *Pax Atomica*—in which the U.S. and Russia remain the globe's only two nuclear superpowers, yet no longer are its overwhelmingly dominant economies. The threat of nuclear war will always remain and even grow as more nations obtain the bomb for illusory security or blackmail. The danger now is more in proxy wars and a grab for resources. Since the U.S.–Soviet showdown over Cuba in 1962, the risks of a superpower confrontation have become but one element of global instability. The world is no longer divided into two hostile power blocs, but instead into a collection of power centers constantly oscillating between cooperation, competition, and potential conflict.

But perhaps the most dramatic difference wrought in the last decade was the rise of key Third World countries to positions of major economic and political power after centuries of subjugation by the industrialized states. Finally, there is the acceleration of government as a force in the marketplace. This is measured in the United States by a public sector accounting for 42 percent of national income, and around the world by an explosion of state-owned enterprises in capitalist and socialist nations alike.

Whatever the individual merits of the changes in the last three decades, an overall problem has emerged that has an analogy in medicine. When the body is administered a number of drugs for different purposes, the result is an unpredictable synergism, a total effect greater than the sum of the effects taken independently.

In their drive to bypass, redress, or absorb obstacles in the classical marketplace of supply and demand, corporations and governments have unwittingly ushered in the age of the globally interdependent "post-market" world.

The development of the post-market society resembles the development of the post-industrial society. The post-industrial society does not mean a society without industry, but one in which a major part of economic life increasingly revolves around nonindustrial activities. A post-market society does not imply that Adam Smith's world of markets with competitive prices have entirely vanished. Instead, within and between societies, most markets are dominated increasingly by new forces and concentrations of power which can overwhelm the laws of competitive markets—the very basis upon which rest government policies to manage the economy.

The race for oil and the wait for gas, the panic in gold, and sustained inflation—all signal markets no longer adjusting fast enough to prevent the widespread discomforts or crises that arise when short-run supply does not equal demand.

The post-market global economy has replaced the national market price system in which numerous buyers and sellers compete on the basis of prices. Concentration is now the rule. The laws that explain short-run adjustments in supply, demand, and prices have been transformed. The new unpredictability of those transformed laws—the seeming inability to make the economy adjust as it once did—has created deep uncertainties about the course of American politics in the 1980s.

Now, the ascendency of these post-market forces is so complete and the classical laws so blunted that the American economy enters the 1980s like a rudderless ship broken loose from its once-stable moorings and pitching in directions that no one can predict. The once-sure remedies for inflation or recession have only made the problems worse. Our once-sure allies in Europe, the Middle East, and Asia feel splintered by contradictory economic and military necessities. The future of governments and societies hangs on this very uncertainty. The United States and the other nations of the world may be buffeted by short-lived booms and busts, and even tumble together into a global depression.

Under present economic policy, the booms are only sustainable by continued escalation in defense and other government expenditures. This brings even more inflation. Policy is then wrenched to engineer credit crunches and other controls that risk national economic busts as the only alternative to rampaging inflation.

This does not have to be. Innovation in foreign and domestic economic policy to match the realities of a post-market world could make the 1980s a "golden decade" of growth, keyed to hundreds of billions of dollars of backlogged investment in the U.S. and around the globe. Yet nothing the economists might suggest will lead to rebuilding America unless politicians and society itself grasp the necessity for political reform and experimentation, both within the United States and internationally. Can national and global politics quickly enough innovate cooperative programs to stabilize the post-market economy? Or will we regress into the use of force in the quest for stability? Because these are still open questions, the 1980s are, as one survey of futurists put it, "the most unpredictable decade of the century."

III

The dominance of post-market forces over the remnants of competitive markets was signaled in 1970. For the first time in

U.S. history, a recession did not halt inflation. The decline of the classical marketplace laws was confirmed again in the 1974–75 recession. It took almost two years for a severe drop in demand and rising unemployment and excess capacity in supply to bring the adjustment to slower inflation. Even then, price rises continued at more than just a brisk gait. By 1980 the malfunctioning of markets appeared permanent. Stagnation was coupled with hyperinflation. Price rises approached the 20 percent rate, generally agreed as perilous to democracy. The 1980s began as the 1970s had, with stagflation the most festering economic by-product of a post-market world.

The vast majority of transactions in the United States and other industrial economies are now controlled by the power of concentrated forces: giant corporations, banks, unions, and government agencies or enterprises with a heavy dose of state control. With the exception of unions, the same is true for the Third World. The rise of these globally linked post-market forces has stripped from our economic managers their policy tools for fighting inflation and unemployment and for bringing about the adjustments for providing a stable supply of basic resources—energy, food, water, and minerals.

Replacing the competitive market economy in the United States is an economy in which more than 70 percent of all private economic activity—production and finance—is controlled and operated through 800 multinational conglomerate firms, while another 14 million firms struggle over the remaining 30 percent. Measured another way, the 400 top firms account for about 50 percent of the GNP, while government accounts for about another 25 percent.

The giant conglomerates have not only become more concentrated, but have spread their global reach. Somewhere between one-third and one-half of world trade now consists of nonmarket transactions between subsidiaries of multinationals from all home nations. A circular process takes place. Profits earned abroad by major corporations are returned home and invested in the acquisition of other companies, further increasing concentration. The 1970s spread of the oil giants into other areas, energy and nonenergy, was a classic example.

Banks followed the same pattern of concentration through global expansion. Foreign dollar deposits of U.S. banks were less than 10 percent of their domestic holdings in 1960; by 1980 they were more than 65 percent. The top 50 of America's 13,000 banks control more than 48 percent of all bank assets and virtually all the foreign deposits. Fueling the surge in domestic concentration was the growth of the so-called Eurocurrency market, the "offshore" haven of dollars and other currencies. In 1980, estimates of the gross size of this unregulated stateless pool of money were reaching one trillion dollars. Multinational banks and corporations thereby gained an edge over smaller domestic businesses, a new source of cash. This advantage grew wider during periods when national governments tried to cut inflation by tightening money and squeezing credit at home. Government's major weapon to control inflation has been effectively blunted even as interest rates reached record levels.

Even the stock market—the fountainhead of capitalism—underwent a major change. As management theorist Peter Drucker explained in his *Unseen Revolution,* disillusioned small investors all but abandoned the exchange. They yielded to the relatively few institutional investors such as pension funds, whose money managers control vast sums and blocks of stocks. In 1976 alone, the pension funds of public and private employees and the self-employed owned 35 percent of equity capital. By 1985, Drucker says, they will own at least 50 percent.

Labor also grew more organized and institutional. Although unions in the United States represent an ever-diminishing percentage of the total work-force, they are concentrated in the basic industries such as steel, automotives, and chemicals. Their wage bargains can set the pattern for the unorganized sectors. Like those of business, labor's demands became less a function of the marketplace and more a function of labor's size and its traditional bureaucratic and political leverage combined with its newfound "pension-fund power." Moreover, the structure of labor changed dramatically and so did attitudes toward work. Women and youth swelled the labor force, pressuring the economy to create hundreds of thousands of new jobs.

But globally, the most dramatic surge in post-market forces is government itself. As economist Kenneth Boulding points out in *The Economy of Love and Fear,* the government sector in the United States, from the Pentagon to the local public hospital, does not need to play by marketplace rules. For example, when the

Federal Reserve raises interest rates to cut inflation, these agencies need not curb their demand, as private industry is supposed to do.

The role of U.S. Government agencies is still small compared with the explosive growth of state-owned enterprises in other countries. Such enterprises, many of them multinationals as well, are now dominant actors in the world economy. State-owned or state-controlled enterprises now produce 85 percent of the oil of the non-Communist world. The control of oil production has passed from the Seven Sisters to OPEC.

The same thing is true of other vital commodities and industries. State enterprises produce 40 percent of the non-Communist world's copper, 35 percent of its iron ore and bauxite, 54 percent of its steel, 35 percent of its polyethylene, and 20 percent of its autos. Of 18 major industrial nations, 16 control their airlines and telecommunications; 14 control their auto industries and shipbuilding. In 1978, governments and state enterprises accounted for 65 percent of all borrowing on the Eurocurrency markets, up from 20 percent only three years before.

Even those figures mask where the trend is leading. In virtually every country, government aid is behind new ventures in capital-intensive technology and, with the exception of the United States, the systematic promotion of exports. For new industries, government is necessary to provide capital, especially during a decade of private capital shortages. In addition, government is increasingly being called on to bail out or take control of old industries. Finally, in the Third World, the planet's new growth frontier, much of new industry is state-owned or state-controlled.

Historically, reliance on markets has always led to an uneven flow of investment, to the booms and busts that have characterized the history of capitalism. The late Stephen Hymer referred to this as the "law of uneven development." Moreover, market economies distributed the benefits unevenly. Marx and his followers blamed the uneven effects on the market system of capitalism itself. And both Marx and Schumpeter and later writers associated with development economics ascribed to the market system another law, that of its inherent instability and momentum toward self-destruction. They foresaw power concentrations inevitably evolving to erode competitive markets. And with the erosion comes economic and then political instability.

What is different now is that no one is willing to accept the dictates of the marketplace. Everyone is determined to control the outcome. This determination is shared equally by voters and consumers of the Western industrial democracies, by governments, corporations, and labor, and by the buyers and sellers of oil, minerals, food, and fiber in rich nations and poor alike.

As this post-market world has emerged, the U.S. Government has tried and still tries to make economic policy by the old vision and rules of a national market economy. Policy functions as if prices were the result of relatively free market competition, as if the expenditures of government were still a controllable policy tool, as if world trade were still free trade, as if labor and capital were still operating at their old rates of productivity.

Clearly, this is no longer the case.

IV

If there is one word that characterizes the state of mind of present economic managers, it is befuddlement.

"Our old rules of thumb no longer work," a member of President Carter's Council of Economic Advisers told *Fortune* magazine. "And we haven't been able to develop new ones."

The problem is bipartisan. "The economy is no longer working the way it should," said former Federal Reserve Chairman Arthur Burns.

Former Treasury Secretary Michael Blumenthal, himself an economist and corporate executive, was even more blunt. "I really think the economics profession is close to bankruptcy in understanding the present situation—before or after the fact."

What he told the President was even more discouraging. "I tell the President when we come to him with predictions about how a certain tax cut will affect unemployment, to listen—then forget it. We can't predict with any certainty what will occur, for the models are as confused as we are about the trade-offs."

So much for "fine-tuning." The government, once capable of fueling expansion while restraining prices, has recently shown itself capable only of perpetuating stagnation and inflation simultaneously. A decade ago, economists would have said this was impossible. The question for the 1980s is whether stagnation and inflation are locked in each other's grasp or whether politics can engineer new economic policies for a better economic order.

So far, no new political and economic vision has developed to bring government into line with the realities of the post-market world and to reverse the course of stagflation. Instead, American government and society are forced by stagflation to play the politics of a shrinking economy, or, as it is more politely called, austerity. This becomes the politics of economic and social tension. As *Business Week* warned, "America could be heading into the worst period of economic and social dislocation since the Civil War."

Within the U.S. and other post-industrial societies, Daniel Bell sees both democracy and its economic base threatened by what he termed "the revolution of rising entitlements." The demand of citizens is for ever more services. They expect the government will eradicate social, economic, and class differences. When growth has become linked with inflation, no government can politically afford to wipe out inflation. Thus growth continues, but more people become dependent on the state. Economic decisions that once were made in the marketplace—on such matters as energy, property, and food—become political decisions.

Bell developed his thesis before the collision of two obviously incompatible political demands: more government programs and lower taxes. Inflation has been a generator of new tax revenues by pushing wage earners into higher brackets. The money encourages more government largess, regardless of the philosophy of the party in power. The voting public rebels against the taxes but still expects to receive all the new programs. The conflicting demands reflect a diffusion of political power among the traditional interest groups of big business and labor now joined by "single-issue" newcomers such as environmentalists, consumers, and balanced-budget proponents. Even while it fulfills demands for entitlements—pensions, social security, food stamps, unemployment compensation, product safety, clean air—the government shortchanges economic and social investment programs. Productivity growth plummets, force-feeding more inflation; cities suffer fiscal crises; the transportation and water systems crumble.

And for all the rhetoric of less government, we are clearly on a course of more government. The windfall oil profits tax alone will bring in more than $200 billion over the coming decade, money already earmarked for a variety of Federal spending projects. There will be more and more energy and conservation incentive taxes, the promises of the politicians notwithstanding. Credit and other controls are increasingly being used. In the 1970s, government grew almost as much under the two Republican Presidents as under the one Democrat. The demands for new programs and regulation are endless. Opposition to the dismantling of existing programs is even more intense. The real issue for the 1980s is not more government versus less government, but effective government that can implement noninflationary policies to encourage investment and employment.

What has happened in the United States is the clashing of antiquated policies (and the outmoded economic theories that continue to propel those policies) with the unattainable demands of voters and the new realities of global interdependence and post-market economics. For the last quarter-century, governments and advertising agencies have promoted the promise of increasing wealth and comfort, of expanding opportunities for generations to come. Stagflation now means the deferral of dreams, a fight to stay even, a skepticism about the rewards for either work or savings, and an almost speculative plunge deeper into consumer debt to buy houses and expensive gadgets because they will be too expensive next year. As the pie shrinks, everyone scrambles harder to grab his share of it. Social tensions increase. And amid the scramble, American politics have become grounded in stalemate.

The result has been a widening lag between what columnist Joseph Kraft referred to as "politics not catching up with economic realities." The political stalemate is reinforced by the intellectual stalemate among economists who are supposed to advise Presidents and Congress on policy. It appears that they have simply run out of ideas, or, as Harvard's Nathan Glazer put it, "the cupboard of ideas is bare." Ironically, the economist John Maynard Keynes, whose pioneering vision in the 1930s still lingers among contemporary economists and policy makers, prophesied today's problem: "Practical men, who believe themselves to be quite exempt from any intellectual influences, are usually the slaves of some defunct economist."

The Keynesian vision of demand management—the concept

of managing the economy's aggregate demand through tax, budget, and credit policy—is the basis of the economics of the industrial democracies. It was enshrined in this country in the Full Employment Act of 1946, the government's acknowledgment that it had to avoid anything like a repetition of the Great Depression. Threatened with slow growth and unemployment, governments can increase budgets, cut taxes, or ease credit in order to raise demand. Under the rules of the competitive market economy, businesses should then respond by increasing investment and supply. In theory, inflation also could be contained by demand management and its "fine-tuning" techniques in restricting fiscal and monetary policy. Competitive markets were also supposed to act as a check on rising prices.

Though held simultaneously by two warring camps, demand economics survives. The disputes between the conservative "monetarists," led by Nobel Laureate Milton Friedman, and the liberal "fiscalists," led by another Nobel laureate, Paul Samuelson, are exaggerated. For all their theoretical differences, their policies result in many of the same things, especially their reliance on demand management of a market economy. Only after the mid-1970s, when stagflation began taking on a permanent character, did some economists begin to doubt their theoretical tools and the vision of a market economy on which they were built. And even then their numbers were few.

"The economics profession is in a crisis," wrote Myron Sharpe, editor of *Challenge* magazine. "Keynesian economics has held the stage for quite a few years, but we have a new set of problems now that it doesn't seem to cope with."

Walt W. Rostow, an economist now more than a decade out of government, has said, "I sense that the economists—be they Mr. Friedman, Mr. Greenspan, or what have you, Samuelson and Shultz—are obsessed with what worked in the '50's and '60's, and they are in great danger of producing a protracted period of stagflation, with a loss of social and political cohesion that will damage the prospects for our own society, as well as the prospects of the developing world."

Peter Drucker observed that "the impact of societal transformation on theories always, in the past, has given birth to a new economic theory. We know we need new economic theory that focuses on the world economy rather than on the national economy alone."

Even Henry Kissinger, who used to profess his boredom with economics, acknowledged by the end of his term as secretary of state that his world of *realpolitik* had been changed by economic developments. "The political evolution and growth of the last 30 years have brought about a new diffusion of power. No nation or bloc can dominate any longer. Economic issues are turning into central political issues."

Acknowledgment of the problem, if not agreement on the solution, is generally bipartisan. Senator Adlai Stevenson III (D, Illinois) perhaps voiced the consensus when he said: "The collapse of the post-war monetary system, the growth of the Eurocurrency market, the emergence of new forms of money, the expansion of multinationals, the accumulation of vast monetary reserves in the Middle East, the rise of new centers of power, and the decline of others—all signal a fundamental shift in the world economic and political order."

V

Globally, two principal changes have produced an impasse similar to the stalemate in domestic politics. In international politics, as in domestic politics, a diffusion of economic power has created a diffusion of political power and the creation of new power centers in the non-Communist and Third worlds. Even more dramatically, international economic arrangements holding these countries together have broken down. The Soviets have become the strategic equal of the United States and spread their military power on the oceans. A new competition for economic spheres of influence also has begun among all varieties of nations. Sometimes it has been pursued with force, as in Afghanistan or Zaire or Angola, but more often through a combination of diplomatic and economic pressures. And the new element to the geopolitical equation is that the nations in the south of the globe now have their own bargaining power to employ.

The international economic system created and dominated by the United States after World War II has been coming apart. The

Bretton Woods agreement and the supremacy of the dollar collapsed in 1971. As the dollar continued to fall through the decade, Western Europe sought protection in its own recently evolved European Monetary System. In the absence of new global monetary rules, 1930s style interest-rate wars are erupting between industrial nations as each tries to battle its own national instability. Similarly, the free trade rules of the General Agreement on Tariffs and Trade (GATT) have been under protectionist siege for more than a decade and are disintegrating into something called "fair trade" or "orderly trade."

Part of this is the price of success. Our postwar economic and diplomatic policies helped create the prosperity and economic integration of the Western world. But now our foreign policy must face a fundamental fact: Whereas in 1945 the U.S. constituted one-half the capitalist world economy, today it is one-third, and by 2000 it will be down to one-fifth. Our allies doubt but still seek our military protection, distrust our political skill and staying power, and seek their own economic and diplomatic advantages when necessary or possible. The bonds of postwar cooperation began fraying as Europeans grew concerned that we were exporting our Vietnam deficits and inflation to them. The oil crisis of 1973 and the subsequent contest for influence in the Persian Gulf have intensified that process.

As Chairman Frank Church of the Senate Foreign Relations Committee said, "If we are seeing the end of 'the American era' it is not because we have lost the superpower race with the Soviet Union for strategic superiority, but because we are losing our capacity to compete with our own allies."

The diffusion of economic power to part of the Third World is symbolized most dramatically in oil. The oil price increases alone have produced a shift of hundreds of billions of dollars from the industrial world to the oil nations. The impact on the world's banking and investment systems has yet to be understood. Meanwhile, other Third World nations are increasing their wealth either through selling their natural resources or through industrialization. New industrial powers, such as Brazil and South Korea, are rising to challenge the established nations for shares of world trade.

The developing nations are a potential "new growth frontier," but the industrial democracies have failed to respond to it with coordinated or systematic approaches. Instead there is intensified competition among the industrial nations for new supplies of natural resources and new export outlets in the Third World.

This competition also has little to do with Adam Smith's free markets. Now there are government-led "swaps," and advanced nations outdo each other in offering technology, finance, and weapons deals in return for Third World resources. The U.S. has been slow to learn this post-market game for expanding its civilian technology exports. When we understandably hesitate to provide nuclear technology to the Third World, the French, Italians, and Germans eagerly step in. With no new rules for this new game, the result could be that Brazil, Argentina, and Iraq will have home-grown atom bombs within a decade.

The Third World nations have become increasingly sophisticated in bargaining with multinational corporations and Western governments for economic benefits. The result: when the lag in United States foreign policy makes us continue to treat Mexico as if we were both in the 1950s, the Japanese and Europeans move in quickly for the immense oil and gas supplies south of our border. The direction of our own foreign policy helps breed the kind of rivalry that creates new tensions among the industrial democracies. There are obvious and immediate benefits for the Third World, but the infusion of wealth to these countries is still lopsidedly distributed within societies and between nations. The gap between the world's very poor and everyone else grows wider. Meanwhile, Iran has become the seminal example of how rapid new wealth can boomerang into political instability. But as the U.S. reacts with single-minded focus on the Persian Gulf, it fails to ask how it can help prevent the Iranian experience from taking place in our immediate neighbor to the south.

World economic instability in the past has led to political instability and wars. The Great Depression prompted a series of protectionist measures and countermeasures among the great industrial powers which exacerbated the conflicts already existing. Today, new kinds of global schisms are beginning to appear. Throughout the postwar period the industrial democracies have held together in the bipolar divisions of the world, first between Communist and capitalist blocs on an East-West axis and later between the rich of the North and the poor of the South. New alignments, however, are appearing as economic problems become more pressing, as new holders of economic power arise and political divisions in the world become more skewed and complex. The diplomatic self-interest of the industrial nations is beginning to revolve increasingly around their raw-material, financial, and export dependence on the Third World.

The challenge for diplomacy in the 1980s is to prevent these global economic schisms from creating global political turmoil as they did in the past. The challenge for international economics will be to provide sufficient growth to give diplomacy a "breathing space," to reduce pressures for protectionism and "beggar thy neighbor" pursuits of bargains for Third World resources and export outlets. This is a challenge difficult even when tensions between the military superpowers are abating, as in the 1970s, far more so when military force is used or threatened to gain geopolitical advantage. As events in the flashpoint of the Persian Gulf demonstrate daily, the task of diplomacy will grow more perilous as the world's supplies of vital resources continue to shrink in the coming decade.

Oil is only the first of many vital commodities that in the 1980s will reach what Robert Heilbroner has termed "cross-over points." At these junctures worldwide demand will permanently outstrip supply unless societies undertake massive adjustments in technology and even consumption styles. The same is true in strategic metals. These shortages will lead to a "threat every bit as damaging as the energy squeeze," according to a 1979 survey of international experts. The American West is but one of many spots on the planet where water is reaching its cross-over point. And to that can be added food and ecological cross-overs in clean air and thresholds of irreversible climatic changes. In global manufacturing—steel, ships, and chemicals, for example—the most efficient centers have shifted from the industrial world to the Third World, creating immense political and economic adjustment problems for labor in the North and for world trade in general. All these cases are living evidence of massive failures and imperfections among crucial markets that are no longer performing their classical role for society: the "automatic" adjustment for balancing supply and demand.

The problems are starkly clear. The resource scarcity demands technological innovation to fill the gap. But science and engineering breakthroughs have been lagging. In the United States especially there has been a bewildering absence of a government commitment to invest in research and a demise of the pioneering spirit in both corporations and government as they grow larger and more bureaucratized.

The stagflation realities of resource scarcity, slow growth, and inflationary instability will intensify the demands for better global distribution, or even a basic redistribution, of income and wealth among rich and poor nations. There will also be competing demands for the physical and psychological humanization of work in the industrial world and for any kind of work in the developing world.

Without sufficient economic growth, economic instability threatens political stability in the industrial world and enhances the spread of authoritarianism in the developing world whether it takes the form of Marxism, Islamic fundamentalism, fascism, or some curious mixture of them all in the guise of nationalism. And the most fearful dimension of the eighties is the almost lawlike proposition of history that when peacetime economic remedies fail, nations resort to military action.

The 1980s must be *the adjustment decade,* a time of social and economic reconstruction and conversion, both globally and domestically. What is needed is a resumption of relatively stable growth, but a growth geared to conversion rather than only more consumption in the resource-short industrial world and directly aimed at improving living standards in the developing world. This new global growth pattern is a medium-term objective, giving countries a chance to experiment and adjust for meeting the threat of the multiple cross-overs of the 1990s. Without this economic breathing space, democracy will be a very limited commodity by the end of this century.

VI

The dramatic changes of the 1960s and 1970s have created their own agenda for the 1980s. The decade will become a critical juncture for the industrial world and developing worlds alike as they move together toward new relationships in a post-market world. The purpose of this book is not to project the world of the year 2000 but to dissect problems and to explore programs of a politics for prosperity in the 1980s. For it is the decisions of the decade ahead which will largely determine what kind of world exists by the year 2000.

In the United States and around the world, new economic approaches require new political approaches—essentially an adaptation of existing political structures and sometimes the creation of new ones to adapt to the new diffusions of economic power. There are new players demanding to be let into the game, or, once in, demanding new rules. To continue to ignore or brush aside those demands runs the risk of war abroad and social strife at home.

Internationally, the key to restoring security and economic stability rests on a U.S. foreign policy that could take the lead in forging political reforms in the management of international economic policy. These reforms would include a revised version of *détente* which would regulate military superpower competition in the Third World and set limits on the geopolitical maneuvering for resources. They would include readjustment of major international organizations to give the new power-holders of the South political weight equal to their economic strength. Only such political reforms will make possible the cooperative and technically feasible economic programs that can stimulate and revitalize the growth links between the North and the South and on which we and the rest of the globe all are actually dependent.

The failure to adapt our policy to global interdependence during the stagflation decade has produced a fundamental obstacle to beginning the growth tasks of the adjustment decade. Investors are holding, but are afraid to commit their global cash pool, approaching a trillion dollars, to "productive" investment.

The result is a perverse *anomaly:* a reluctance to invest at a time when the United States and other advanced nations have massive needs for capital formation and new technologies and for plants to create growth and jobs. And, at the same time, the Third World countries of the South have even more obvious and massive needs for investment transfers to buy capital goods and technology from the industrial North. Without those investments their poverty will deepen and their foreign debt, much of it owed to private banks in the industrial countries, will reach explosive levels that threaten an already teetering international financial system.

In the U.S., as in a Third World economy, the country's infrastructure of railroads and transport is crumbling. It will cost $400 billion in the late 1980s just to replace, restore, or repair existing railways, highways, and bridges, much less add to the network. On top of this, investment needs in the private manufacturing sector are estimated for the adjustment decade to be in excess of another $200 billion.

Western Europe and Japan are also suffering a capital formation crisis. Their productivity growth is declining, though not at such an abrupt rate as in the U.S. In Europe, middle-class university graduates are swelling the ranks of some 6 million unemployed. Even in Japan, layoffs, once unheard of among paternalistic companies, have become more common since the midpoint of the stagflation decade. And social investment, bypassed in the rush to supergrowth, will make housing and pollution control top priorities in those overcrowded islands.

Whatever the difference in their political systems and levels of economic development, the nations of the world are sharing a capital formation crisis that is compounding their failure to cure stagflation. Economic managers in the last decade have tried to induce growth and investment through the postwar Keynesian prescription of expanding domestic demand. The hope was that new demand would encourage new investment, as it has in the past. For a decade now, a post-market world has transformed that prescription into a placebo. The remedies of the 1950s and 1960s no longer are drawing investment money out of its shell. Rich Americans, rich Europeans, and rich Arabs no longer have the confidence to place their money long term into new factories or new technology. Instead, they are buying real estate, gold, or commercial paper, or acquiring each other's corporations. None of these "nonproductive" investments expands growth or creates jobs.

Only now are conventional economists beginning to see the other side of the problem, the economics of supply. Long observed in poor nations, a "vicious circle" has also emerged in the industrial countries: inflationary fears discourage investment, which reduces productivity growth and therefore profits, further decreasing investment and adding to inflation even more. The spiral, begun in the mid 1960s, is now accelerating because of higher energy and raw materials costs. The confidence of investors has been sapped by a decade-long fear of unstable currency markets, protectionism, future inflation, and uncertain government policies and regulations that despite their social value divert potential investment capital to such goals as pollution control.

In early 1980, a prestigious international commission, headed by Willy Brandt, released its long awaited *North-South: A Program for Survival.* Noting that survival refers equally to North and South, the report "sets out to demonstrate that the mortal dangers threatening our children and grandchildren can be averted." But the commission also concluded: "It would be dangerous and insincere to suggest that they can be overcome with the conventional tools of previous decades."

We in the United States are, to some degree, at the same stage of impatience and frustration which we faced in the late 1940s, in the years before the Truman Doctrine and Marshall Plan and before we set out robustly to reestablish confidence in our leadership of the Western world. In those few impatient years, we fretted about European instability and the risk of war, about inflation and a postwar depression. We wanted to know why few would invest in the immense capital formation tasks of rebuilding Europe and its still stagnant economies.

At this parallel point in the early 1980s, it is time to rediscover and expand upon the political and economic principles of global interdependence. There is the need for an international action program to bring alive the many proposals for the modern equivalent of a global Marshall Plan. It should be adopted, not as a gesture to demonstrate idealism, but because it is needed, as the original Marshall Plan was, by donor and recipient alike. It offers a political means to attack both the supply and demand blockages of the global economy which are contributing so much to the persistence of each nation's stagflation. It could spark confidence among disillusioned and increasingly fearful global investors and restore, not only the spirit, but a pragmatic basis of cooperation among the U.S. and its allies. It would not be a one-shot cure-all but a catalyst for growth as its European predecessor was.

This is not charity. It is a matter of putting the right resources in the right place and negotiating the right return in order to gain the participation of industrial, OPEC, and Third World nations alike. The postwar era of interdependence has opened to all three groups of nations a clear road for pursuing a newly defined vision based on a sharply honed policy principle of mutual economic interests in reviving the globe's growth machinery.

One benefit for the U.S. and the industrial world would be the cracking of the supply blockages to the mineral and natural resources of the Third World. Another would be the freeing up of new demand sources for our exports in the globe's South. Without new sources of demand, the prospect that the industrial economies will resume growth is dim. And unless we invest in Third World growth, the development of the planet's last great geographic frontier for new sources of both supply and demand will not take place.

Most OPEC nations, and particularly the important ones, have mutual interests in setting stable growth again in motion. Continued instability brings daily both mounting military and economic threats to their newfound wealth.

Yet sitting alongside these needs, the trillion dollar global cash pool of the Eurocurrency markets is used less and less for productive investment. It remains outside national controls, fuels inflation, and has become a source of speculative dynamite to be bought and sold against the dollar, other currencies, and gold. It harbors a lot of nervous OPEC oil money vulnerable to political threats of seizure. It also includes the monies of equally jittery corporations and other private investors of the North. Only a concerted effort among nations can defuse this transnational financial time bomb to restore stability where none exists now and to direct its monies to the purposes of real economic growth.

Just as the United States financed its technology exports to Europe through the original Marshall Plan in the late 1940s and early 1950s, the industrial world can now export its technology to the developing world, financed by its money and OPEC's. For what is different now is that the United States is no longer the West's economic superpower. It is rather a first among equals. But U.S. leadership is still necessary for a global Marshall Plan that could be a platform for rebuilding global growth.

What is lacking to launch this international experiment are the political principles and mechanisms of decision making and participation that match the revolutionary shifts in global economic power. The International Monetary Fund, the World Bank, and other international organs still largely reflect the world of the 1950s and 1960s. In any effort to break open the blockages of the global economy, these organizations need to revise their voting shares and other power arrangements, or create new ones, to gain the effective participation of not only the industrial world, but OPEC and the developing world. Just as the original Marshall Plan demanded participation from donor and recipient, the United States will once again have to accept the principle of voluntary power-sharing.

And just as the Marshall Plan was inspired by a Cold War stimulus, the 1980s revival of tensions makes more starkly clear the implications of economic interdependence and its central role in developing policies to reduce those tensions. *Détente* collapsed in the absence of rules to govern superpower competition in the Third World. But the American attempt to respond unilaterally to events of 1979–80 with economic weapons showed how the dualism in our foreign policy rendered it ineffective. The threats and the applications of weapons of "economic warfare" such as embargoes and seizures of bank deposits frightened our allies more often than they scared our adversaries. And big increases in military spending threatened bigger deficits and a weaker dollar, diminishing even further our capacity to provide global leadership.

The starting point of a new U.S. foreign policy would be the recognition of this dichotomy: that the U.S. and the Soviet Union are still the globe's only nuclear superpowers but are no longer the only dominant economic powers. A revised and updated *détente*, providing rules of the game for military superpower competition in the Third World, needs to be coupled with new rules governing economic competition among all nations in the development of the Third World.

The Third World is obviously more vital than ever before to the economic and, therefore, national security interests of both Russia and the United States. As in the U.S., Russia's economy is stagnating and approaching its own cross-over in oil, perhaps as soon as 1982 or 1983. And the Soviets will be facing this cross-over as they are making their unpredictable transition to a post-Brezhnev era. Amid such instability the two nuclear superpowers play their bluff and counterbluff over Third World countries with standby military weapons that can annihilate each superpower. Just as they formalized principles to govern their postwar *realpolitik* in Europe, the U.S. and Russia must now quickly evolve explicit "rules of the game" in the Third World.

The most important element of these national security principles is a recognition that national liberation, not capitalism versus communism, is the driving force in Third World politics. Neither the U.S. nor Russia has an enviable or successful record in the selection of regimes they have installed or systematically helped stay in power. Soviet inroads in Guinea, the Sudan, Somalia, and Egypt have all been rejected. U.S. efforts to manipulate the internal policies in Third World nations from South Vietnam to Iran have also backfired. For most of these countries the freedom from foreign domination, including the freedom to choose their own "model" for economic development, is the dynamic of their politics. Regardless of which "ism" and sphere of influence a Third World nation appears to lean to, as we describe in Part II, its economic policies increasingly reflect a synthesis of insights taken from both Adam Smith and Karl Marx and a capacity to trade with both the U.S. and Russia.

A new U.S. foreign policy must encompass the economic dimension. It must address the failures of market links among industrial, OPEC, and Third World nations. Coordinated and negotiated action by governments is necessary when competitive global market mechanisms are nonexistent, as in oil, or are adjusting imperfectly, as in food and other commodities, or are inherently unstable, as in finance. Post-market global interdependence makes not only mandatory but also operational the economic policy principle of mutual interest coupled with the political principle of voluntary power-sharing.

Finally, there must be a more prominent role in U.S. foreign policy for bilateral and regional economic cooperation, especially on a North-South axis and coordinated internationally. To avoid even more costly schisms with such vital neighbors as oil-rich Mexico, the U.S. needs to act on their demands for regional cooperation. In the past, Latin Americans have complained that we treat them like any other Third World nation. The special geographic links with Mexico and the unique regional bond with Latin

America should become an opportunity, not a burden, in our foreign policy. The global economy is complex and rich enough and the rigidities of traditional international bureaucracies paralytic enough for experiments with global decentralization to commence.

VII

At home, as in the world, U.S. politics must adapt the principle of checks and balances, the foundation of our system of government, to the new profusions of economic power-holders that have been created in the post-market economy. Stagflation has many roots and causes in the global revolution and is not merely the creature of OPEC and high oil prices, whatever some politicians say. The actions of OPEC have turned some problems into full-fledged crises. Higher oil prices have certainly complicated economic management, especially in the last two years. But stagflation had already taken root by the end of the 1960s. Serious supply-side problems, such as declining productivity growth, worker alienation, and capital shortages, were already surfacing by the mid-1960s. Inflation has been ravaging the economy since the Vietnam War. If OPEC vanished tomorrow, many of these problems would still be with us in acute form.

The stagflation decade was far more seriously the product of an outdated econopolitical vision. Political stalemate contributed to the failure of conventional economic remedies to work as they once did. In turn, that failure produced even more stalemate. Our politics must create more effective mechanisms to generate whatever consensus is possible in a vast, sprawling, heterogeneous land. We must return to its central place a politics capable of making decisions rather than postponing them. Consensus mechanisms need to be built, not only in Washington, but at the grass roots of the economy, the corporation. Reform in this country needs also to come from the bottom up to head off increasingly expensive and often counterproductive federal attempts to manage and regulate economic activities. Actual examples of innovation and reform abound. Some examined later include a cooperative government, business, and labor attempt to revive a major U.S. industry, the efforts of American corporate managers to develop new relationships with Third World governments as their European and Japanese counterparts already have, and the efforts of labor and business leaders to humanize the workplace and reform the boardroom.

At the national level for energy and industrial development, there need to be experiments with the self-financing capability that quasi-public, quasi-private mechanisms offer rather than the creation of more bureaucratic line agencies of government. Our future energy and industrial policies need to be keyed to such consensus-building *and* self-financing mechanisms if we are ever to contain inflation while breaking out of an energy deadlock of nearly a decade's duration.

America's reindustrialization represents the technological and social frontier for the pioneering of new sources of growth at home. In this respect, it parallels the Fourth World, which represents the globe's last geographic frontier for the tapping of new growth in the 1980s.

The pioneering of new policies for energy, for industrial development and against inflation, will require experiments with new political mechanisms and economic policy principles. In Part III, we explore these new ideas in considerable detail. Among the most important are proposals for a political mechanism for determining an agenda of national development priorities. This goes beyond the shopworn Presidential commission to which this task has been relegated. A national development program also provides safeguards against the overlap and boondoggles that sometimes afflicted the New Deal and the Great Society. The reindustrialization of America must be based on development priorities that reflect a political consensus and a government commitment. As the European experience has demonstrated, an effective incomes policy, including price and wage controls when needed, also calls for a new consensus-generating political mechanism. Without it, we will repeat the 1971–73 experience when prices exploded after the controls were lifted.

In 1974 the authors of *Global Reach* used the metaphor of "the Latin Americanization of the United States" to describe a process already well underway in the U.S. economy. Until 1970, only Third World nations were affected with stagflation. Now the United States is burdened not only with stagflation and a crumbling transportation infrastructure, but with other symptoms of underdevelopment as well. The middle class is pinched by inflation; productivity growth is plummeting; structural unemployment deepens; and job opportunities in an increasingly sophisticated economy shrink for the very poor, who fall behind in education and skills. Like a Latin American banana republic of old, the U.S. is coming to rely on agricultural exports to cover its trade deficit in oil, consumer goods, and, increasingly, industrial products. This trade pattern is causing sporadic food shortages, higher prices, and unemployment and is fueling protectionist pressures reminiscent of the 1930s.

These symptoms are similar enough to those of the developing world to bring about a certain similarity of antidotes. As much as they would not want to admit it, other governments of the industrial world have begun taking the first tentative steps toward a "development economics," integrating supply and demand economics, a major management principle in the Third World.

Other industrial democracies are coming more quickly to recognize that conventional demand management remedies have not been able to break the vicious circle of sagging investment, diminishing productivity growth and rising inflation. The reason is that domestic economic blockages, like global ones, are not only in demand but in problems of supply. The elements of a supply policy are stimulating technology and innovation, eliminating the bottlenecks in the flow of raw materials and energy and helping old industries adjust to new competition from abroad. This element of economic management has been almost totally ignored in the U.S. government except by a few lost souls in the Commerce and Labor departments. In Europe and Japan there has always been more emphasis on industrial supply policy—the targeting of money, technical assistance, and, at times, regulatory relief to priority industries. Targeting seeks to capture future export markets before they are lost and to program the adjustment of declining industries and firms before they reach the "status"of a national catastrophe.

In the United States, we abhor planning and end up bailing out Penn Central, Lockheed, and Chrysler. *Planning* as a word and concept strikes terror in many Americans who tend to equate it with Moscow economics, and therefore remains politically impossible as an economic remedy. In high contrast, the Europeans, especially the West Germans, are devoting more attention to the supply economics of fostering new technology. (They spend 2 percent of domestic output on R&D. We spend half that.) The Europeans are also devoting more money and attention to programs to improve productivity through the humanization of work. In other private-enterprise industrial democracies, their government planning mechanisms make it easier to spot future growth areas that need encouragement and investment. What is politically feasible and essential for America this decade, is a policy for industrial development that learns to draw both from the successes and from the failures of the experiences of other democracies.

Some politicians and their advisors are beginning to budge from their fixation with demand economics, but most remain basically prisoners of bureaucratic and academic rigidities. In early 1979, there was finally an official recognition, at least on Capitol Hill, that the United States had to follow the other industrial democracies and actively pursue policies based on supply economics. The major and unanimous conclusion of the Annual Report of the Joint Economic Committee of Congress was that "the Arab oil embargo and subsequent behavior of the OPEC cartel suddenly and dramatically began to force the attention of the country and its economic experts on the supply side of the economy."

As significant a breakthrough as this committee report was, it still reflected the problem of political perceptions lagging behind economic realities. Even the growing Washington vogue of supply economics with its call for across-the-board tax breaks rests on an outdated market vision. This point was made by economist Robert Nathan as he observed the expanding interest in supply economics:

"Many economists, including liberal economists, can't stand the very thought of questioning the functioning of the marketplace.

"I'm convinced that the deterioration of the marketplace is a serious contributor to inflation, but almost no one is willing to whisper such a conclusion."

For post-market America, supply targeting should mean tax breaks selectively aimed at where they will most stimulate productivity and thus fight inflation. But across-the-board, quick-fix tax breaks are an inflationary perversity explainable only by politicians in desperate need of votes. Similarly, targeting is an alternative to the across-the-board credit crunches and budget cuts that now seem the only gamble left for beating inflation but that risk wreaking havoc upon America's blue- and white-collar classes alike. Wherever these bludgeons of a free market approach have been tried—from a beleagured Britain to a dictatorial Chile—the success has been long in coming if at all. It is a last gasp effort to seek salvation, not in science but in the religion of "monetarism and free markets," and a confessional of the now-defunct vision of demand economics.

To raise doubts about market mechanisms, however, is not to challenge private enterprise. In the post-market era, the art of economic management will be to leave healthy markets alone, but to create cooperative business-government-labor mechanisms for promoting efficiency where markets no longer exist. It will also target temporary selective policies to adapt, revitalize, or close down industries where persistent unemployment and low productivity reflect markets incapable of automatically adjusting to new forces of supply and demand.

VIII

To look beyond the conventional wisdom, to leapfrog bureaucratic barriers and economic rigidities, is the role of the pioneer. In government, in some corporations and unions, and in some evolving relationships between corporations and Third World governments, we are seeing some examples of pioneering approaches. Those probed later in this book are offered, not as panaceas, but as testimony that we do not need to remain in the thrall of past failures and the mindsets often responsible for producing them.

Some academics are trying to throw off the shackles of dogma. Like Keynes and his colleagues in the 1930s, they are seeking to develop a new analytical vision for government policy—in this instance, one that does not discard entirely the past vision of demand economics. Rather, the attempt is to modify demand economics with a new supply economics, the conceptual cornerstone of development economics, and an integration essential to creating a national economic development policy.

Past transformations, such as the one leading to the Great Depression, ultimately produced a new policy vision, in that instance the programs of the New Deal. The present transformation similarly requires a new vision (what the Germans call *Anschauung*), but this time based on the principles of development economics.

The post-market economy that continues to emerge from the global economic revolution will not go away. The 1980s, like the 1930s, will be a critical juncture. Keynes was perhaps premature when he said then, "intellectual solutions will make the difference." They do, but it took more than a decade and a world war before the new theories replaced the then-existing conventional wisdom and became the foundation for new policies. Ever-rising frustrations in both rich and poor nations deny governments in the 1980s the luxury of that much time if they want to maintain political stability and international order. A continuation of the conventional wisdom and of conventional foreign and domestic policies promises more stagflation, punctuated by periodic booms and busts. And the dangers and temptations of war grow with each bust—whether triggered by a disruption in the flow of oil or other vital commodities, a breakdown in international financial stability or the sheer persistence of inflation.

Still, the 1980s need not repeat the 1930s. The global economy offers vast opportunities for trade, investment, and growth, a chance to bring about a golden decade. We are really striving for time, for a breathing space, for an opportunity to make choices. Before long, that time will run out, and the choices will no longer be ours to make.

The problems do not stem from a single cause, and the challenges will not be met with a simple prescription. The politics of the stagflation decade has been too often characterized by the quest for single villains. This has been coupled with the messianic sloganeering of the dime-store free marketeers, and their political acolytes, who want to take care of everything with only quick-fix tax breaks. The answers are much more complex: creation of a modified demand policy with new emphasis on supply policy, development of new approaches in diplomacy and international economic policy, and a realization that these two are really now one.

As immense as the challenges appear, their technical economic cures are not that difficult, at least in theory. The challenge is as much one of politics as of economics, and this is true both domestically and globally. The key to the technical economic approaches is political reform of international organizations and political and government innovation at home. In both instances the essential task of a politics for prosperity will be to adapt to the new diffusions of economic power wrought by the global revolution.

The question for governments, especially democratic governments, is whether they can move with enough speed and agility to catch up with the new economic realities. For democracy, the question is whether politics will be the master or the slave of economics.

CHAPTER 2

The Politics and Economics of Stagflation

I

STATISTICS LEND DREARY confirmation to the unhappy designation of the 1970s as the *Decade of Stagflation*. The average unemployment rate for the industrial democracies of North America, Western Europe, Japan, Australia, and New Zealand reached 3.9 percent in this decade, compared with 2.5 percent in the 1960s. That figure disguises the real impact. In the 1960s, U.S. policymakers were dissatisfied with a 4 percent jobless rate; the figure has not gone much below 6 percent in the last decade. Even the Europeans, whose politics could never tolerate American levels of unemployment, are now accepting them as a matter of course. Their economies are proving less resilient than the U.S. economy in adding new jobs to absorb the flow of postwar babies and women into the work force.

The figures for inflation are equally dismal. U.S. inflation, after the Korean War price-burst, held below 2 percent until the mid-1960s. The Vietnam buildup, financed through budget deficits rather than new taxes, pushed it beyond 3 percent. By the end of the decade, it was approaching 6 percent. That figure was considered so alarming that President Nixon reversed his self-professed "free-market" ideology and imposed wage and price controls to ensure his reelection. By 1979 the nation was in its second bout of double-digit inflation in less than five years. Meanwhile, the inflation rates of our European allies have, at times, resembled football scores. In such countries as Italy, a 30 percent or 40 percent inflation rate and the social and political disruptions resulting from it have threatened the existence of democratic government. And this may be only the beginning. Some studies project an overall U.S. inflation rate of more than 140 percent over the decade of the 1980s. And some important individual items like a $6,000 car would cost $12,000 and a 1990 loaf of bread $2.00.

Inflation and the attempt to impose the temporary antidotes of fiscal and monetary austerity have produced either sluggish growth rates or none at all. The growth rates of the industrial democracies, which were the engine of the world economy in the 1950s and 1960s, stalled in the 1970s. The 5.5 percent growth rates in the 1950s and 1960s sagged to 3.3 percent in the 1970s. The American drop was less precipitate, from 3.9 percent to 3.2 percent, partly because our economy was not coming off the steep incline of a postwar recovery program.

Stagflation has persisted in the United States and the other democracies through changes in leaders and political parties. The intractability of the problem helps create an illusion, or dangerously cynical attitude, that it is beyond the capability of government or politics to solve or ameliorate the problem. This in turn gives the politicians of the moment a convenient out, but begs the question: If government is not responsible, who is?

The answer rests not in the pursuit of villains, even the convenient villain of OPEC. The OPEC oil-price hikes of 1973–78, by the highest estimates, accounted for no more than one-third of the increase in the inflation rate. And even the big increases of 1979 were not the sole cause of the 13 percent inflation rate, the White House notwithstanding.

What needs to be acknowledged instead is that political and economic forces are pushing the props out from under the foundations of economic policy-making. Essential to the successful management of aggregate demand, the basis of Keynesian economics and the policy of the last four decades, is that government be able to control its budgets and fiscal policy and the supply of money. The emergence of the post-market global economy has now made obsolete these conventional tools of government economic management. How and why this has come about is the subject of this and the next three chapters. They lay the basis for exploring the new national and international policy tools to restore stability in the 1980s, the domain of the book's concluding chapters.

II

The fundamental dislocations that have become apparent in the last decade are characteristic of important turning points, or critical junctures, as they are described in economic history. Between two stages of economic development, instability rules and leaders grope for a new policy vision. There are struggles, sometimes epic, between advocates of the new and defenders of the old. For the unfortunate majority who are neither economists nor intellectuals, there are often depressions or other upheavals.

In England, for instance, in the late eighteenth and early nineteenth century, there was a struggle between the *laissez-faire*, free-trade principles of Adam Smith and the entrenched policies of mercantilism, designed to keep out imports. The battles between Whigs and Tories, between new factory owners (whose cheap labor needed cheap food), and old landowners, finally peaked with repeal of the Corn Laws in 1846. At that time, Britain became a free trader with all nations except its colonies.

On the Continent, France tried to catch up with England's industrial revolution. What emerged over the protests of the landed gentry and regional interests, was an amalgam of free-trade economics and a uniquely French alliance of centralized government and big industry. Germany, united after the 1870 Franco-Prussian War, expanded the Prussian practice of government-bank interlocks to steer credit and build up chosen industries. This was coupled with Bismarck's victory over small business interests in enacting a social security system of minimum wages, pensions, and medical care to quell labor unrest.

Industrialization spurted in the United States after the Civil War, led by a technological revolution in transportation and communications. Small family firms, usually regionally based, transformed themselves into nationally integrated companies. The groups that did not share fully in the transformation, farmers and labor particularly, reacted to the abuse and expansion of corporate and financial power. Government intervention came with the Sherman Anti-Trust Act and the creation of the Federal Reserve System. Industrial and financial transformation and growth continued into the twentieth century, cresting and then collapsing at the end of the post–World War I boom of the Roaring Twenties.

There are almost as many theories of how and why the Depression took place as there are economists and historians. But as Charles Kindleberger wrote in his much acclaimed *The World in Depression, 1929–1939,* there was more involved than any single cause or even a series of historical accidents. "Great depressions recur," Kindleberger wrote. He said the European crisis of 1848 and the 1929 Depression "both represented failures of the economic system at a transitional stage from one set of institutions and forms to another."

The Keynesian economic vision emerged from the crisis of the Depression. The then prevailing "classical" theory had no explanation for the Depression. It held that sustained unemployment was impossible in a market economy. Yet the continuing downward spiral of wages and prices in the early thirties did not produce the desired result of increasing employment, output, investment, and purchasing.

Keynes and others observed a phenomenon alien to classical theory. In situations of persistent uncertainty, low interest rates could not induce industrialists to borrow and create new investment. Nor would low wages effect more hiring, because companies were convinced no one would be buying up their products. The possibility of a persistent recession or depression scared off potential investors. No matter how low interest rates dropped, and they fell precipitously in the Great Depression, companies were still too frightened to invest. There was a "crisis of investor confidence" based on the fear of insufficient demand. Keynes argued for a "revolutionary" new role for government economic managers: the use of fiscal policy to lower taxes, increase government spending, or do both, and thereby stimulate enough consumer demand to spur new investment and employment by private enterprise.

The Keynesian revolution represented a dramatic change in the government's role in managing the economy and did so without interfering too deeply in private enterprise, despite all the pained howls of anti–New Deal industrialists of the time. By the 1950s this major management innovation of industrial democracy acquired the name *fine-tuning* of aggregate demand. Government could smooth the inevitable business cycles that occurred in private enterprise economies every four to eight years. During the downward phase of the cycle, as unemployment started growing, the government could "prime the pump" through increased spending or lower taxes or a combination of both. During the upward phase of the cycle, when prices started rising, government could take the opposite course. The deficits incurred during the down phase would be made up with the additional revenues and reduced expenditures of the up phase.*

After World War II, the institutional cornerstone of Keynesian domestic policy was laid with the Full Employment Act of 1946, establishing in law the vision of the Keynesian revolution. The followers of Keynes felt that government had a political responsibility to "fine-tune" the economy to attain stable economic growth with full employment but without inflation. Later, equity, or the wider spreading of benefits, was included. The analytical basis of government's new role was demand economics, a mixture of the tax, credit, and spending policies capable of producing all these desired results.

Through the 1950s and 1960s there were political refinements of Keynesian theory along the lines described by John Kenneth

* There is one interesting footnote to the slow and sometimes troubled birth of Keynesian economics in this country. Franklin Roosevelt in the 1932 campaign attacked President Herbert Hoover as a profligate for budgeting a total deficit of slightly over $3 billion for the years 1931–32: "I accuse the present Administration of being the greatest spending Administration in peace time in all our history," said Roosevelt to an audience in Sioux City, Iowa, in September 1932. Upon assuming office, however, Roosevelt promptly doubled the Hoover deficit, and more than doubled his predecessor's spending by 1936.

But by the 1936 election Roosevelt proved, in the words of Robert Lekachman, that he "was in his heart a true descendant of thrifty Calvinist forebears." A balanced budget again became the Democratic party platform plank for the 1936 race. In 1937–38. Roosevelt reduced deficit spending by nearly 50 percent. On October 19, 1937, ominously another "Black Tuesday," the stock market experienced its second great crash within a decade. It signaled the beginning of the recession within the depression that continued into 1938. In June 1938 the Roosevelt Administration finally returned to the Keynesian policy tool of deficit spending, pushing through Congress an emergency Omnibus bill to authorize spending of $3.75 billion.

Roosevelt's ambivalence was symbolic of the caution and brief return to conservatism that has marked many critical junctures. These junctures take place amid great instability. There is an initial tendency to pioneer and then to pull back. When the return to old ideas fails to work, the pursuit of the new ideas resumes.

Galbraith's concept of countervailing power. The politics of "fine-tuning," practiced by big government, the third agent of countervailing power, also became the art of balancing off and reaching consensus between the competing claims of big business and labor on the social contract governing the economy. Although Galbraith, Michigan State's Walter Adams, and others warned that concentrated power could disturb the price system and economic stability, the growth spurt of the sixties masked the problem, and the message went unheeded.

The "new economics," the vision of countercyclical action by government in a competitive market economy, grew increasingly detached from reality as the mid-1960s, marked by the Vietnam deficits, wore into the 1970s. By the early 1970s the Keynesian economics were coming full circle as President Nixon, of all people, declared himself a Keynesian and primed the pump with huge deficits before the 1972 election. At the same time, he disavowed the doctrinaire Republican faith in free markets and imposed wage and price controls.

III

The present transformation has been characterized by the development of a global, interdependent, post-market economy dominated by government, multinational conglomerates, and, in the industrial democracies, unions. Policy has yet to catch up with many of these changes. What once worked no longer does.

Keynes originally designed his policy tools to combat the Great Depression. Yet since World War II they have been used almost exclusively to correct cyclical problems: short-run bouts of either too much or too little demand over the business cycle. Since the mid-1960s, however, new crises have been developing on the supply side of the economy: in productivity, investment, energy and other scarce resources, and bureaucracy. These are deeply structural and not merely cyclical problems. The global crises of finance and protectionism are also tied to cyclical problems to some extent, but have other and more fundamental causes stemming from the neglect of the new strains in supply.

Keynesian economics and the ability to "fine-tune" the economy rely on three fundamental and interrelated assumptions about the links of political and economic power in a society: a political consensus or rationality sufficient to allow correct economic policies to be put into effect in good times and bad; government control of its spending, taxing, and money supply; and a competitive market economy with a flexible price system responding to short-run changes in supply and demand. The post-market economy of the global economic revolution has shattered these links, these fundamental assumptions of Keynesian economics.

There are three basic assumptions of Keynesian policy dependent on one another. The first is that government has the ability to control its spending through the existence of a collective political rationality, or consensus. The second is that government tax and monetary policy is controllable and effective. This hinges on the third assumption, the existence of a classical competitive marketplace. Understanding why these assumptions no longer reflect the reality of a post-industrial post-market global economy explains why the continuation of our almost sole reliance on demand management policies will yield but more instability and dangerous turmoil.

IV

The main political problem for Keynesian economics during the stagflation decade has been the tendency of the political consensus to collapse under stress. During expansionary times, consensus is comparatively easy, as the period of the early and mid-1960s demonstrated. Voters feel that they are at least sharing in the gains of an expanding economy. The lower the rate of inflation, the lower wage demands are likely to be. When productivity is rising, wage demands are viewed as moderate and reflect the feeling that no particular group of workers needs to jump ahead of the rest. The consensus is solidified as prosperity allows government to expand programs without raising tax rates or creating inflation. But during stagflation, voters and consumers begin to feel they are falling behind and push for new programs and higher wages in order to catch up. The consensus is further fragmented as government tries to curb inflation by raising taxes and holding down spending. The final breakdown of consensus erupts in the likes of Proposition 13 and conflicting demands for lower taxes and more programs, whatever the economic conditions and consequences.

Keynesian economics assumes that budgets are flexible, turning down as well as up. But during the decade of stagflation, budgets were going only up. The revolution of rising entitlements has been translated into unending expectations of more for everyone, an expectation fed by the boom period of the 1960s. An increasing share of the federal budget, which itself has risen from $100 billion to $400 billion a year over the last fifteen years, is going directly to payments for individuals. A higher and higher proportion, now 76 percent, of the budget is coming under the category of "uncontrollable" items with built-in or open-ended increases. The budgets of such civilian agencies as the departments of Health and Human Services, of Transportation, and of Education are on the same upward spiral as that of the Pentagon.

One dramatic indication of this inability of government to control costs—even if it wants to—is the increasing cost of its own pension systems. The government is locked into generous pension benefits to military and civilian workers, generously offered years ago when government salaries were very low. The salaries have since gone way up—in many middle and low-middle categories to higher levels than comparable industry rates—and the pensions are still magnificent. The result: The government has an unfunded pension liability, in a variety of pension programs, of more than $300 billion.* Military pensions, at more than $10 billion annually and paid out of current funds, are nearly the largest item in the Pentagon budget. A small proportion of government pension benefits comes from employee contributions invested in stocks and bonds, as is the case in private plans. Most pension benefits, however, come out of current revenues, assuring that the government in the future either will be deeper in hock or will have to renege on obligations to its employees.

In January 1979, President Carter submitted a so-called "austerity" budget to Congress. He claimed a triumph in bringing down the deficit to $30 billion at the peak of a business cycle, when

* The government pension system does not even meet the standards of soundness demanded by the government for private plans. The situation in many state and local systems is more precarious.

conventional Keynesian economics would have called for a budget in balance or in surplus. Yet even the President admitted it would be a short-lived triumph: "The inevitable pressures to spend just a little more here or a little more there—for someone's pet project or for someone's favorite interest group—have begun."

The collective political rationality, or consensus, of the Keynesian economic vision has become the politics of single-interest groups and special interests. The trend has been intensified by the almost complete breakdown of the already weak bonds of party loyalty and, in Congress, of party discipline. The few cohesive elements that used to keep the parties together—regional, class, ethnic, and family loyalties—are being eroded in a mobile society. In their place are single-interest groups, relying on the power of public relations and the modern techniques of electronic organization and mass communication to push forward their demands.

Programs once initiated never die. Instead, they expand through informal alliances of often interchangeable congressional staff members who draft the laws, executive branch staff members who administer them, and lobbyists who manipulate them. When a special interest is threatened, it makes *ad hoc* alliances with others, swaps computerized mailing lists, and with other electronic miracles of the 1970s creates a barrage of reinforcements overnight. Presidents, senators, and congressmen are confronted with mailbags of identical telegrams. If big money is involved—an effort to change oil company taxes, for example—the Lear jets carrying corporate vice-presidents will be stacked up over Washington's National Airport.

Special interest groups are as old as democracy itself, but their struggle for power has become more intense in an economy in which 42 percent of national income flows from the government. The Keynesian notion of flexible budgets tends to become lost, especially as stagflation heats up the competition for government largesse. Added now to the traditional interest groups of farmers, the Chamber of Commerce, the American Medical Association, and the labor unions, are new single-issue groups—environmentalists, consumers, teachers, aged, handicapped, and pro- and anti-abortionists. In the scramble of all these competing interests, there is little room for "fine-tuning" budgets and fiscal policy.

But this new process of econopolitics is reflected most dangerously in a major postwar phenomenon called the political-business cycle. The latter is both bipartisan and international. In years between elections, efforts are made to hold down the money supply and reduce deficits to curb inflation. As elections approach, politicians opt for a quick fix and allow expenditures to go up to help reduce unemployment. Increased federal outlays or across-the-board income tax reductions are used to put dollars in the hands of consumers and stimulate demand. With each successive Presidential campaign, the incumbent in the White House, regardless of party, increasingly resembles a traveling Santa Claus doling out gifts to primary and caucus voters. In 1976, facing a crucial test against Ronald Reagan, President Ford crisscrossed Florida handing out subway grants in Miami, an interstate highway in Tampa, and a veterans' hospital in St. Petersburg. In 1980, President Carter did not even have to leave the White House to play the role of the gift giver. According to CBS News, federal outlays in Maine doubled in January 1980, the month before the caucus, above their level of January 1979.

In his seminal work *The Political Control of the Economy,* Yale's Edward Tufte noted that "two of the biggest mistakes of recent economic policy came about as presidents pursued covert economic policies with concealed priorities.

"A perverse policy replaced economic good sense in both—the cover-up of the cost and postponement of the financing of the Vietnam War from 1965 to 1967 and the all-out stimulation of the economy for the 1972 re-election campaign."

In both cases, noted Tufte, voter myopia cannot be blamed. "There was, in fact, deliberate concealment of the economic agenda by the White House," he observed.

The Johnson economic policy cover-ups were not directly tied to an election-year cycle, but rather were part of the larger cover-up of the growing war effort. But the Administration waited until after the 1966 congressional elections, which produced huge losses for the Democrats, to introduce the surtax to help pay some of the war bills.

But the economic expansion preceding the 1972 election represented the classic case of political-economic stimulation. Many were surprised that Nixon was taking an expansionary route, but they should not have been. His course of action was clearly anticipated in his own memoirs, *Six Crises*. Describing his 1960 election loss to Kennedy, Nixon, in large measure, blamed it on President Eisenhower's refusal to prime the pump before the balloting. Nixon recalled the Eisenhower cabinet's refusal to accept the prognosis or the suggestions of economic advisor Arthur Burns that a recession was coming, that it would hit in October right before the election, and that stimulation was required.

"The bottom of the 1960 dip did come in October, and the economy started to move up in November—after it was too late to affect the election returns," Nixon wrote. And all the speeches, television broadcasts, and precinct work could not "counteract that one hard fact," he concluded.

And while Nixon may have been acting in 1971 and 1972 in response to his bitter lessons of 1960, his pump-priming policies were hardly unprecedented. As Tufte's statistics show, between 1946 and 1976 the "median rate of growth in real disposable per capita income was 3.3 percent in years when the incumbent sought re-election compared to 1.7 percent in all other years."

One quick way to achieve this is to increase Social Security and veterans' benefits. In 1972, Nixon was only slightly more obvious about it, having the Social Security Administration send out letters with the 20 percent increases, reminding recipients the extra money was enacted by Congress and "signed into law by President Richard Nixon." As Tufte points out, nine of the thirteen Social Security increases voted by Congress since 1950 have come in election years. The increased benefits usually arrive in November; the increased payroll taxes follow in January. And veterans' benefits increased by an average $660 million in election years and only $220 million in off years.

As was true in numerous Nixonian endeavors, the excesses of his economic policies were not as much in kind as in degree. The Social Security splurge was so big—$8 billion—that Congress later rescinded that gift-giving power by indexing Social Security to inflation with the increases to take place in June. And Nixon's pump-priming also coincided with the imposition of wage-price controls—through the election year. In other words, he turned on the heat under the pot and at the same time bolted on the lid.

What really turned out to be new about Nixon's economics

was their post-election severity. Controls were lifted and inflation boiled over. There was already a bonfire raging when OPEC poured on more fuel at the end of 1973. And the Nixon Administration, then fighting for its survival at Watergate, was the first to be confronted by that perverse phenomenon of the stagflation decade: despite the presence of rising demand, investors refused to invest in expanding supply—with the upshot being even more inflation. In a post-market economy the classical laws of short-run market adjustments had not responded.

Investor uncertainty about more inflation is further reinforced as prices and wages begin to rise in the conglomerate and unionized sectors. These set in motion still other "cost-push" inflationary precedents, such as the need to raise legal minimum wages, for less concentrated sectors. Insufficient investment also means insufficient supply expansion in energy and other sectors, thereby adding a "demand-pull" rise in prices. The vicious circle of the quick-fix stimulation entails a tremendous cost: it worsens the fundamental causes of inflation.

In the early 1970s the convergence of the political-business cycles among industrial democracies brought disastrous results as several major nations all geared up for elections. The entire industrial world was already suffering from the lingering consequences of Vietnam deficits. They all began to increase spending at about the same time. By 1973 the economies of all the industrial nations were experiencing accelerated inflation. The confluence of events was described in an OECD report as "the most important mishap in recent economic policy history."

But the work of Tufte indicates there was more involved than a mishap or a random "anomaly," as mainstream economists are fond of calling it. In fact, a pattern, with consequences still not entirely understood, is developing.

Like the United States, other industrial democracies have indulged in their own political-business cycles. But until 1971, their elections more frequently (thirteen of twenty-two) took place in odd-numbered years, while those of the United States took place in even-numbered years. The result was that the cycles of the U.S. and Western Europe tended "automatically" to offset and restrain each other: foreign politically inspired economic expansion helped limit off-election year doldrums of the U.S. economy, and vice versa. But between 1971 and 1976, eleven of the twelve elections in Canada, France, Italy, West Germany, Japan, and Britain took place in even-numbered years.

"With the synchronization of electoral calendars in large capitalist democracies," concluded Tufte, "we have a recipe for an international boom-and-bust cycle."

V

Equally critical in the government's diminished ability to "fine-tune" the economy is the transformation of the classical competitive marketplace. The old marketplace has been supplanted by a combination of political and economic forces. A dual economy has emerged in the United States in which some 800 U.S. multinational conglomerates now account for 70 percent of private sector domestic business and some 14 million smaller firms compete for the remaining 30 percent of the domestic business. The present theories of demand economics, still resting fundamentally on the Keynesian vision of the 1930s, have largely ignored these new forces, at their peril.

For more than thirty years economists and politicians have been debating the effects of corporate concentration. Since Berle and Means broke the theoretical ground in their classic study *The Modern Corporation and Private Property,* the debate over what they called administered prices has waxed and waned. Only briefly in the 1950s and, more recently and more intensely, in the 1970s did the debate begin to focus more on the question of whether concentration and administered prices contribute to persistent inflation and instability.

At one extreme are the unabashed conservatives of the University of Chicago, such as George Stigler, who maintain that such oligopoly industries as steel set prices in the same competitive manner as the local machine shop. Most conventional economists and most Washington policy-makers recognize the existence of oligopoly pricing but assert that there is price competition among the oligopolies. For instance, J. Fred Weston of the University of California argues that the growing presence of foreign multinationals has rejuvenated the price competitiveness of the U.S.

multinationals even in concentrated sectors of the American economy.

This contention is valid to a point. The crucial issue is whether the post-market economy has frustrated classical demand management of inflation by creating a form of "aggregate" price rigidity that prevents the general price level from going down even in the face of falling demand. Prices eventually do respond downward to precipitately falling demand, but by the time they do, the horses are already out of the barn—plants are closed, jobs are lost, and the recession is well underway. In the 1970s, prices fell so slowly in response to falling demand that governments had to induce deep recessions to cool the inflationary fevers of their economies.

The behavior and timing of price changes in the post-market economy have been crucially affected by four things: administered prices in the concentrated industries, such as steel or automobiles; the spread of administered prices to unconcentrated industries, such as food retailing, as multinational conglomerates buy companies in these industries; the effect of nonmarket transactions by governments and between subsidiaries of multinationals; and the impact of government as a buyer and seller in the marketplace. Individually, these factors could not account for the slow response of prices to changes in demand in the past decade. But the cumulative and synergistic effect of all four has been a thwarting of Keynesian policy by a post-market economy. An analysis of this synergism must begin with each factor.

Competition among the oligopolies of concentrated industries was characterized as the "herd effect" by Peter Gabriel, former dean of Boston University's School of Management. They all must administer prices because they have similar problems and advantages. Their flexibility is limited by the very bigness of their projects and sales and by the long lead time required to put their products on the market. They all face similar wage demands.

The modern "megacorp," as post-Keynesian theorist Alfred Eichner described it, "sets a price, then produces whatever quantity the market will take." But while such corporations may dominate an industry, they have little independence. If one were to lower its prices, the others would follow and none would gain. If one raised its prices ahead of the others, its share of the market would fall dramatically. Market shares thus change because of breakthroughs in advertising, marketing, and product innovation, not because of what one of the founding fathers of a modern corporation once called "ruinous price competition." Administered pricing is a logical outcome of a post-market economy.

Various studies have shown that where a few oligopoly firms dominate an industry, they can ignore supply and demand conditions for as long as six months or more. Price levels persist in the absence of competition; buyers have nowhere else to go. For example, the big four U.S. auto companies together controlled more than 75 percent of the American market in 1974. During the steep recession that began that year, they steadily increased their prices even though sales demand dropped precipitately and hundreds of thousands of potential car buyers began having second thoughts about purchasing a Detroit gas-guzzler. Only by early 1975, when unemployment and excess capacity in the auto industry exceeded 20 percent, did the American companies react in the classical manner, lowering prices through the gimmick of highly advertised rebates. By then, however, the inflationary damage had already been done. Prices had reached new high levels at a time of deep recession and came down only temporarily, basically because the industry wanted to be rid of excess inventory.

The entry of foreign competition has not really affected the price behavior of the U.S. multinationals in general and the auto industry in particular. The most recent success of foreign cars in the U.S. market was due to their design and fuel efficiency rather than their prices. Volkswagen and Toyota pursue oligopoly pricing, as do Ford and GM. In the summer of 1978, the slide of the dollar and the sharp appreciation of the mark and the yen forced up the U.S. selling price of popular German and Japanese cars. The American companies, instead of capitalizing on this price advantage, raised their own prices. Their belated production of competitive fuel-efficient cars has been more a response to pressure from Washington than to pressure from the marketplace.

Even Harvard Professor Raymond Vernon, an authority on the multinationals, has noted this lack of competitive response. Commenting on a "painstaking study of the world tractor industry," Vernon observed that "even with the appearance of new entrants, the leaders have managed to retain their share of the market and to resist the pressure on prices by skillfully using product differentiation and distribution structures as their mechanism." Kenneth Boulding identified the same phenomenon in the steel industry. "A fall in the demand for steel and consequently surplus stocks of steel," he said, "may not result in falling prices at all." It appears easier for steel companies to lay off workers or to reduce production than to lower prices in the face of falling demand.

The price impact of concentration is felt not only in the concentrated industries. The giant corporations, in the two waves of conglomerate-spread in the late 1960s and mid-1970s, have been buying into unconcentrated industries. According to a pathbreaking study for the Joint Economic Committee of Congress by Professors Peter Adelsheim and Howard Wachtel, administered pricing has spread to various previously unconcentrated industries.

When a multinational moves into an unconcentrated industry, say the ITT purchase of the National Baking Company and Wonder Bread, it brings to that industry all its accounting, advertising, and managerial expertise. By official government statistical measure, the bread industry remains unconcentrated. Yet the corporate giant has existing financial and advertising power to discourage new competitors from entering the field as they normally would in such a high-turnover unconcentrated business. As economist Corwin Edwards put it, "the big company can outbid, outspend, or outlose the small one." Clorox, for example, was the leading firm in the bleach industry. But after Procter & Gamble acquired it in 1957, smaller competitors became, according to a Supreme Court decision, "more cautious in competing due to their fear of retaliation by Procter." Similarly, after Philip Morris took over Miller Brewing Company, its share of the beer market went from 5 percent to 18 percent in nine years. "Dozens of small brewers," observed an *Economist* writer, "unable to keep up with the giants' advertising expenditures in the transformed market have gone to the wall."

When prices and the business cycle move up or down together, this means prices are flexible and competitive. But when prices keep going up, regardless of the state of the economy, this signals price rigidity, the opposite of classical market behavior.

In 1950 only 40 percent of the U.S. manufacturing sector showed rigid prices in the face of falling demand. By 1974, after two intensive rounds of conglomerate mergers, the estimated figure had risen to more than 70 percent, even though many of the industries in that sector were still officially labeled unconcentrated. As Adelsheim and Wachtel found, oligopoly companies during the 1960s "went fishing in the low concentration sectors, acquired firms and created conglomerates." They wrote that the process of evolving mature oligopolies out of infant ones was just beginning and asserted that the trend "can account for the type of price mark-up behavior we witnessed in the most recent recessions in the sectors of low and medium concentration."

The third and most important measurement of post-market pricing by the private sector is "transfer pricing." That is, literally, nonmarket pricing. The term is used by the Internal Revenue Service to cover transactions between subsidiaries owned by the same parent corporation. More than 70 percent of total U.S. exports and more than 50 percent of imports are "intra-firm subsidiary transfers" between subsidiaries of U.S. and foreign multinationals. These transfers are made for a variety of legal and, in most cases, legitimate business reasons—to take advantage of or to protect against rapid changes in foreign exchange valuations; to use offshore tax havens; and to "cross-subsidize" an overseas subsidiary entering a new country and trying to rapidly gain a large market share.

The transfer price attached by a multinational to such an export or import has little or no relation to classical marketplace laws of supply and demand. Numerous nonmarket considerations can determine the price that conglomerates attach to transfers between subsidiaries, whether across national boundaries or across industries in the same country. Conglomerates transfer not only products but services and intangibles such as personnel, advertising, and finance. Such a corporation is very likely to "cross-subsidize" a new subsidiary in order to expand the subsidiary's share of the market.

Finally, local, state, and national governments, as buyers and sellers in the economy, also contribute to price rigidity. Governments are increasingly buying products and services on the basis of long-term cost-plus contracts with single suppliers. The practice was begun by the Pentagon in purchasing billions of dollars' worth of ships, aircraft, and missiles. The practice has now extended to civilian agencies, and to state and local governments as they buy $5 billion subway systems, for example.

Alone, any of these post-market forces might not have enough effect to thwart Keynesian demand management. But taken together, they have a cumulative and reinforcing effect on inflation, making the price system more rigid and pushing prices in an upward direction when they should be falling. Thus the second basic assumption of Keynesian policy, flexible prices through competitive markets, no longer holds except sporadically, and usually only during periods of prolonged and high unemployment.

Corporate concentration, however, is a fact of life in the post-market global economy, in the U.S. and around the world. As we will see in later chapters, it is not at all clear whether new U.S. policy can, and to what degree it should, mount an all-out attack to reduce the size of our conglomerates. Returning wholesale to the American populist tradition of trust-busting is hardly possible in an interdependent global economy in which other nations will not do the same. Traditional notions of corporate reform will have to give way to new ones. And the task of policy for restoring the price stability of the overall economy will have to be adapting new tools of both aggregate demand management and a new supply economics.

VI

Similarly, global interdependence and post-market forces are eroding the effectiveness of tax and credit policies for "fine-tuning" the economy. The last decade saw a shift of the tax burden away from corporations and toward individuals. Government revenue has grown to meet rapidly rising expenditures (minus the deficits) only because inflation has bequeathed higher salaries and higher tax brackets.

Between 1958 and 1973, corporate income remained a relatively constant proportion of national income in the United States. But during this heyday of global expansion and mergers into conglomerates, corporate taxes (not including Social Security payments) fell sharply as a percentage of total federal revenues—from 25.2 percent to 15 percent. At the same time, the proportion of federal revenues coming from personal income taxes rose by 12 percent, a substantial shift of the tax burden from the large to the small.

The disparity is true even among the corporations. Smaller companies paid an average 44 percent tax rate in the late 1960s and 1970s. The big corporations paid a 24.9 percent rate in the same period. And the more a corporation spreads around the world, becoming a multinational, the lower its tax burden can become. Numerous devices, all clearly within the law, give the multinationals tax breaks that are not available to others. Among them are foreign tax credits and the use of offshore tax havens. These advantages are reinforced by the inability of the government to effectively monitor and calculate actual profits on billions of transfer-pricing transactions on exports and imports with overseas subsidiaries of multinationals.

In the light of such inequality, the traditional attempt to build equality into the tax laws is perverse. A corner drugstore has stayed the same in the eyes of the law as the Pfizer Corporation, a small town bank the same as Citicorp or Bank of America. Unequal players in the economic game are formally treated as equals. The result is a widening of inequality and an increase of instability.

The continuing existence of these inequalities, even as they contribute to a growing tax revolt, is an indication of how government's sovereign powers are being eroded in a globally interdependent post-market economy. Corporate tax reform, for all its campaign-year appeal, runs the serious risk of imposing a unilateral disadvantage on U.S. firms competing against foreign multinationals for exports and markets. The first result of a tax reform on U.S. multinationals—at least without harmonized tax rates and laws among all industrial nations—could be a loss of American exports and a further drain on the U.S. balance of payments and trade, which would only serve to weaken the dollar further.

But it is at the heart of the third assumption underlying demand management policy—the ability of government to control the domestic money supply and credit—where the forces of the post-market global economy have inflicted the most damage. The impotence of monetary policy, the nation's most often used "big gun" to fight inflation, has come about because of dramatic postwar changes in domestic and offshore finance.

Starting in the late 1960s, the government's conventional monetary tools came into direct conflict with the new realities of the Eurocurrency market. The activities of this market were once described by Princeton's Fritz Macklup as "the mystery story." It is a story of three parts—the government's efforts to control inflation, which is taken up here, and parts two and three, the stability of the dollar and the international banking system, to be covered in subsequent chapters.

By 1980, the Eurocurrency market had become a trillion-dollar pool of unregulated "stateless money," as *Business Week* called it, "run by a few dozen giant banks that now operate in every corner of the globe." Their depositors are primarily multinational corporations and OPEC petrodollar holders, their loan clients, other corporations, and governments. In 1978 the *Business Week* survey concluded, "this stateless financial system that is a blessing to business may in the end turn out to be a peril for the world at large."

How the globalization of finance crippled national monetary tools was first demonstrated in a 1968–69 anti-inflation attempt by the U.S. Government. In 1968 the Federal Reserve tried to take some of the steam out of an economy overheated by Vietnam War deficits. It implemented a standard anti-inflationary measure, lowering interest rates on private certificates of deposit. The hope was that CD holders would cash them in and put their money in higher-yield Treasury bills. The Fed would then be able to hold these monies and restrict new credit expansion from adding to inflationary pressures. It was a tried-and-true measure that had often been used in the past.

But in 1968 and 1969 the money from CDs did not go into Treasury bills. Instead, investors pulled their money out of CDs and placed it in the higher-yielding Eurocurrency market. Via instantaneous electronic transfer, the money was borrowed from the foreign branch offices of U.S. banks by their parent banks in New York and then lent to prime corporate borrowers who could afford to pay the higher interest rates. The Fed had lost control of the money supply and its ability to restrict new funds from being loaned to corporate borrowers.

Before the advent of Eurobanking, domestic money often had been drawn offshore by higher interest rates. But the amount of overseas money, seventeen times greater now than in 1968, and the speed of the electronic transfers, are wholly unprecedented. What were once minor and regular flows have become unpredictable tidal waves of global money, quite beyond the control or surveillance of any government. Thus a principal defense against inflation—control of credit and the money supply—has sprung huge leaks. And the leaks are growing larger as the Eurocurrency market expands toward the trillion-dollar point. In 1979, Federal Reserve Chairman G. William Miller admitted, "One of the Fed's big problems is the alternate sources of money and credit which come into our own economy."

More to the point, and with rare candor, a Swiss banker observed, "Our political forces are a bit obsolete and old-fashioned for today's financial world." Dr. Hans Mast of Crédit Suisse added, "The Eurodollar market is a child of modern communications. But it has grown so fast because of two reasons: the increasing speed of information transfer, and the need to work around many national rules that don't recognize the demands of world trade."

The Eurodollar currency pool has wrought havoc on a rational price system's ability to adjust supply and demand. Higher interest rates to fight inflation have not led to contractions of domestic credit and business expansion. Instead, exactly the opposite has occurred. The ease of unregulated Euroborrowing by multinational banks and corporations "is similar to that encountered by consumers in the United States," noted Washington *Post* financial writer Larry Kramer. It is "the largest banks and multinational companies in the world who are juggling the billion dollar Euromarkets the way the average citizen shifts funds between his or her bank accounts." The result, concluded Kramer's international survey of expert opinion, is "an almost helpless interdependence. No single country now has the power or the funding to stop the kind of rampant inflation that could occur because of the huge amount of money around the globe."

It is, however, only the big banks and corporations that have been able to exploit the more costly but available offshore credit. The companies forced to slow their growth and expansion are the smaller, more numerous, and more competitive firms that were less able to pass on higher costs directly to buyers. The same phenomenon takes place in banking, widening the gap between big and small operators. During the credit contractions, global banks managed to grab a larger share of the available credit through their access to the Eurocurrency market and through their foreign branches. The market share for the smaller U.S. banks has been increasingly eroded and the process of concentration accelerated.

The Wall Street Journal quoted a Federal Reserve official who remarked, "This avenue of extra competitiveness and profit isn't open to the great majority of U.S. banks that don't have branches in London or in other financial centers." As one official told the *Journal,* "it's a problem of equity."

The classical policies end up as "dual" policies with perverse outcomes for the "dual economy." For at least the 70 percent of the economy controlled by the giant corporations and banks, the Fed's "anti-inflation" measures led in the last decade to short-run credit and demand expansion when their aim was the opposite. The remaining 30 percent, the thousands of small businesses and banks, do end up following the dictates of classical competitive markets. They do reduce their lending and investment plans when credit becomes scarce. As one Fed official acknowledged, the effect is to "press down harder" on the smaller banks as the Fed loses control over the money available to the big ones. In short, the post-market global economy forces thousands of smaller firms to subsidize the profits of the few big ones.

The 1968–69 experience and its numerous repetitions in the 1970s dramatized the shrinkage of competitive markets and the emergence of the post-market global economy. The multinational banks loan their offshore money to their favorite customers—the multinational corporations. (By the early 1970s, nine New York global banks, including Chase Manhattan, Citicorp, and Morgan Guaranty, held 90 percent of the debt of the U.S. petroleum and gas industry, 75 percent of the chemical and rubber industries', and 66 percent of the machinery and metal products industries'.) The oligopoly-conglomerate borrowers do not need to worry excessively about the higher costs of borrowed offshore money: they can pass the costs along to their customers.

This phenomenon was fully documented by 1971. The cure, however, was far more than the system could absorb politically. Economist George Budzeika, in his pioneering study, reached the conclusion that "the only way to restrain [big banks] efficiently is to reduce the overall liquidity of the banking system." But such radical surgery would have forced politically unacceptable levels of unemployment. The political reality, the compromise, has been the pursuit of moderate monetary policies; the result, to kill or seriously injure many of the patients, the smaller firms, and thereby increase concentration without doing much to cure the disease of inflation. Concentration, which initially weakened monetary policy, is intensified by globalization, which, in turn, brings more concentration and further emasculates anti-inflation weapons. The clash between a post-market global economy and conventional management tools of government has produced a classic vicious circle of policy erosion once known only in Third World countries.

Guido Carli, former governor of the Bank of Italy, has tried to emphasize the need to regulate Eurobanking: "I believe that we have reached a point which necessitates that a worldwide action be taken." By 1976, Carli's proposals were supported in public by West German Chancellor Helmut Schmidt.

But no other nation can afford to take action unless the United States exercises leadership and offers support for a harmonized international approach. America's failure to push for permanent multilateral reform has deprived the industrial world of perhaps its most important policy tool for controlling inflation.

In fact, it took a second collapse of the dollar and an international rush to gold in late 1979 before the U.S. instituted any measures to curb the flow of Eurodollars into the American domestic banking system. With inflation at 13 percent and with gold breaking what was then the historic $400-per-ounce barrier, the Fed finally imposed a stiff but temporary reserve requirement for American banks on Eurodollar borrowings. Yet this was not part of a concerted multilateral program to control the Eurodollar market permanently, but a one-time unilateral move to restrict domestic credit and the U.S. money supply.

In 1979 a *Wall Street Journal* report from the Middle West noted how the Fed's efforts to restrict monetary growth had promoted a redistribution of financial power to the rich. "Tight money is here," the *Journal* reporter wrote, "not in New York or the other big financial centers. But here in Western Illinois and in many small towns across the country, the Federal Reserve's gradual credit squeeze is finally starting to be felt. Washington's inflation fighters may be pleased, but folks out in the hinterlands aren't."

This perverse "anomaly" of the post-market economy is also the result of domestic credit innovations that are reinforcing the globally induced negative effects of unregulated Eurobanking. Big companies, in contrast to small business, have now refined the art of borrowing from one another as a further means for sidestepping contractions in bank credit. Commercial banks are still the primary source of corporate borrowing, in 1978 to the tune of $141 billion. But corporate financial managers, with their computerized information flows, have learned how to borrow from one another, particularly when bank credit is contracting. At any given time, one large corporation is likely to have excess cash and another to be in urgent need of money. Their device for passing the money around is the commercial paper market. In 1978, borrowing through the commercial paper market reached $88 billion.

Other recent conglomerate innovations in domestic banking have further eroded the Federal Reserve's ability to control money and credit and helped to fuel the 1978–79 round of double-digit inflation. Invading the banking business have been such companies as Sears Roebuck, American Express, and some brokerage firms. They offer many banking services, especially credit. Unlike regular banks, they can operate across state lines and are not subject to many state and federal regulations. While interest rates have been going up to record levels, these so-called near banks keep churning out money to keep the consumer boom alive. Despite record interest rates, by 1979 consumer debt reached record levels, and debt service averaged more than one quarter of disposable income. The creation of near banks, new savings and loan certificates, and other changes in banking and bank regulation have "allowed lenders to flood consumers with easy money," commented *Business Week,* adding what had become all too obvious: " . . . inflation has become institutionalized and the ability of the Federal Reserve to manage the money supply has been impaired."

Inflation is thus being force-fed not only by global but also domestic transformations in finance and attitudes toward credit. Yet the Federal Reserve professes to raise interest rates to protect the dollar and to show both foreigners and residents that we are serious about holding down inflation.

It has taken nearly a decade for policy makers and mainstream economists to admit that these various episodes have been more than "transitory anomalies." In 1978 outgoing Fed Chairman Arthur Burns warned a congressional committee that the economy could no longer be explained by the conventional laws of economics. His successor, G. William Miller, when asked why monetary policy was taking so long to work, responded: "Monetary policy is certainly more difficult." According to *The Wall Street Journal,* a Fed official who was asked why interest rates could not be raised faster, replied, "We're afraid to."

If candid admissions were heartening, they still brought no new policy breakthroughs. Having failed to act on the many proposals for an incomes policy and for domestic and global financial reform (summarized in later chapters), the spring of 1980 saw both inflation and bank lending rates approaching the 20 percent mark. These opportunities lost, the only thing left the demand management fraternity was the overkill of credit controls—even at the risk of triggering an economic bust into a steep and prolonged recession.

VII

In 1970, as the stagflation decade was beginning, Yale economist Carlos Díaz Alejandro surveyed the political and economic trends in the United States—from campus riots to regional stagnation—and coined the phrase "Latin Americanization of the United States." As the decade wore on, the concept turned out to be far more powerful than Díaz Alejandro or others who had picked up the phrase imagined.

In 1968 economist Robert Averitt had anticipated this theme but in slightly different terms. In his widely used textbook *The Dual Economy,* Averitt described the coincidence of corporate concentration and regional imbalances in the United States. He was taking up a favorite theme of development economics, pioneered by scholars in the industrial world and the Third World. This branch of economics was designed to deal with reconstruction tasks after World War II and refined to deal with the underdevelopment problems of the southern part of the globe. In the United States, development economics has been applied sporadically, and with mixed results, to the problems of urban blight and regional stagnation in such places as Appalachia.

The decade of the 1970s magnified the most glaring similarity between the U.S. economy and the economies of the Third World—the persistence of stagflation. Stagflation brings other similarities into clearer focus—frequent balance-of-payments crises, energy shortages, a declining currency, uneven regional development, productivity problems, inadequate capital formation, government aid to inefficient industry, and profound changes in attitudes as consumers borrow more and save less in a frenzied race to stay abreast of what they now believe is institutionalized inflation.

Neglect of this correspondence by many conventional economists helps explain why their most recent forecasts have been so wide of the mark. Their models anticipated certain results from certain actions: for example, a near unanimity existed that President Carter's emergency measures of November 1978 to stem the slide of the dollar would accelerate the economy into a recession. What happened instead was a further heating-up of inflation. Less than a year later, the dollar had plummeted again. To shore it up, another record-breaking interest rate hike was imposed, accompanied by new, but again incorrect, predictions of a heavy recession.

What went wrong? Nothing—except that times had changed and the models had not. U.S. corporations and middle- and upper-income consumers, after a decade of stagflation, had learned how to adjust, or so they hoped. Their reactions bore a striking resemblance to the reactions of the middle and upper classes in the cosmopolitan centers of Latin America after a decade of stagflation in the late 1950s. A New York shopper in April 1979, at a sale of winter clothes, was overheard saying, "I'm going to buy as much as I possibly can now. Who knows if next year I'll be able to afford anything." (How often had I heard the same comment in Bogotá, Buenos Aires, or Rio!)

Consumers, anticipating further inflation, gobble up more goods and services and usually plunge deeper into debt to do so. Oligopoly conglomerates follow the consumers with further price increases. In fact, they use what has become time-honored behavior in passing on to consumers increased costs, from higher interest rates to higher union wages. Corporations, like consumers, begin stockpiling commodities to avoid anticipated higher prices in the future.

As in Latin America, although not in quite the same fashion, more wages and pensions are being indexed to inflation, with the result of making the short-run costs of inflation less painful, but complicating the search for a long-run cure. Social Security is officially indexed to inflation. Congress has reduced federal income tax rates as inflation pulls more people into higher brackets. As *Business Week* noted, those two adjustments, especially in the upper-middle-income class, allow real income to keep pace with inflation. By 1978 more than 60 percent of the workers covered by large union contracts had automatic cost-of-living adjustments. And as we have already seen, corporations have learned how to sidestep credit restrictions through commercial paper, Eurobanking loans, and such new exotica as "financial instrument futures." They move with such speed and innovation that banking authorities are left breathlessly behind.

VIII

In August 1979, Washington *Post* economics writer Art Pine noted that the latest round of recession forecasts had been made by mainstream economists for two years. "They've been predicting the downturn for so long it had to come true eventually." And he, like others, recalled what had become the stagflation decade's most popular joke about a demand management fraternity in disarray: "Lay all the economists end to end around the world and you still won't reach a conclusion."

The limitations of demand management in a post-market global economy have perpetuated throughout the stagflation decade what is in fact a shallow debate between the two warring camps of mainstream demand economics.*

* Professor Robert Lekachman wrote of his profession: "Minor adjustments in tax, monetary, and spending policy, practically the entire content of the New Economics (Keynesian demand economics), are, as recent events ought to prove, incapable of resolving intertwined dilemmas of inflation, unemployment and energy supply." To this description he added, "For mainstream economists to accept 5.5 to 6 percent unemployment as a permanent inflation barrier is to confess intellectual bankruptcy."

For more than a decade an economic debate has been carried on between the conservative "monetarists" who advise Republicans and the liberal "fiscalists" who advise Democrats. The monetarists stress tight credit control and austere government budgets to reduce inflation. They believe the problem is excess demand, that inflation is of the "demand-pull" variety. The fiscalists advocate stimulation to reduce unemployment and wage-price guidelines or controls to curb inflation. For them, the problem is "cost-push" inflation coupled with insufficient demand.

The lines of the old debate were once described by political consultant Michael Rowan, who quipped: "Things would be easier if you could breed a Democrat with fiscal responsibility and a Republican with a heart." In reality, as this and the next chapter show, both arguments have a grain of truth. The failure is one of synthesis. Both sides can dodge blame for the results of the stagflation decade by averring that their policies have not worked because political pressures have prevented their theoretical notions from being enacted in their pure form. But whatever the rationale, the end result has been a one-sided combination of inflation and unemployment, capped by the admission at the decade's closing year that neither side's policies are working anyway.

For all the heralded differences between the fiscalists and monetarists, between the Democrats and the Republicans, both sides have shown an almost total preoccupation with demand economics. In this debate over fine points in what has become an antiquated vision, very little has been done about the supply side of the economy. Major problems afflicting the American economy—especially inadequate energy production, diminishing productivity, the failure of industry to adjust to new competition, and protectionism—are the problems of supply economics and the result of malfunctioning supply forces. These problems have until very recently been lost in the debate over Keynesian demand management, which assumes that, because of automatic adjustments in a competitive market system, the supply side of the economy will take care of itself.

Western European governments, which were forced by the devastation of war to establish national industrial development policies, are hesitantly shifting the emphasis of their policy making from a total reliance on demand management back to renewed interest in supply problems. While memos have circulated at the Commerce and Labor departments proposing a national industrial policy and development agenda, these have long been ignored by the White House. In the Washington economic lineup, the power hitters are not in the Commerce and Labor departments, which are being ignored these days even by their business and labor constituencies. They are in the White House Council of Economic Advisers, the Treasury, the Federal Reserve System, and the Council on Wage and Price Stability, what the late Stewart Alsop labeled "The Center." There, officials remain preoccupied with the problems and failures of demand management, the only tools their agencies have. "They are frustrated and frightened," wrote Richard J. Levine of *The Wall Street Journal,* "and many concede they have run out of answers."

CHAPTER 3

Vicious Circles

I

THE ECONOMY OF THE UNITED STATES is caught in a vicious circle, unable to reverse the decline in capital formation and investment in new factories and equipment. On the path of the circle are the signposts of the post-market world: declining productivity; problems of outdated industries; protectionism; currency and financial instability; and bureaucratic rigidity in government and corporations. The solution to these problems lies in supply and development economics, long ignored in the quest for "fine-tuning" aggregate demand.

Capital formation, measured by the fixed investment in new factories and equipment, is the basic prerequisite to growth. Unless a portion of a nation's output and wealth is devoted to productive investment, economic policies aimed at expanding growth, jobs, and income are doomed to ultimate failure, even if they achieve short-term successes.

The figures for fixed investment in the United States are particularly dismal. Since 1971 the rate of fixed investment in new factories and equipment has been running 30 percent below the annual average of the 1960s. Even that figure is misleadingly optimistic because it includes increased capital formation in food and service industries. In the basic industries, such mainstays of the American economy as steel, electronics, computers, and autos, there has been virtually zero growth in capital formation. And there has been an alarming decline—28 percent between 1960 and

1975—in the crucial component of fixed investment that is actually devoted to constructing new factories and plants.

There are now signs that this trend, too, is catching up with other nations, another indicator that slow American growth can slow down the rest of the world. An OECD report of 1979 showed a downturn in capital investment in Western Europe, Japan, and in the Third World as well. The distance between the United States and its industrial partners is still wide, however. One measure is the percentage of gross national product devoted to investment. Since the mid-1960s the United States has been running 25 percent behind West Germany and 50 percent behind Japan. In the 1970s capital formation was running at less than 10 percent of GNP in the United States. Just to catch up with our industrial partners would require raising that figure to 12 percent (according to the Joint Economic Committee) or 16 percent (according to many private economists).

Capital formation is declining just at the time when many economists are anticipating a need for record rates of investment. The United States needs to overcome the past decade of neglect and to meet new investment demands. This translates roughly into a $600 billion agenda for fixed investment, some to replace aging machinery and buildings, and the rest for new plants and machines and such capital-intensive projects as transportation, energy development, and new water development. Whatever the needs, surveys of business investment decisions show more investment going toward the modernization and purchase of old plants and machinery than toward new plants.

These figures suggest both enormous economic opportunities and political and economic risks for a democratic government. Government's contribution to investment will be limited, especially as long as its budget is locked into social and entitlement programs on the one hand and unproductive military expenditures on the other. Most of the money, if it is to be found at all, will have to come out of private capital markets. The object of government policy will be to draw the money out of its current shelters, to end the blockages and bottlenecks to increased capital formation.

When the American investment needs are added to those of the rest of the industrial world and the Third World, there is a massive demand for capital formation throughout the 1980s. If this capital is not forthcoming, the 1980s will make the 1970s pale as a decade of inflation, unemployment, and slow growth. If this capital does emerge, the 1980s can become what Marshall Loeb of *Time* magazine called "a golden decade."

The other side of the capital formation slump is a worldwide loss of investor confidence. People with money are not placing it in such long-term investments as new plants and new technologies. Stagflation discourages this kind of "productive" investment and encourages investors to put their money into shelters against inflation, either real estate, commercial paper, or exotica ranging from gold coins to art. Investors are not investing, for two reasons: uncertainty about the ability of governments to restore economic stability and, equally important, because they are not receiving a good return on fixed investments.

Between 1970 and 1978 the rate of return on fixed investment in the United States was running 30 percent below the average for the 1950s and 1960s. The same decline is beginning to appear in other industrial nations, even in West Germany.

The quarterly and annual reports of corporate profits are a misleading indicator of return on investment. As dazzling as those nine- and ten-digit numbers sometimes appear, especially in the case of the oil companies after 1973, for most industries there has been a decline in the real corporate rate of return on fixed investment, especially after adjusting for inflation and inventory accumulation. The profitability problem is debilitating productive corporate investment. It has become a major contributor to the capital formation and growth slumps. Corporations, like other investors, have begun putting their money into "nonproductive" investment.

The most common form of nonproductive corporate investment is acquisition of a firm in an unrelated industry. Even President Carter criticized the oil companies for this kind of merger investment and expressed hope that their new profits from decontrol "will not be used to purchase hotels or stocks as they have in the past but will be committed to the needs of ensuring a plentiful supply of oil." Even in their internal investments, corporations are too often buying used equipment rather than new equipment and technology. A steel company, for example, may purchase machinery from a plant closed by a competitor. Whatever the short-run business wisdom of such decisions, they do little to create new plants or new jobs.*

At the peak of the 1960s conglomerate merger movement, the Federal Trade Commission estimated that manufacturing and mining companies were devoting almost 60 percent of new investments to corporate acquisitions. Since late 1973 a second conglomerate merger movement has been accelerating in the same direction.

Clearly, stagflation and the loss of investor confidence feed each other. Businessmen hate uncertainty, especially when they think government is contributing to it. The single-minded reliance on "fine-tuning" of demand management during a decade of stagflation has brought swings between expansionary policies to promote employment and deflationary policies to curb inflation. The response of investors has been a justified and growing lack of confidence in the ability of government to do either.

II

The transformation of the global economy has contributed both to problems of supply and to missed opportunities for capital formation and investment. The Western industrial nations saw billions of dollars drained away to the OPEC nations after the 1973–74 price hikes. But these accumulations of petrodollars could have been returned as investment capital had not the oil nations, like private investors in the West, also suffered a loss of confidence. Between 1974 and 1977, according to some studies, OPEC nations placed less than 35 percent of their 170 billion petrodollar surpluses into fixed investments anywhere in the world. But for OPEC there were political as well as economic reasons for this hedging of bets.

Even prior to the U.S.–Iran confrontation, the oil countries worried about the potential seizure of their foreign assets by industrial nations desperate to regain bargaining leverage over energy prices. Their way of reducing this threat and giving themselves counterleverage has been to place their money in the Eurocurrency system. The OPEC nations have been equally hesitant to invest in

* Federal tax policy implicitly encourages this diversion of investment capital. It makes no distinction between "productive" investment and acquisition investment.

the developing nations, and this is largely because the industrial nations have failed so far to offer the right inducements, such as more voting power in the World Bank and the International Monetary Fund.

The problem of oil is symbolic of the problem of escalating commodity prices in general, which cut into profits, raise costs, and contribute to inflation and decreasing productivity. To some extent, these higher prices have been induced by resource producer cartels. They are also part of a historic pattern, ignored by many conventional economists. The Kondratief cycle is a well-established pattern of forty-to-fifty-year cycles in the prices of raw materials. Walt Rostow, in his book *Getting from Here to There,* dates the current Kondratief upswing from 1972. Some of the initial price explosions were temporarily capped by the 1974–75 recession, but the outlook is for fifteen more years of rising prices and shortages in food, water, metals, and energy.

At first glance, this prospect poses the likelihood of fifteen more years of inflation, declining investment, and declining productivity. But the causes of the current productivity and investment slumps go beyond just changes in raw material prices and the questionable notion that a bloated government financing its deficits in the capital markets is largely responsible for draining off investment money. There are other causes for the productivity slump: declining investment, declining technological innovation and research and development, new government regulations, crime, and changes in the work force and attitudes toward work. Whatever the causes, the statistics are dismal. Between 1948 and 1965, the conventional measure of productivity growth in the United States averaged 3.2 percent. From 1965 to 1973 it fell to an average of 1.3 percent. From 1973 to 1978 it dropped to below one percent. In 1979 productivity barely grew at all. This current slump is worse than the one that occurred during the Depression. In the industrial world only Britain, which some feel has gone a long way toward abandoning both work and investing, had a lower productivity growth rate.

The American phenomenon, moreover, is beginning to spread. Productivity growth rates throughout the world have dropped dramatically since 1973. Set against the productivity growth rates of 1964 to 1973, Japan's rate fell by 63 percent, West

Germany's by 32 percent, France's by 33 percent, Canada's by 75 percent, and Italy's by 80 percent. Even so, the United States remained the loss leader at 94 percent. Commenting on these figures, a 1979 OECD report asserted that the slowdown could not be explained solely by the 1974–75 recession and that other factors must have been involved.

The effect of post-market forces on productivity is most evident in shrinking research and development and technological innovation. The classical prescription for a company suffering declining productivity and profits is to increase research and development. Since World War II, oligopoly companies have often put off making the sometimes risky investments needed to increase productivity. Instead, they have tried to create new market demand by going overseas, creating subsidiaries, and often licensing their technology to foreign firms.

Frederick Knickerbocker, a deputy assistant secretary of Commerce and former Harvard Business School professor, drew the link between the global spread of companies and declining productivity. Knickerbocker's thesis, now widely accepted, is that U.S. multinationals can delay technological innovation by extending the profitable life of their existing production know-how when they transfer technology abroad and introduce old products to new customers. Until the early 1960s this transfer was confined to Western Europe and Japan. Since then it has spread to the Third World.

There were other devices whereby the multinationals put off the day of reckoning for new technology investment. A favorite one, perfected by the mid-1960s, was to increase profitability by buying up other corporations rather than by reinvesting profits in the existing corporation. The conglomerate trend was profitable for the companies involved but, like new investment overseas, did little to create new plants, new technologies, and new jobs. In our judgment, it is no coincidence that the downturn in American civilian research and development and technological innovation occurred at the same time American corporations were spreading overseas and becoming ever larger conglomerates.

This spread and growth also coincided with another phenomenon—a significant decrease since the late 1960s in scientific and technological breakthroughs in such key areas as metallurgy, non-fossil fuel, chemicals, and many forms of electronics other than miniaturization. There are a variety of causes, as documented by Edward Renshaw in his book *The End of Progress*, including the pattern in scientific history of pauses in the theoretical advancements behind new technology; the late-1960s drop in military and space research; and the Nixon Administration's deep cuts in basic research, which are only now being slowly reversed.

Michael Boretsky, the Commerce Department's technology expert, was among the first to sound the alarm. His figures show how dramatically and dangerously this slide has occurred. There are two measurements, the first being research and development expenditures as a percentage of GNP. Since the mid-1960s the U.S. figure has been 80 percent of that for the Common Market and Japan. A more important indicator is the measure of R&D dollar expended per professional employee. The U.S. rate is only 35 percent of Japan's, and some 30 percent smaller than the European nations'.

The trend in the 1970s, says Boretsky, was more alarming. "Growth in total U.S. civilian [-financed] equivalent industrial R&D in that period might, therefore, be assumed to have been about zero."

Another measure of American product and technology innovation is the number of new patents issued and applications received in the U.S. from Americans and foreigners. Compared with 1961 figures, foreigners had more than doubled their innovation efforts by the early 1970s.

This slowdown has been coupled with the diffusion of advanced American technology to the rest of the world. Boretsky refers to these "naked transfers" as a major cause of the slowdown in U.S. productivity compared with that of other nations. The transfers include the sale or licensing of patent rights, instructions, blueprints, and other technical assistance that allows the buyer "a quick and full exploitation of the know-how."

Again, this diffusion of technology was accompanied by the spread of U.S. corporations into global multinationals. They are by far the most important U.S. transfer agents. A classic example of the impact of technology transfer is in the electronics industry. The large corporations spread the technology to Japan in the 1950s. Since the 1960s, RCA and Zenith have been haunted by what they helped create, the flood of Japanese electronic imports into this country.

The corporations are now running to Washington for protection against imports, just as they successfully ran to Congress a decade ago for the tax breaks that made it cheaper for them to export technology rather than to invest in new technology at home. Some of the tax breaks have since been curtailed, but the process of technology transfer continues almost unabated. The buyers are no longer Europeans and Japanese, who instead have become competing sellers with the Americans in the race for Third World markets. The big customers are now, more often than not, the state-owned enterprises of the Third World. And it does no good for Congress to try to lock the barn door after the bolting horse, as some have suggested. The only result of new tax laws to discourage technology transfer would be the loss of U.S. business and trade to European and Japanese competitors in the growing and important Third World market.

Bigness and bureaucracy are two other important factors behind the dismal figures on technological innovation. Long ago, the German sociologist Max Weber predicted that controlling bureaucracy would be a major problem in a modern industrialized state. Weber was one of the first to see bureaucracy as a problem both for government and corporations. The effects of bureaucratic rigidity on declining R&D and technology in the large multinationals are now becoming apparent. In a survey for the American Management Association, Louis Sultanoff described how once vital and sacrosanct research budgets have become victims of a form of Parkinson's Law within the large corporations. Managers want stability and not risky research. The incentives for scientists are weakened, and their results are sometimes killed inside the bureaucracy. So-called practical people in line jobs resist innovation and new products.

"Few new products . . . ," the Sultanoff study remarked, "can defeat a combined attack of manufacturing engineers who object to any disruption of production, sales people who do not want another product for their overstuffed catalog, comptrollers who do not like to spend money, and general managers who avoid taking career-periling risks."

The result, according to the Commerce Department, is that

"most genuinely new inventions are generated by small companies and individuals rather than major companies. (Kodachrome, for instance, was not a product of a large Kodak laboratory, but the invention of two laymen.)" As Sultanoff noted, companies prefer to obtain new products through the acquisition of innovative companies or through licensing arrangements. Scientists in research and development in corporations are drawn away from a general and entrepreneurial direction and toward increasingly esoteric technologies. The process feeds on itself as corporate managers, worried primarily about bureaucratic stability, resist new and potentially risky and costly product development. They opt, instead, for acquisitions, which can be made with little risk and, when accomplished through stock transfers, even less cash.

All these add up to an alarming erosion of U.S. technological leadership and a decline of productivity. One example is in the machinery and transportation-equipment industries. The U.S. held a commanding lead through the 1960s. By the early 1970s, before the huge jump in our fuel import costs, we were spending more on imports of machinery and transport equipment than we were for imports of petroleum.

III

The problem of declining investment is compounded by government policy and regulation that diverts investment into socially beneficial but not necessarily "commercially productive" directions. It is impossible to measure the effect of government regulations on productivity, partly because there has not been devised a measurement of the economic benefits of clean air and water and healthy and safe workers. But two studies prepared for the Joint Economic Committee of Congress by economists Michael Evans and Edward Denison estimated that government regulations and the shifts in spending priorities they entailed for corporations accounted for at least one-third of the total drop in productivity since 1968.

First, corporations are simply spending vast new amounts of money that might have gone to other investments in order to comply with federal regulations. Second, a climate of increased regulation adds to investor uncertainty and probably inhibits some risk-taking investment. Finally, environmentalists have used new laws either to block or to delay projects all around the country, ranging from power plants to dams to shopping centers. As Robert Kahn, a Pulitzer Prize–winning environmental correspondent for *The Christian Science Monitor,* wrote in April 1979, the trend may be going too far. The early laws, he wrote, "were enacted in the heat of aroused public concern and were based on insufficient scientific data." One example is the demand of environmentalists to set aside vast new wilderness areas in addition to the millions of acres already allotted. The result is to reduce further the supply of timber, raising the prices of lumber and, therefore, of housing.

There are other causes of the productivity decline, partly social and only partly economic. One of these is crime. Business loses an estimated $2 billion a month in shoplifting and another $5–6 billion in employee pilferage. Shipments have a way of getting lost at the nation's mob-dominated major ports and airports. The problem does not stop near the executive suite. The U.S. Chamber of Commerce estimates $44 billion is lost in white collar crime. In addition, potential investment money, as much as $6 billion per year, is diverted to private security measures. All this, according to the Chamber, adds 15 percent to retail prices.

New attitudes toward life and work are having an unmeasured effect on productivity as well. There are no statistics to buttress what is already known: that more people are more concerned about their life and leisure time than about their job or career. This is coupled with growing demands by some workers for more humanized work, whether on factory lines or in offices.

Two decades of affluence and job security produced an explosion in demand for consumer goods and services. After two decades of improving their level of living to the point where they could buy boats, workers now want more time to use them.

Nixon Administration advisor Herbert Stein sees the change in worker attitudes as part of a more significant social change, reflected in rising divorce rates and new attitudes toward children and families. Management professor James O'Toole of Southern California University sees another ominous trend. He told a gathering of management and business leaders that "short-sighted labor demands are leading American workers towards the 'irresponsible' work ethic of the Italians and British rather than the committed discipline of the Germans and the Japanese."

The attitudes toward work are part of the emergence of the post-industrial society. At the same time, the development of a post-industrial economy turns standard measures of productivity on their heads. In economic history there is a "law of motion" of industrial development. According to this law, based on the studies of British economist Colin Clark, the demand for services grows proportionally larger than the demand for industrial products once an economy reaches a certain level of industrialization. By the year 2000, estimates pollster Louis Harris, 80 percent to 85 percent of the nation's workers will be performing services or selling information rather than making products. The problem now is that the service sector of the economy is expanding rapidly while the industrial sector is barely holding its own or actually contracting.

This change in the economy is reflected in the change in the work force. A service economy is providing more job possibilities for the thousands of women entering or returning to the work force. It also provides jobs at the lower end, at fast-food shops, for example, for the growing number of teenagers looking for work. Or at least white suburban teenagers. A rapidly expanding service economy has not come close to replacing the massive losses of jobs once available to urban minorities in factories and industries that have either shut down, modernized, or moved to the suburbs. Equal employment laws try to square the circle, providing job opportunities for often inexperienced or untrained minorities. All these developments, given the current statistical devices, contribute to the figures that show declining productivity growth.

The vicious circle in productivity meets itself in the phenomenon of a reduction of new additions to the nation's capital stocks. The global economic revolution, as we have seen, has magnified a variety of economic and social problems into a cumulative and serious decline in productivity which further reduces real profits, which leads to a further decline in capital formation. The process comes full circle, after a decade, when the relative reduction in new capital stock due to the investment decline contributes to yet a further downward push on productivity.

As "The 1979 Economic Report of the President" noted, "slower growth in the capital stock . . . could well have reduced productivity growth by up to one-half a percentage point a year from earlier trends."

From the vicious circle of productivity and investment, another, grander vicious circle has emerged. The global economic revolution, characterized by the worldwide spread of government and corporate concentration over the economy, and changes in the work force and work attitudes, has eroded the basic prerequisites of growth on the supply side. When this process takes place, it also wipes out the fundamental conditions that make demand management work. The impact is especially noticeable on prices and inflation. When the supply side of the economy is functioning poorly or not at all, standard measures to stimulate demand end up adding more to inflation. In the last two decades most Keynesian economists have so ignored supply economics in their pursuit of demand management that their policy efforts have been contravened by the development of these new vicious circles. Problems on the supply side have bottled up the workings of classical demand economics and rendered the usual policy tools either ineffectual or actually counterproductive.

IV

Another severe supply problem began to emerge with the mid-1970s recession—the problem of global gluts in such basic products as steel, shipbuilding, textiles, chemicals, and electronics. (The gluts had only a little to do with conventional business cycles and sometimes ran directly against them.) These adjustment failures in production were the outcome of years of corporate global expansion, especially in the Third World, and the drive to industrialization in that part of the world. The emergence of these gluts has turned into yet another monumental example of the impact of post-market behavior by corporations and governments, of supply being fostered and encouraged not by economic demand but by the bureaucratic and political imperatives of corporate managers and state planners. The consequences, however, are suffered by steel and shipyard and textile workers in the industrial world thrown out of their jobs by cheap imports and eventually by consumers who end up paying higher prices as those industries and workers successfully push for protectionist legislation.

In such basic industries as steel and chemicals, technology was standardized and diffused during the 1960s. Every country took the opportunity to create its own industries, sometimes more as a matter of national pride than through economic sense. Other more labor-intensive industries such as shoes and textiles pursued cheap labor markets the way hounds pursue foxes. In the developed nations both sets of industries were subject to declining productivity growth, and the battle for survival soon came to be a battle of productivity.

One example is the $300 billion global chemical industry. Notwithstanding growth rates of almost 10 percent annually in the boom years, forecasters told corporate managers to begin even more expansion projects. And "once underway, they could not be stopped," as one corporate chief noted in an interview. With growth in demand cut in half since 1974, the investments nevertheless continued. Post-market impacts on classical supply and demand adjustments were all too apparent. Many projects were initiated by state enterprises in socialist East Europe. In oil and non-oil Third World nations, private multinationals eagerly offered equipment and contracting services to new state enterprises there. Expansion was lopsided. There was excess capacity of more than 30 percent in Western Europe's core ethylene production, but naphtha was overlooked, and scarcities pushed up plastic prices by 50 percent during 1977 and 1978. "Technology has reached a plateau . . . the men in the white lab coats warn the world not to expect many more miracle products in the coming 10 years," observed an *Economist* survey. "The political era has begun for the chemical industry. The entry of new state-owned producers is the obvious sign," the survey concluded. "The risk of dumping on the one hand and protectionist barriers on the other is growing."

Similar patterns appeared in steel. Multinationals, especially Japanese ones, transferred technology or participated directly with state-owned enterprises in the Third World. In the shoe and textile industries, multinationals and foreign investors brought machinery from the North to operate in the cheap labor markets of the Philippines, South Korea, Taiwan, and other nations of the South.

The developments in these industries were, from the Third World's point of view, a successful application of sophisticated supply economics and planning. As long as there was global economic expansion and as long as the established rules of free trade worked relatively smoothly, the glut or excess capacity was pretty well hidden. A proper working of conventional free trade and market economics should have led to a gradual reduction in production in high-cost countries as more production moved to the cheaper South.

But when jobs and political futures of democratic governments are at stake, conventional economic laws do not stand up very well to the pressure. The post-market combination of the power of multinational companies and Third World governments has drastically altered supply patterns in the world, at historically breathtaking speeds. This development brought a political response—a return of protectionism in the industrial world. In the shoe industry in Europe and the United States, more than 300,000 workers had lost their jobs by 1976 because of imports. There were layoffs in almost equal numbers in the textile and steel industries. Only in the last two years has there been some effort in Europe, and, with the exception of shoes, even less in the United States, to try to modernize these industries and to make them more competitive, either in their productivity or in the product they sell. The instant and easiest response is to call for measures to block Third World imports.

As an OECD report of 1978 commented, "Governments will not watch their industries go under, even though they rationalized their action as only a tactical retreat on the way to liberalization; the danger is that protectionism threatens to freeze the West into ever-descending patterns of growth and higher unemployment." *

Despite all the recent self-congratulation, there is no guarantee, and there will not be for several years, that the new GATT

* This tendency is most notable in the defense industry, and the two results, according to former Deputy Assistant Defense Secretary Jacques Gansler, are growing inefficiency and a weaker national defense. The industry, relying on government contracts, is obviously a post-market creature, but the government often fails to acknowledge this reality. For instance, when defense procurement spending fell in the early 1970s, little was done to help the industry to adjust, to convert to civilian products or to use the interlude to improve productivity. The result, according to Gansler's forthcoming book on the defense industry, was overcapacity, debt, pleas for government help and increased efforts to sell arms abroad. But there was no concerted program for structural adjustment of the industry. Now that defense spending is on the increase to match a continued Soviet arms buildup, the contracts are going to the same firms and are being piled on the same but increasingly less productive industrial base. The result is more money buying less defense.

multilateral trade agreement, signed by twenty-two industrial nations and one developing nation, will reverse this pattern of creeping protectionism. It took considerable statesmanship and courage for the nations of the industrial world, in the face of overwhelming protectionist pressures, to sign an agreement committing them to even lower tariffs and expanded free trade. The new agreement represents a successful defensive effort, after five years of negotiations and increasing protectionism, to maintain free trade. But like previous agreements, it is full of loopholes. Given the liberties already taken with existing trade laws and given the spread of so-called "organized fair trade," the world trade system is functioning far differently from the free trade model espoused by conventional economists and politicians.

The agreement also buttressed criticisms that free trade mainly helps the rich. Third World nations are now the most important buyers of exports from Japan, Western Europe, and the U.S., but all but one of the sixty developing countries at Geneva refused to sign the final agreement. The biggest cuts in tariffs were in items traded between the industrial nations. Their cuts were some 50 percent greater than those for Third World exports and 100 percent greater than those granted for poor nations' labor-intensive mainstays in shoes, textiles, and leather goods.

At the signing ceremony, the Common Market's chief negotiator, Sir Roy Denman, said that without the new pact the West would have experienced again "the economic blizzards of the 1930s." Neither Denman nor any other Western official mentioned that there also are storms in the southern part of the globe.

The crisis of trade and rising protectionism are symptomatic of more severe problems in the international pricing system and in the division of the world's labor. During the growth decades of the 1950s and 1960s there was enough flexibility for imperfect markets to adjust to the dictates of demand economics. As the noted British economist Lord Thomas Balogh wrote in 1974, "At the precise time when markets were being increasingly dominated by national and international oligopoly power, theoretical orthodoxy ensured that the very problem to which this would give rise would be ignored or dismissed."

By the early 1970s this margin for maneuver had been eliminated as investor-confidence waned, productivity gains declined, and the downturn in capital formation became more pronounced. In 1971 the United States imposed quotas on textiles. Later that year, as part of the Nixon-Connally New Economic Policy (NEP), a 10 percent surcharge was imposed on all imports. In true retaliatory tradition, the Europeans devised protectionist measures on steel. By the late 1970s the United States had responded with the protectionist mechanism of trigger prices on foreign steel (a minimum import price barrier) and limits on imports of Asian shoes and television sets. Despite the efforts to keep out foreign steel, and even though the price of imports was raised by 20 percent, foreign manufacturers were still able to penetrate the American market. Competition came not only from Japan but from India, South Korea, and other Third World nations that employed the most modern technology and the clout of their cooperative business-government arrangements.

The crisis of imports proclaimed by the U.S. steel industry and its labor allies was really a demonstration of how protectionism worsened an already serious problem in productivity. Thanks to the protection, American steel companies by 1979 had increased production and reached levels in excess of 90 percent of capacity. Profits were booming after years of low profit margins. U.S. consumers, in this case as purchasers of cars and every other product made with steel, paid the price. Domestic steel prices rose 34 percent in two years and were 20 percent above world levels.

At the same time, the U.S. Government began a program to subsidize new investments in steel mills. It was a classic case of an industrial democracy running to the rescue of an inefficient industry, attempting to preserve with limited resources a major source of jobs and an industry considered vital both to national security and to national pride.

In an article, "Steel Industry a State Ward," Robert Samuelson, an economics writer, described the process: "Having fought for years with the government over prices and over environmental and safety rules, the steel companies now see regulation as inevitable and have decided to twist it to their advantage." The $500 million of loan guarantees included $150 million to finance a new rail mill, a sector already experiencing excess capacity. As Samuelson noted, "the loans will support investments that wouldn't be made otherwise, and, in a few cases, may prevent—or, at any rate, delay—firms from going bankrupt. If the protectionist barriers were ever removed, the industry would be in as bad, if not worse, shape than it was in the mid-1970s.'' But the chances that this will happen are remote, since the U.S. Government is now ''acquiring an increasingly large steel investment that it will need to protect.'' When governments subsidize inefficiency, the follies tend to compound themselves. The one company that did invest its own funds to modernize its rail plant, according to Samuelson, ''now fears a government-subsidized competitor will steal part of its market.'' One month after the ground-breaking ceremonies of the government-subsidized rail mill of the Wheeling-Pittsburgh Steel Corporation, there was a new twist to the folly. Nippon Steel in Tokyo announced it had agreed to sell ''technological cooperation . . . in constructing and operating [the] rail production plant.''

Steel thus becomes a classic example of the vicious circle of supply-side causes of the capital formation slump. The process of concentration—oligopolies turning into conglomerates—siphons off investment in technology which is needed to overcome earlier problems of productivity. There is a drain on capital needed for adjustments to higher energy and raw material costs to maintain competitiveness in world markets. Added to this are new environmental and safety regulations. But only the American firms are forced to pay these extra costs; foreign governments are imposing few, if any, of these regulations on their exporting corporations. (There has been no effort at international coordination of environmental and safety standards.) Thus, when the American steel firms begin losing business to foreign competitors, they and their unions call for protection, which only pushes prices higher. Once protected, the companies put off the day of reckoning and the new investment in modernization and the shift to new and competitive products. Productivity is further impaired. What little investment there is goes to propping up outdated industries and jobs rather than to fostering new and job-creating technology. The spiral of capital formation is pushed further downward.

All these developments have resulted in a spectacular competitive loss for U.S. industries and products in the world economy. And the loss comes at a moment when the United States is more dependent than ever on exports. Between 1968 and 1979 the number of manufacturing jobs in this country directly or indirectly tied to exports jumped from one out of fourteen to one out of six. Even in the stagflation decade, one of three dollars of profits for American corporations came from exports or from foreign investment. One out of three acres of U.S. cropland is growing products for export. While this dependency on exports was growing, the U.S. share of world trade declined from 15 percent in 1965 to less than 11 percent in 1978.

The figures for manufactured exports point to a more serious development. From 1965 to 1978 the U.S. share of manufacturing exports of industrial nations slid by 25 percent. According to studies of Labor Department expert C. Michael Aho, the ratio of exports to imports in such high technology industries as chemicals, machinery, transport equipment, and scientific instruments fell from 3.8 to 1.5. Aho found that this precipitate drop occurred even though the declining dollar had made the exports cheaper than those of many foreign competitors.

In a post-market world it should not be surprising that price is not the major factor in the U.S. export decline, but what is? Studies by Aho and others suggest that competitors are offering better quality, more aggressive marketing, easier financing terms. U.S. business and labor argue that they are being undercut by foreign governments offering hidden and direct subsidies to private and state-controlled exporting enterprises. But one country's subsidy may be another's trade promotion policy. Foreign governments, far more than the U.S. Government, have become directly involved in export promotion, which sometimes skirts the edges of the world trade rules. Whatever the legality or ethics of these policies, the actions of foreign governments and business reflect a tradition tempered by the reality of a greater dependence on exports than has been the case for the U.S. until recently.

In contrast, at the economic power centers of the U.S. Government—the White House, Treasury Department, State Department, Council of Economic Advisers, and the Congressional Ways and Means Committees—the peculiarly American attachment to "free market" principles is all too obvious. The almost exclusive reliance on demand management ignores supply economics as well as a coherent synthesis of both. Nowhere is this truer than with the U.S. export policy and the lack of industrial development programs; inactivity in both areas hobbles the economy's response to the new realities of post-market competition in the era of global interdependence. In the absence of what in other nations is called a national industrial policy, there are no criteria for production, and, therefore, there is no systematic evaluation of the effects on exports of the plethora of social and economic measures taken. Whatever their individual merit, new regulations and laws on antitrust, taxes, corporate bribery, human rights, the environment, and job safety all have an effect on the competitiveness of U.S. companies and labor and on our standing in the international economy. The result of the supply "blind spot" in policy making is that decisions are made without the information to gauge the trade-offs between what are often conflicting social and economic goals.

The Foreign Corrupt Practices Act passed by Congress, and the Carter Administration's human rights policies, are examples of admirable measures with disastrous consequences because they were implemented in contradiction of the reality of our economy's new vulnerabilities to interdependence. One Administration official estimated privately that U.S. statutes outlawing corporate bribery and denying aid to countries violating human rights have cost the American trade balance $12 billion a year in forgone exports snapped up by our industrial trading "partners." These, like other policies, reflect an early postwar tradition when U.S. unilateral actions were both necessary and effective.

The United States is one of the most progressive nations with regard to social, environmental, health, safety, and other regulations. It has failed, however, to pursue the principle of global harmonization of these regulations as an essential aim of its foreign economic policy. And its failure is costing the economy jobs and billions of dollars.

In the 1976 Presidential campaign, Jimmy Carter frequently complained that Republican foreign policy was being made with little consideration for international economic issues, a state of affairs he has only partially moved as President to correct. While policy makers talk of the importance of economic issues in diplomacy, our policies reflect economic considerations much less than do those of the Europeans or Japanese. This has been historically true: the Marshall Plan had as its main objective the shoring up of Western Europe against Communist political penetration. Compared with our allies, we have been far less dependent on foreign trade and foreign commodities. Our dependency and vulnerability increased dramatically in the 1970s, but the policies still lag behind those realities.

This policy lag in the government's economic power centers frustrates officials in lesser agencies directly responsible for trade and export planning. Various new export promotion schemes have been proposed, but they often get lost in the block and a half between the White House and the Commerce Department.

As one assistant secretary claimed privately in early 1978, "It's difficult to get people to believe that the decline of the dollar has so increased the price of manufactured imports that this contributes to inflation as much as the oil price hike." As to a thwarted plan for export tax incentives to match those of other governments, he added, "No matter how much we demonstrate the need for export tax incentives, the White House insists that both unions and national business firms would claim favoritism to the big multinationals while arguing about undue government intervention in the market."

The White House resistance stems from the opposition of labor and smaller businesses to the export rebate program of the Nixon years, which did turn out to be a gift to the multinationals. White House officials have refused to push labor and business groups to consider a better designed and more equitable program of export tax incentives. One obvious reason, for any who have witnessed the maddening pace of the White House, is simply a lack of time. In the economics sphere, the mainline agencies are engulfed with GATT negotiations, voluntary wage-price guidelines, and raising or lowering interest rates, all of which are beside the point, delay new policy tools, and fail to stem the capital formation slump and its impact on U.S. global competitiveness. Meanwhile, the nation's unprecedented balance-of-trade deficits go from bad to worse.

V

The currencies of the industrial states have been suffering the jitters since the late 1960s as the United States balance-of-payments deficits have increased. The jitters turned into a global financial crisis when, in 1971, President Nixon abrogated the Bretton Woods agreement of 1944, untied the dollar from gold, and thereby devalued the world's trading currency. The slide of the dollar contributed to protectionism, which compounded the global financial crisis. Between June 1977 and November 1978 the dollar declined by almost 18 percent, with two-thirds of that drop taking place in the last six months alone. The West German mark and Japanese yen reached record highs in the same period. The Common Market nations sought refuge in a hurriedly established European Monetary System pegged to the deutsche mark, turning it into a *de facto* reserve currency. By the spring of 1980, the sporadic plunges of the dollar followed by "emergency recovery programs" had become too numerous to recount.

The financial crisis of unstable exchange rates and rapid movements of money in the Eurocurrency system is the final link in the vicious circle of supply problems and slumping capital formation and investment. Volatile exchange rates create havoc for investors who want to commit their money across borders to long-term capital formation projects in various countries. Confronted with uncertainty, investors tend to put their money into gold, real estate, or financial futures rather than into the building of new factories with uncertain prospects because of stagflation and protectionism.

The trillion-dollar Eurocurrency market, while a source of instability, is the largest potential source of long-term investment capital. Its two major depositors are the multinational corporations and the OPEC nations with their petrodollar surpluses. Some bankers and financial experts argue that this vast pool of money is being committed sufficiently to worldwide capital formation. Others, like Yale's Robert Triffin, are not so sure. They contend that the major borrowers on the Eurocurrency market are industrial and Third World governments, accounting for 60 percent of all loans and using the money to finance balance-of-payments deficits. To whatever extent the money is being used for investment, an anomaly still exists. As a report of the Swedish Foreign Ministry and International Development Agency notes, there is "an enormous cash pool of hundreds of billions of dollars coexisting in a world of both rich and poor nations in urgent need of capital formation."

Contributing to the global financial crisis have been excessive growth in world money supplies fed by government deficits and the uncontrolled credit expansions financed by borrowing from the unregulated Eurocurrency market. Protectionism has added to uncertainty, especially to the fear of heavy Third World borrowers that they may not be able to sell their exports and receive foreign exchange to pay their massive debts.

Finally there is the failure to address the fall of the dollar. Until the 1960s the U.S. multinational companies and banks profited from the dollar's position as the world reserve currency. As long as the dollar was overvalued, U.S. multinationals could buy assets abroad and at low prices compared with local competition. The dollar's preeminent position gave U.S. bankers a head start in creating the Eurocurrency system. The arrangements worked as long as the dollar remained strong. As it started sliding, problems developed, but the lobbying in Washington for the reserve currency status continued. The problems were compounded by the failure of the United States to push for an orderly replacement of the Bretton Woods system that would reflect the new international economic realities and the new sources of financial strength in the global economy, from West Germany to Saudi Arabia. The United States continued to play the role of the world's central banker, even as it went deeper in debt to do so. It continued to play central banker even as stagflation, growing balance-of-payments and trade deficits, and a deteriorating competitive position in world export markets turned the dollar into one of the industrial world's weakest currencies.

After years of prodding from other members of the International Monetary Fund (IMF), the United States finally agreed in September 1979 to a partial substitution of dollar reserves by Special Drawing Rights. (These SDRs, pegged to a "basket of currencies," are issued for use between central banks.) But many foreign central bankers wondered if it was not already too late.

"I can't understand why the Americans let it go on this way," a Bank of England official commented. "It smacks of 1929 the way they run it."

To sustain the dollar's international role, the U.S. Government twice within a year had to resort to the demand management bludgeon of severe monetary policy. After the shock therapy of October 2, 1979, Wall Street did suffer "The Great Crash of '79," as *The New York Times* described it, with bond markets experiencing their largest single fall in the nation's history. And the Fed's chairman, Paul Volcker, made no qualms about the broader costs of letting interest rates skyrocket when he said, "The American people will have to be prepared to accept a lower standard of living." But as great as the costs were, credit bludgeons alone would not bring stability. The dollar's real weakness was rooted in persistent inflation that defied demand management in large part because it grew out of supply-side problems, a waning trade competitiveness, and an American politics unable to initiate institutional reforms, domestically or internationally.

"The tail wagging the dog" is how one economist described the American efforts to defend our international position at heavy cost to the domestic economy.

VI

The problems of supply economics, for all their complicated ramifications, are as simple as the reality of two-dollar-a-gallon gasoline. The crisis of oil is the most dramatic and pressing crisis of supply. It represents the failure of too much reliance on demand economics in a post-market world. It has been exacerbated by attempts to apply political solutions to economic issues and demand management policies to supply problems, and by the growing interdependence and vulnerability of a post-market global economy.

The Arab oil embargo of 1973 and the subsequent quadrupling of oil prices accelerated the inflation of 1973 and deepened the recession of 1974–75. In many minds, in many political speeches, and in many columns of newsprint, OPEC and oil became synonymous with stagflation, a convenient single-villain explanation for a problem of many origins. Stagflation was already well entrenched by 1973. Yet OPEC would become, in the words of columnist George Will, "an alibi for politicians eager to export the blame for the inflation manufactured in Washington." The embargo and price hikes merely dramatized and speeded up a supply crisis that was already gaining momentum before the first shot was fired in the 1973 Middle East War. World demand for oil had been booming since the late 1960s, American production was falling, and the Arab oil producers were making up the difference, supplying 92 percent of the newly increased demand. Prices were already going up, although obviously not at such dramatic rates as they would later, and the producers were being pushed to expand their pipelines, docks, and drilling to meet the demand.

Even before 1973, oil experts and the oil companies, perhaps to some degree in a self-fulfilling prophecy, began warning that the postwar era of cheap energy was sooner or later coming to an end. But the warnings of the companies were accompanied by encouragement of more driving and consumption. The events of 1973–74 and all the subsequent price hikes made it sooner. An extremely brutal process that began feeding on itself as inflation, indecisive U.S. energy policy, massive balance-of-payments deficits, and a sliding dollar pushed OPEC to maintain the real value of their new petrodollar wealth. Nevertheless, between January 1974 and December 1978 the cartel showed restraint as the real purchasing power of their petro-revenues declined by 22 percent because of inflation and the eroding value of the dollar. But between the two springs of 1979 and 1980, with the curtailment of Iranian oil production, OPEC's frustration exploded with successive price hikes.

Confronted with a shortage since 1973 of its most vital industrial commodity, the United States could have allowed classical marketplace economics to operate in the hope that higher prices would stimulate new investment in oil and gas production and force consumers to switch their demand to other forms of energy. Politically, such conventional economics were impossible because they would have enriched the oil companies, put the worst price-squeeze on the poor and middle class, and widened the existing inequality between the rich and everyone else. The day of reckoning was postponed with an econopolitical mishmash of controls on the price of domestic oil and gas and the use of deficits and easy money policies to accommodate the OPEC price-hikes. Only in 1979 and 1980 did the government back into price solutions with the decontrol of domestic oil prices and the passage of a windfall profits tax.

In oil as in other sectors, the real failure of U.S. policy has been to ignore supply: the opportunities of global interdependence to expand oil and gas production in non-OPEC countries. Again, only in 1979 did the U.S. Government give grudging support to plans of the World Bank and other institutions to finance new oil production and exploration. The U.S. Geological Survey has estimated the potential reserves of the non-OPEC Third World countries double those of the OPEC countries and triple those of the United States. Yet drilling density is less than one percent of the U.S. figure, and there are more wells in Kansas than in Latin America and more in Arkansas than in all of Africa. As Senator Edward Kennedy noted, "the failure to exploit new oil sources heightens our dependency on OPEC. Our policy has been tied to production by the major oil companies in the OPEC countries. It is time to let a hundred oil fields bloom." With current policy this is unlikely, Kennedy said. "The oil is there. The capital is not."

At the same time, the United States was falling behind its industrial world partners in making deals with Third World oil nations involving swaps of finance and technology for oil and gas. This policy lag became dramatically apparent when the U.S. rejected a Mexican gas deal and suddenly found the Japanese and then the French making swap arrangements with the Mexicans. President Carter's ill-fated trip to Mexico in early 1979 was an effort to play catch-up. By failing to keep up with its industrial partners in the pursuit of energy deals, the United States is losing not only potential supplies but potential export markets for technology and capital. This further worsens a balance-of-trade deficit, created in part by rising oil imports, but also by declining competitiveness in the export market and the absence of industrial development and export promotion policies to offset increasing imports of items ranging from luxury goods to heavy machinery.

When the oil crisis erupted, Secretary Kissinger tried to respond by lining up the industrial nations as a consumer bloc to stand up to OPEC. The response, however, of other governments, far more dependent than we are on raw material imports, was to take over and centralize their negotiations for oil purchases while forming new business-government arrangements to pursue post-market swap deals with not only OPEC but also other resource-rich and -poor Third World nations. This approach reflected an awareness of their own vulnerability and was an effort to offset their oil and raw material trade and payment deficits by exporting capital and technology. These swaps have now become a $20-billion-a-year business, with little of it going to the United States.

If the oil crisis has failed to produce an oil supply policy or an export promotion policy for the United States, it has at least educated Americans to the existence of a globally interdependent economy, the diffusion of economic and political power from the United States to other industrial nations and to the Third World, and the vulnerable links between our economy and those of other nations. A world economy once dominated by the dollar and U.S. multinationals has been replaced, as analyzed in the next two chapters, by a world economy of intense competition among industrial nations for the resources and markets of the Third World, and of new relationships between the multinationals and foreign governments.

But the drama of global interdependence has yet to give way to the requisite understanding and accommodation. And not until American politics—whether in energy, finance, or trade—adapts to the new diffusion of global power and the intensity with which the global economy affects our own can the nation hope to break some of the most vicious circles perpetuating stagflation.

PART II

Global Econopolitics

CHAPTER 4

Third World Pioneering

I

THE WORLD ECONOMY is becoming a global supermarket. Arab, African, and Latin American oil fuel the industrial world. South Korea sells its steel not only to Europe but to Japan. Brazil sells its machinery to Europe. European couture houses make high fashion items from Asian fabrics. The Japanese devour McDonald's hamburgers, and bartenders in Montgomery, Alabama, mix bourbon with Perrier water. What was once a novelty or luxury is becoming commonplace, drawing nations of the world more deeply into one another's economic web.

International trade has been growing and spreading at unprecedented rates since World War II, doubling in volume in the last decade alone to $2 trillion. The growth of trade spurred the postwar economic boom, expanding national wealth as well as consumers' tastes and appetites. But in the decade of stagflation, the preeminent trading position of the United States, its industrial allies, and the Western multinational corporation is being challenged by new buyers and sellers from the Third World. The challenge and the industrial world's response to it are shaking the old order of the world trading system. Nations and corporations are being forced into a new array of political and economic relationships.

The postwar global trading system has depended on a continued stability and expansion of trade and international finance, and a continued stability of international politics. Its principal engines are the multinational corporations with their worldwide staffs, finances, and management expertise to carve the world into markets. The multinationals now account for more than 70 percent of the trade, technology, and finance flows between non-Communist nations. This relatively orderly arrangement of buyers, sellers, financiers, and workers provided the organizational innovation for the revolution of the postwar period. The multinationals—first the Americans, later the Europeans and Japanese—helped engineer twenty years of global growth despite great controversy over their accumulation of power and over who benefited from their exploitation of labor and resources.

In 1967 the French journalist and politician J.-J. Servan-Schreiber wrote the best-selling *The American Challenge,* which predicted that U.S. corporations would soon take over the world economy. This prediction has not come to pass—global reach is turning out to exceed global grasp. The once-lopsided relationship between the corporations and Third World nations is slowly becoming more balanced as the governments of those nations acquire new wealth, power, and sophistication. As these relationships evolve, they create new post-market forces in world trade and the global economy. More and more economic decisions are made through political negotiations between governments and corporations instead of being based on traditional marketplace forces.

The global economy is now a far more diffused economy. Japanese and European multinationals are challenging the American corporation, especially in the Third World. And there, in the South, a new class of nations, the newly industrializing nations, is becoming a force in the world economy. These countries are creating their own multinationals that are beginning to compete with corporations of the industrial world.

Brazil, Taiwan, South Korea, Venezuela, and Mexico are some of the more prominent members of the newly industrializing countries. Their economic success is a mixed blessing for the rest of the world. Their exports are adding to new and more dangerous protectionist pressures in the industrial world, putting the exporters in a no-win situation. Their economic future hinges on the elimination of stagflation in the industrial nations that buy their products. But, at the same time, the growth of the newly industrializing nations contributes to the forces behind protectionism, instability, and stagflation in the industrial world. (For example, the United States and the Common Market countries are blocking competitive Third World textiles and other goods. These barriers add about one percentage point to the U.S. cost-of-living index.)

The dependence works both ways, however. The industrial world's reliance on Third World oil and raw materials is more, not less, acute, and the industrial world increasingly needs Third World export markets to sustain its own prosperity.

This chapter and the next focus on the forces that have led to this impressive turnabout. The multinational corporation, in its rapacious need for raw materials, labor, and new markets, has exposed its Achilles' heel to the Third World, which needs the corporate technology and capital know-how to pursue its own development and industrialization. The economics of mutual needs, what economists call "interdependence," is slowly replacing the antagonism and acrimony of the "Ugly American" era. What once was a David and Goliath contest is being transformed as Third World nations load their slingshots with vital minerals, markets, and a new political and economic sophistication. The developing countries are also able to exploit the new competition as Japanese, European, and even Third World multinationals join the American giants in an intense pursuit of the resources and export outlets of the nations to the South.

The native wealthy often benefit more than the native poor when a Third World nation extracts new concessions from a multinational. And, of course, this contest for influence is far from painless. These bargaining-power victories are also not irreversible. In Chile, for example, under a repressive junta, it is back to business-as-usual for the returning U.S. corporations. "I don't think we spent five minutes talking about human rights when the board made the decision to invest in Chile," said a Goodyear manager about their recent investment. "We don't mix business and politics," added a U.S. branch bank executive about their Chilean reopenings. Such remarks smacked of the early 1950s, of naiveté or hypocrisy, depending on one's view. Similarly, Dan Morgan's *Merchants of Grain* documents how across the globe these multinationals have escaped the control of their home country governments, let alone those of the Third World. Yet for a different industry, Morgan reports how even Morocco is learning to pit one multinational against another. There, as in other countries, the government raises its bargaining power by taking advantage of a bitter fight among firms for control of the tire industry. It reflects the trend, albeit uneven, toward the new corporate relationships being established in the Third World. Not all the developing nations have shared in this spreading of wealth and power. For every Brazil, Qatar, and Korea, there is a Chad, a Bangladesh, and a Uganda falling deeper into poverty and misery. A so-called "Fourth World" has emerged, even poorer than the Third World. This is one of the global schisms that we will discuss in chapter 5, schisms that contribute to economic and political disorder in the world.

II

The evolving relationship between multinational corporations and Third World governments is a triumph of ingots over ideology. Some corporate leaders are putting aside some of their beliefs and rhetoric about the incompatibility that exists when private enterprise does business with governments and state-owned enterprises. Many socialist governments have had to discard their ideas about the incompatibility between capitalist and socialist institutions. What some Third World governments have attempted to do is to use multinational corporations to achieve their highest priorities of independence and development. The admittedly reluctant but nevertheless marked flexibility and adaptability of more and more multinationals are becoming more pronounced, as is the ingenuity of governments in turning these corporate profit motives to their own advantage.

The distinction between socialism and capitalism has become blurred as new partnerships form between governments and multinationals in countries as ideologically diverse as Brazil, the Philippines, Algeria, and now China. The avid courtship between governments and corporations has rendered meaningless the rhetoric of a decade ago about their basic incompatibility. As John Kenneth Galbraith has said, "To see economic policy as a problem of choice between rival ideologies is the greatest error of our time. Only rarely, and usually on matters of secondary importance, do circumstances vouchsafe this luxury."

There have been other dramatic changes in the Third World

economies. By the mid-1970s, Third World nations accounted for 10 percent of world trade in manufactured products, compared with a miniscule 4 percent a few years before. India's steel industry, nonexistent two decades ago, has become an exporter. In fifteen years war-torn South Korea had engineered a truly equitable agrarian reform and matched it with an export drive that set the country up as a feared competitor of Western Europe, the United States, and even Japan. South Korean multinational corporations operate in the same arena as the giants of the industrial world. Hong Kong has instituted social and economic reforms, and it is now a financial and commercial center. Brazil, suffering its own brand of stagflation and economic collapse in 1964, is pushing toward the ranks of the leading industrial nations. But its growth "miracle," engineered without reforms, still leaves the majority of its inhabitants in dire poverty. Even in Africa, the world's most underdeveloped continent, some countries are pulling themselves into the ranks of the newly industrializing countries. The Ivory Coast, Kenya, and of course Nigeria have become significant exporters, especially to Europe.

All these countries, despite their diverse political and social systems, had one thing in common—a development strategy that emphasized the mobilization of finance (domestic and foreign) and the targeting of it into investments that raised productivity. Regardless of where their economists were trained, they brought home the lessons and theories of Western and Marxist economics and turned them on their head. They all embraced development planning and development economics. This was just as true in South Korea and Brazil, which proclaimed themselves capitalist and supporters of free markets, as it was in Algeria, which proclaimed its adherence to socialism.

Development economics has turned out to be a bouillabaisse of Keynesian demand economics with a heavy seasoning of supply economics. In the industrial sector, this has meant a "coordinated national industrial policy." The Keynesian demand approach assumed that credit and tax policies could be used to adjust the level of demand in the economy and that the supply and production side would rise automatically to meet the new level of demand. Development economics recognized that the automatic adjustment is unlikely even in productive sectors because market forces were either weak or perverse. The countries making the leap to industrialization had to concentrate on improving production and setting goals to strengthen such sectors as agriculture and such basic industries as steel and capital goods.

This adaptation of foreign economic theory was not limited to those trained in "market" economics. Local needs also led to innovation in countries whose young economists were trained in the Soviet Union and Eastern Europe. Just as the Third World graduates of Harvard, Yale, and the London School modified the lessons of capitalist demand economics and "fine-tuning," so too did the graduates from Moscow and East Berlin modify socialist lessons of supply economics. For one thing, the Third World nations lacked the huge central bureaucracies of the COMECON nations to administer elaborate national production plans. The response that evolved was as pragmatic as that of their counterparts in nominally capitalist countries. The market mechanism and multinational private enterprises were actively exploited in sectors where they were effective.

A combination of policies was pioneered in these developing countries during the 1960s. Such strongholds of capitalism as South Korea, Brazil, and Venezuela developed state-owned but profit-motivated enterprises that reflected a mix of East-West lessons. They also targeted new kinds of credit and tax incentives to the sectors in industry and agriculture which most needed them.

A big problem confronting Third World nations was a shortage of investment capital. They were short on both foreign exchange and tax revenue and could not pay for foreign steel to build factories and foreign machinery to set up mass production lines. Something had to give, a problem not considered in conventional demand economics. Poor countries had to create medium-term development plans, an agenda of development priorities, and then stick to them. These were not, as Americans might imagine, huge bureaucratic enterprises on the Soviet model, controlling all aspects of the economy. Instead, from Brazil to Malaysia, these were limited programs of tax and credit incentives targeted to priority private sectors buttressed increasingly with wholly or partly state-owned enterprises. The initial aim was to substitute for imports and to expand labor-intensive assembly production of durable consumer goods, such as cars and household products. The second phase was to begin local manufacture of some basic items of the assembly operation. The third phase was to build capital goods, such as machine tools.

In this fashion, the development programs of the Third World confronted the complex set of major and interrelated problems called the "vicious circle": inadequate capital stock, undereducated labor forces, and other factors generating low productivity, yielding low income, creating low levels of savings, which in turn meant low levels of capital formation, which finally led to low productivity and a continuing cycle of low income.

In the 1950s, capitalist-oriented Third World countries found that reliance on traditional market forces had helped perpetuate the cycle. The rich dominated these forces. Acting as traders, they were intermediaries in the export of raw materials and the import of foreign luxury goods. Investment and productivity both suffered.

The object of the amalgam of altered demand economics and altered supply economics was to eliminate the bottleneck in productivity and to break the cycle of low income, low levels of savings, low investment, and low productivity. Productivity became the linchpin, not only because it was part of the investment cycle, but because as long as productivity was low, so was a country's capacity to bring in vital foreign exchange through more competitive exports. Increasing exports meant taking advantage of a country's low-cost labor and producing exports at prices competitive in world markets.

In countries rich in natural resources this meant getting off the yo-yo of world commodity prices. They fluctuated wildly in the short term but over the long term declined relative to the worldwide prices of manufactured goods. Even when the prices were high, much of the instant wealth was skimmed off by the wealthy few and deposited in such foreign tax havens as Switzerland, Monaco, and Panama. The lack of investment opportunities at home perpetuated the flight of investment capital from the countries that most needed it.

The basic problem of the resource-rich nations was to create the first stage of industry to process those resources and to keep more of their wealth at home. This was the aim, often ill explained or misunderstood, behind the threats and nationalizations of oil and mining industries. During the tumultuous "adolescent phase" of Third World multinational relationships of the 1950s and 1960s, some countries not only attempted nationalization but tried to establish their own processing industries independent of the multinationals. Nationalizations did take place, but they often failed. The industries suffered for lack of skilled management and advanced technology. Other early efforts at extreme regulation of the multinationals succeeded only in driving corporate investments to other countries.

This form of development through confrontation with the multinationals began changing and evolving by the late 1960s. The change started with new relationships based on new objectives of both the resource-rich Third World nations and the corporations. Its outcome in the Third World increasingly has been to transform multinational capitalism from an enterprise based on ownership to one still based on the profit motive of global corporations but exercised through the sale of management, marketing, and technology services. The ownership of resources and capital is increasingly of secondary importance and is held through a variety of new forms, including state enterprises and joint ventures between government and local private firms.

The classic case study of the new government-multinational relationship is the oil industry and the formation of OPEC. All the important elements are there: new knowledge, the postwar spurt in industrial nations' consumption and strategic dependency, global competition among multinationals, and innovative leadership.

"It was the entry of the oil independents, what you call the 'latecomer oligopolists,' like [Amerada] Hess which gave us the power to prick the Achilles Heel of the Seven Sisters," OPEC-founder Juan Pérez Alfonso related in an interview. "The independents' absolute need to get access to foreign petroleum to survive against Exxon and the other six, forced them to outbid the Seven —whether in terms of the percentage tax paid or the degree of ownership given up to the government." Pérez Alfonso, now hailed by Venezuelans as "our Old Wise Man," went on to convey an essential element for the exercise of bargaining power against the "global oligopolies" as he describes them: "Regardless of their home origin or industry, they must be analyzed worldwide, for the globe is their profit horizon. When some of them fall behind, either on the supply or sales side, then that may make them all vulnerable to government bargaining. We [in OPEC] were patient and studied; when the time came, we seized it." What other multinationals and their home nations in the industrial world have increasingly come to experience in the 1970s, the Old Wise Man noted, is that "other poorer nations are learning and struggling to apply this lesson. We are not quite so dependent as we once thought."

In this often-told tale, even the best chroniclers, such as Anthony Sampson, have underestimated the influence of Pérez Alfonso. It took the weight of the vast Arabian reserves to convert his ideas to reality and then to economic power, but Alfonso was the first to foresee, as far back as the late 1950s, both how absolutely dependent the industrial nations were becoming on foreign oil and the prices they would pay to obtain it. He also saw how existing arrangements and low prices benefited the industrial world at the expense of producer countries. It took a misguided effort by the oil corporations in 1960 to lower the posted price of oil before the Arab producers became sufficiently enraged to form the producers' group that Pérez Alfonso said was necessary to match the collective power of the major oil corporations.

Every effort of the oil-producing nations to coalesce on prices, output, and control was resisted by the corporations. As long as there was an oil surplus throughout the 1960s, the corporations could play the producers off against one another. A worldwide oil shortage developed as American oil production fell behind American demand and as European and Japanese consumption also grew exponentially. The producers of OPEC began gaining more bargaining power. Even before the cataclysm of October 1973, the demand for oil had pushed the market price beyond the posted price established by the major corporations. As Raymond Vernon points out in *Storm over the Multinationals,* the Venezuelan determination to gain bargaining power was strengthened from the Middle East by "a new generation of well-trained and knowledgeable specialists." The cartel of producers had gained the upper hand over the cartel of corporations.

But as events since 1973 have shown, the oil corporations, once effectively pushed, quickly accommodated to the new bargaining rules. Their profits have mushroomed beyond 1973 levels. A marriage of cartels has enriched both partners while making the rest of the world considerably poorer.

The rest of the world suddenly realized the implications of this new post-market relationship after the embargo of 1973 and the subsequent quadrupling of oil prices. For the first time since the end of World War II, a new economic relationship was creating new geopolitical realities in the world and making into a facade the old confrontations of capitalism versus socialism and East versus West. There has been a turnabout of bargaining power, dramatized by the growing and nearly complete dependence of the industrial world on a Third World resource.

Five years later, the fall of the Shah of Iran underscored these new realities. No longer could a foreign corporation (British Petroleum) and a foreign intelligence agency (the CIA) work together to depose an unfriendly government and install a friendly one that would guarantee their economic interests—as was the case with Mossadegh in 1953. Nearly thirty years later, Mossadegh's revolutionary heirs demonstrated the growing disparity between the old sources of power, military, and the new sources of power, economic. Military power—ships, missiles, and well-equipped armies—bears little relationship to what is to be defended. Armies and navies and air forces, even those as well equipped as the Shah's, could neither occupy nor manage oil fields. Nor save his regime.

To some extent the new relationships between industrial world multinationals and Third World governments reflect these new perceptions and sources of power. They reflect as well quantum leaps in the economic and technical sophistication of a growing number of Third World nations that only a few years ago were bogged down in their own stagflation and underdevelopment. Finally, these new relationships between governments and corporations show that handsome, if no longer lavish, profits can be made in an environment of nationalization followed up by management contracts, joint venture partnerships, or other new institutional marriages that give the Third World governments more regulation and control.

III

The new relationships between governments and corporations are the outcome of a bargaining power process. The two sides are, above all, interested in the control of finance, technology, and marketing. In the initial postwar period, while the Europeans and the Japanese were rebuilding from the war, American corporations took the lead in establishing plants and factories in the poor nations. As these multinationals grew and spread, they began financing their overseas investments with money from profits earned there or from borrowings on local capital markets. At the same time, the American multinationals expanded their foreign markets through purchases of local plants and firms. In this initial phase of the relationships, it was the corporations that controlled the flows of finance, technology, and sales (marketing) between branches, subsidiaries, countries, and continents.

By the mid- to late 1960s a reaction began setting in—attempts at nationalization were a frequent response to corporate power. But as the Venezuelans and later the Arab oil countries were to learn, along with the Seven Sisters, ownership was a small prize compared with the vital elements of control. The bargains that began to be struck revolved not so much around ownership or compensation for nationalization as around the divisions between government and multinational control of financing, technology, and marketing. As Peter Gabriel, former McKinsey partner and management consultant, notes, "The basic function of the MNC is shifting from the mobilization of capital, in which the company's reward is an entrepreneurial one for risk-taking, to the sale of its corporate capabilities, in which its reward is a managerial one for services rendered."

In the case of oil, the producer countries were most interested in gaining control over technology and over the intermediate steps of production and refining of oil as well as in the development of a broader industrial base. Left to the oil majors in the bargain was the control of marketing, since they, far more than the producers, were capable of organizing global distribution systems. (There is, however, some evidence that the next test of bargaining power by certain OPEC nations will be to develop the capacity to do their own international marketing.)

The first stage of harnessing the multinationals for development economics, symbolized by the success of Venezuela and some of the OPEC nations in transferring oil money to broader industrialization, was then emulated in a second stage by the efforts of other commodity nations to control and mobilize their resources.

The Third World nations that did not have the good fortune to rest on a bed of oil or other resources prized by the industrial world had to take the best advantage of what they did have in abundance—human labor. The word *underdeveloped* is not just a capsule description of their overall condition but a cause of their low productivity. Illiteracy was high, labor largely unskilled. Their sparse capital stock was composed of old factories and machines. For certain of these nations a third stage of new interactions with multinationals evolved, this time in manufacturing. While short on resources they were long on supplies of labor and offered the multinationals what came to be known as the "export platform."

U.S. multinationals were facing stiff competition in their home markets from Europe and Japan. They were also confronting higher wage rates and a new array of government regulations. They began looking for new production sites. Waiting to accommodate them were such countries as South Korea, Taiwan, Brazil, and Mexico, which welcomed the labor-intensive assembly operations. American firms were not the only ones on the "labor-rich" Third World doorstep. Volkswagen and Toyota learned quickly and became just as anxious as Ford and General Motors to expand into the south of the globe.

Until the early 1960s, U.S. multinationals were dominant in the Third World. But since 1965, Japanese and German companies have been investing at a rate almost triple that of the Americans. In Brazil, Japan has replaced the U.S. as the largest foreign investor. In the late 1960s it ranked sixth. Just as their American counterparts did, European and Japanese multinational banks provided the financing and servicing of this overseas industrial expansion of other home countries. Between 1971 and 1976, Japanese and European banks went from some 48 percent of total foreign affiliates in the Third World to almost 60 percent. This new element of European and Japanese competition gave the export platform countries a bargaining lever. Just as the petroleum and mineral-rich nations learned to exploit the industrial world's growing resource dependency, the export platforms of the Third World began to recognize the dependency of manufacturing multinationals on cheap labor.

The resource nations had sensed the vulnerability of Europe and Japan, with almost no oil and few other minerals, and their increasing anxiety about sure sources of supply. They were able to strike deals that assured, among other things, the import of technology and other development aid at a favorable price. The non-oil and non-resource-rich nations did not have this vulnerability to play on, but they did exploit as much as possible the oligopoly competition among multinationals for global market shares. When one giant firm entered a lucrative domestic market such as Brazil or Venezuela, or attractive export platforms, such as South Korea or Taiwan, the others would soon be on its tail. This gave the governments new bargaining leverage. It also allowed them to exploit the phenomenon of the newer upstart corporations trying to catch up with the older established pioneers among the multinationals. The latecomers, anxious for a foothold, would accept terms that the early pioneers would initially disdain. But if the upstart managed to get into a vital market, then the pioneer would have to catch up.

By the mid-1970s a new *modus vivendi* was clearly developing among a growing number of countries. Corporations and governments were learning to live with each other and were above all seeking stability in their relationships. Many corporations, however reluctantly, were discovering they could become more flexible and adaptable. Many government managers and technicians, sometimes just as reluctantly, were struggling to learn how to fix responsibility for corporate regulation and administration within their own bureaucracies. They were trying to minimize the recurrence of an old game—the outsiders manipulating, bribing, or playing off various elements of a chaotic and underpaid civil service. The successes were uneven from country to country, industry to industry, but the trend was there. Led by Venezuela and followed by other OPEC members in the Middle East, more Third World governments were learning the rules of the new bargaining power games with the corporate giants. The demonstration effects of the early pioneering host governments did not go unheeded.

Ironically, the "demonstration effect"—often correctly seen as the villain in a familiar development economics story ending with a peasant woman buying a transistor radio or Coca-Cola rather than food for her child—in this instance played a positive role. Knowledge has spread with uncharacteristic speed across the Third World. Not only have success stories spread informally; they also have spread through the deliberate technical assistance efforts of international agencies such as the UN and its Centre on Transnational Corporations (UNCTC) and its Industrial Development Organization (UNIDO). As UN contract specialist Thomas W. Waelde observed in his study of mineral contracts: "Access to individual contracts by consultants has helped developing countries gain experience in negotiation and contract bargaining. As more detailed information on contractual arrangements becomes available, the nature of contracts will undergo substantial change toward satisfying the needs of both countries as well as legitimate expectations of the companies." Knowledge has propagated and information has spread among Third World governments. New laws have resulted where formerly there were none, aimed not only at regulation to curb past abuses, but also at systematic promotion policies to foster multinational activity where most needed.

In a UN–sponsored trip to Kenya in 1978 our group witnessed the success of this Third World grapevine. We were amazed at the speed of its development. We were there to initiate the work that would eventually develop a new negotiations strategy for the government's dealings with multinational banks—particularly, how to get them to finance rural development and labor-intensive projects. In addition, the chief economist of an East African government and the governor of its central bank wanted to hear about Botswana's new mining contract. Our briefing turned out to be a lesson on how Botswana gained more control and greater returns from its mining sector. This tiny nation, one of Africa's poorest, had for more than a year been working with a team of private experts and specialists from international agencies. The team's negotiations were based on hundreds of man-hours of study and preparation. They resulted in what ten years earlier would have been unprecedented concessions by international private mining companies, not to mention the particular companies involved, a group from Botswana's not overly friendly neighbor South Africa.

National legislation has tried to curb the tax and transfer price abuses and monopolistic practices of the corporations. Many countries have long barred foreign ownership in such vital areas as utilities and communications. But now there are new prohibitions, with varying degrees of success, on domestic political meddling by companies. Regulations and incentives are aimed at promoting exports, regional development, and employment, and at establishing local technology. Governments are developing more precise and sophisticated long-range economic plans and wedging the multinationals into these plans. The sales, and especially the export targets, pressed on the multinationals are woven into the national export and development plans of such countries as Mexico, South Korea, and Brazil. A Brazilian program provides a case study of the manipulation of corporate giants, of a government turning global oligopoly competition for new markets to its own advantage.

Like all oil-importing Third World nations, Brazil was hit hard by the quadrupling of oil prices in 1974. Its growth rate sagged from its usual 6 percent to 4 percent, and the trade accounts were held in balance only by the big jump in coffee prices. To reverse this situation, the government launched a trade-balancing and export promotion program. There were three elements to the strategy: heavy foreign borrowing to stimulate more investment; an import substitution program to generate self-sufficiency in processing raw materials (including the pioneering of the world's first and most successful massive gasohol program *); and the exportation of more manufactured products, once thought the domain of industrial nations.

The trade-balancing and export program was a refinement of economic plans already in place. The Brazilian model is based on a combination of incentives and penalties, rather than rigid five-year plans, to guide private and state enterprise toward the planned priorities. There is fairly close surveillance of the most important private companies, both foreign and domestic, by a bureaucracy of manageable proportions with clearly defined lines of authority and responsibility. Within the office of the presidency, there is a secretary of planning. Various agencies within this office carry out special studies and research-and-development projects. The State Development Bank is the major financer of projects by Brazilian firms that match development objectives. Other agencies, such as the Industrial Development Council and the Amazon Development Office, grant incentives to projects that conform to development

* Brazil's commitment of $800 million to its gasohol program compares with the U.S. Government's $15 million in 1979.

priorities. "In our medicine bag of incentives," related one technocrat, "are partial or total exemptions from customs duties, rebates on indirect taxes and other tax credits and exemptions, accelerated depreciation allowances and municipal tax exemptions." And he added, "We make many mistakes; the art of guiding imperfect markets is new and experimental. But the secret is finding the right incentive and knowing the trade-offs."

At the heart of the Brazilian export promotion program is the Export Fiscal Benefits Program, which goes by the acronym Befiex. It operates under the Industrial Development Council, whose members include the ministers of the major economic agencies, heads of the central and state banks, and the directors of the national confederations of industry and commerce. Adding clout, both symbolic and real in this established military dictatorship, is the presence of the chief of staff of the armed forces. The council screens investment projects to determine if they should be awarded incentives, and the final decision is made by the ministers of industry and the president. The major element of the program is the requirement for a potential investor to make a *net* contribution, through exports and financing, to Brazil's balance of payments. In return, investors receive a variety of incentives including reductions or exemptions on taxes for imported equipment and tax credits on exports.

These councils and programs, no matter how effective, are only mechanisms. Brazil itself, the largest and richest nation of South America and one with limitless growth potential, was and is a market the global companies could not afford to pass up. It was the lure to establish operations in the Brazilian market and the knowledge of the competitive forces within certain giant industries that gave the Brazilian Government its real leverage to obtain concessions from the multinationals. In this instance, it was the giant automakers of the world, so eager to enter a new market they were willing to make concessions they would have dismissed out of hand a decade before. As each company jumped into the Brazilian market, anxious to join its competitors already there, the government began to squeeze more concessions from them.

"With Befiex we set a new bait and Ford was the first to bite," as the program's architect described it. In 1971 the company told the government it wanted to take over Willys, the old Kaiser operation, and bring Mustangs into the Brazilian market. A year later it signed an agreement to export initially a gross value of $1 billion, which would later increase to $1.3 billion. The terms were relatively soft with no firm commitments on net balance of trade or current accounts. But a major auto company was in the net, and it was only a matter of time before its competitors would be rushing to join. The initial reaction from those competitors was negative and hostile. Some companies even tried to outflank the national government and make arrangements with state governments, which had their own incentives to offer under schemes to decentralize industries beyond the already crowded coast and São Paulo areas. But as Ford, already with a large base in Brazil, began drawing a bigger share of the market, the resistance of the competitors began weakening. Slowly, the supply structure of Latin America's largest automotive sector began changing.

Volkswagen tried first with a modest export proposal, but the government rejected their terms. "We squeezed them," remembered one official, "because we knew they could afford it and would have to follow Ford." Eventually, the German company signed a five-year $1.069 billion export commitment, and the production of Dashers for both the local and export market began. Chrysler came in at the end of 1973 but with a smaller $315 million export commitment. The government was shrewd enough to seek a smaller commitment from a smaller and less profitable company. Other major auto manufacturers have climbed on the Befiex bandwagon since 1974—Alfa Romeo for $400 million, Mercedes for $500 million, Scandia Saab for $415 million, and Volvo for $352 million.

The last to join was General Motors. Its late and reluctant decision followed a pattern in corporate-government relationships. General Motors was the early pioneer in developing its Latin American market, just as it became the giant among giants at home. It was the first company offered and the first one to reject the terms of a Befiex commitment.

The pioneers are often the most resistant to the new proposals from Third World governments. G.M. is not alone in this distinction. Coca-Cola and I.B.M. have pulled up their operations in India because of a refusal to part with know-how, technology, or control. It is often the case that companies that have for the longest time enjoyed near monopolies are those whose organizations and attitudes have become the most rigid and the most resistant to change. This "lag" in adapting to new economic conditions has lost Coca-Cola lucrative business in other Third World countries as well.

Gradually G.M. saw its competitors, anxious to gain a competitive advantage in a lucrative market, accept the export commitments of Befiex and grab a chunk of Brazilian business. The competition for market shares in an oligopoly situation finally forced G.M. to relent. When it finally got around to making the decision to join the Befiex scheme, it ended up paying the stiffest initial price of U.S. auto companies. The Brazilian Government extracted an export commitment from G.M. valued at more than $1 billion.

The Befiex program was showing results three years after the first auto company signed its export commitment. By 1975, Brazil's trade account in automobiles had registered a small surplus of $60.2 million. The overall current accounts deficit had dropped from $179.4 million to $37.1 million. Exports increased by $168 million. By 1976 the capital accounts contribution from the Befiex program was projected at $589 million. And in 1980, Ford, the first to take the bait, had alone committed itself to $1.6 billion in annual exports as it further integrated Brazil into its global network for the production of cars and trucks.

While setting firm goals, the Brazilian Government had given the foreign companies considerable flexibility in reaching them. A company could, for example, reduce imports or expand exports to reach the export surplus goal. The net export goal concept helped eliminate the particularly bothersome problem of monitoring transfer pricing. Similarly, as long as companies reached the targeted net surplus on the nontrade portion of the current account, they were free to determine values for such items as technical fees and royalties. In short, the Befiex agreements reflected what one official at the Planning Secretariat called "the general philosophy of enterprises—decide your strategy in dealing with private vital sectors and establish the goals and the incentives and regulations to match them but minimize interference with as much of the strictly private commercial considerations as is possible."

The Befiex program, within certain limitations, is a model for certain other newly industrializing nations. Its applicability to other countries depends on the size of the local economy, on the product involved, the extent of oligopoly in the industry affected, and the bargaining power of the government involved. It takes some sophistication and good planning to make the program work, but it does not require a large bureaucracy. The Befiex program was started by a professional staff of five. Although the program has worked well in the automobile industry, it has not yet shown results in the textile industry. There the government is trying to deal with an unstructured industry, not one dominated by just a few corporations.

The multinationals have spread their production and financing around the world, but in the process have laid bare some vulnerabilities. To achieve the balance of payments surplus they wanted, the Brazilians had to know where to apply pressure. A Brazilian planner gave this explanation:

> The corporation has a home office; let us call it the sun. They also have plants and subsidiaries located around the world; let us call these planets. They come to see and say we must import, but at the same time I know a piece of equipment produced in Brazil or produced in South Africa or produced in Germany or the United States or France is exactly the same. The same color, the same quality, the same everything.
>
> I understand that the corporation works in a closed universe. In this closed universe the Brazilian planet has a negative balance of payments. I know another planet has a positive balance of payments result. So in my initial negotiations with the corporation, I start with the proposition that I don't want a positive balance, just a zero balance.
>
> I don't care how that balance is compensated or distributed among all other planets. All I want for Brazil, to start with, is a zero balance. It is the Brazilian government who pays me, and I negotiate for the Brazilian government.

The remark shows how far the Third World governments have come in dealing with the multinational corporations. This new brand of business-government cooperation is an essential element of the development economics strategy adopted by newly industrializing nations of the Third World, regardless of ideology.

What a procapitalist government accomplished in Brazil was duplicated with a similar strategy toward multinational electronics producers by the government of Algeria—a banner waver of Third World socialism. Algeria's bargaining objectives were the same—absorbing technology and management skills for high productivity to serve both local and export markets. A $223 million agreement between Algeria's state-owned SONELEC and the General Telephone and Electronics Corporation (GTE) is bringing to Algeria a complete consumer electronics sector. Manufacturing includes final products, such as TVs, tape recorders, and cassettes, as well as components, like cathode-ray tubes and semiconductors.

While GTE assumes early management of the facilities, Algeria is paying them $25 million to train 300 managers and technicians in the United States. Within a few years the complex at Sidi-Bel Abbès will be entirely managed by Algerians, fulfilling another aim—that of minimizing future dependency on foreign multinationals. GTE is selling the best of its technology. Its rewards are export sales and technical fees. Had it not entered, eager German and Japanese firms would have. The creation and modernization of an entire industry, what formerly had taken decades, is now accomplished in less than one.

"The technology sold," finds transfer specialist Jack Baranson, who has studied such cases in aircraft, automotives, chemical engineering, computers, and consumer electronics throughout the Third World, "is increasingly the most sophisticated available, and its release is often under terms that assure the rapid and efficient implantation of an internationally productive capability."

Similar arrangements are the basis of the vast multibillion dollar Guyana (Regional) Development Corporation of the Venezuelan Government. Ten years ago this was the country's most underdeveloped region. It is now harnessing global corporations through various arrangements including tripartite partnerships with local private and state-owned enterprises. The demonstration effects abound. Brazil learned from Venezuela's early mistakes in state-corporation "turnkey operations" and developed the tripartite concept. Venezuela then used it in aluminum, steel, and other basic industries in the Guyana regional programs.

"In South Korea in the late 1960s we did little to regulate and structure the MNCs although we were well aware of the transfer price problem and the use of our own local savings to finance their operations," commented a former member of that country's foreign investment board. "Now that they're established we have better leverage. We're increasingly tightening the regulations, adding to the incentives, promoting our own corporations, using joint venture and [technology] transfer agreements. To both promote and control is more than just the laws; it's a question of the right mix of incentives and organizational innovation . . . only then can we develop our own supply of technology." A few months later the official's comments had become part of a UN round table for Asian nations. At a meeting in Malaysia, they discussed their various successes and failures in designing and administering "the policies to promote, structure and control the transnational corporation."

"It was a little red book that gave us our first breakthrough," a former official of Mexico's foreign investment and technology transfer agencies recalled with a smile. "One of us had acquired a book of prices, licensing fees, and royalty charges of one [home] nation's important industries . . . the comparison with what we were paying revealed the classic 'caveat emptor' that we knew of but could never pin down." Mexico at the time had passed new legislation, and the Mexican–U.S. Chamber of Commerce "reacted with outrage." In fact, it was little different "from many of the statutes in U.S. and other industrial nations' laws except for the 51 percent ownership clause that we've had on the books for years." The effectiveness of the new laws hinges on their enforcement. In that respect they resemble the investment regulations of Decision 24, promulgated by the Andean Common Market over initially bitter opposition of U.S. multinationals. The Mexican laws, noted the official, "while a step in the right direction, could be effective only if we had the capability to enforce them and that meant knowledge and information. The little red book, we jokingly called it 'Mao's book,' gave us the bottom line on how far we could press on negotiating prices. Facts about what the companies were doing worldwide was an essential element of our leverage."

Mauricio Maria y Campos, former director of the Mexican foreign investment commission, noted: "Our new capabilities have saved us millions of dollars, we've created more jobs per dollar of foreign investment and generated more exports. But there are still problems . . . the transfer price question remains, corruption by our own firms, as well as the MNCs, while reduced, still exists . . . [and] the political will of the administration in terms of budget and personnel appointments waxes and wanes depending on other domestic and foreign policy considerations." At the conclusion of the interview, conducted in late 1977, he added: "Soon Mexico will have a lot of oil money. I hope we don't repeat the mistakes Iran is now making. In many sectors, but not all, we need much of what the transnationals have, but on our terms, and which still leave them a profit. Iran has thrown open its doors to the MNCs and lost control in the process. Its poor have benefited little. Our experiences here in Mexico and Latin America should make us know better. I hope we do not forget that."

Another stage in the evolution of the newly industrializing nations (whose impact on the global economy we will discuss in the next chapter) is the development of the Third World multinational. Third World nations are entering such sophisticated manufacturing industries as steel, construction, shipbuilding, and petrochemicals. The image that Americans and Europeans have of Third World sweatshops staffed by dollar-a-day laborers does not match, in a growing list of nations, the reality of increasingly skilled technicians and corporate executives whose enterprises are now competing with Western multinationals. Contrary to a widely held view by industrial-nation scholars, there is no absence of entreprenurial skills in the Third World. As Nathaniel Leff noted in a 1979 survey for the American Economics Association, "experience of the post-war period has not confirmed this view of the underdeveloped countries condemned to economic stagnation because of lack of entrepreneurship."

One statistic, courtesy of the *Harvard Business Review,* tells an important story. By 1978 there were 34 multinationals based in Third World countries which had made it to the Fortune 500 list. These include not only petroleum companies of the Middle East but also major South Korean corporate groups in shipbuilding, electronics, and textiles. There are also Brazilian chemical and auto manufacturers, two Indian manufacturers, and a number of giants from Singapore, Hong Kong, the Philippines, and Malaysia. There are also several Third World multinational banks. The state-owned Banco do Brasil operates globally and is the eighth largest bank in the world, bigger than such giants as the United Kingdom's Barclays, Germany's Dresdner, or the U.S.'s Manufacturers Hanover.

These corporations, if not directly owned by their governments, are all encouraged in their expansion and export programs by government assistance ranging from local development bank financing to tax breaks to state-controlled monopolies. The pronounced trend of Third World nations to do business where possible with other Third World corporations is further aiding their growth.

One of the keys to this growth of Third World multinationals is the global spread of technology. Many of the agreements between Third World governments and multinationals are technology transfer agreements. Other countries are developing technology appropriate to their labor-intensive economies in such areas as agriculture, textiles, construction, and housing.

The results of all this can be seen around the world. As the *Harvard Business Review* noted, South Korea did not have a shipbuilding industry as recently as 1972. Now it is turning out supertankers, and its Hyundai Group shipyards can build thirty-five ships of various sizes all at one time. Taiwan has an advanced electronics industry and is building steel mills in Nigeria. Philippine companies are providing services to multinationals all over Asia; the SGV accounting group now competes with the Big Eight accounting firms of the world.

The Third World multinationals are beginning to penetrate the industrial world, as well as competing with American and European firms for Third World business. Stelux Manufacturing of Hong Kong bought into Bulova and pulled that American watch company out of a slump. A Hong Kong bank bought a 51 percent controlling interest in Marine Midland, the twelfth largest bank in the United States.

IV

Third World multinationals, both private and state-owned, are the most novel element in the evolving bargaining-power strategy in the Third World nations. These newest of the multinational firms provide another means for Third World nations to gain access to technology and to widen their export opportunities. *Diversification* is a favorite word among Third World technocrats; for them it means the opposite of dependence. The fear of dependence characterizes all developing countries, regardless of whether their individual economies tilt toward capitalism or socialism.

The multinational happens to be the most visible daily reminder of the Third World's historical legacy. This legacy includes great-power military intervention, foreign profiteering, and the exclusion of Third World nations from real power in the postwar international institutions such as GATT, the World Bank, the International Monetary Fund, and the United Nations Security Council. It is not surprising, therefore, that the first measurable signs of the shift from dependency to interdependence can be seen in the day-to-day dealings between multinationals and Third World governments. A transition is taking place from "adolescence" to "maturity." The many innovations in the relationships were initiated largely by the Third World governments, which took advantage of changing global conditions. But the pioneering, however reluctant, by the multinationals to accommodate themselves to these new relationships was very real. It was, in fact, living testimony to the many writers who describe the multinationals as the most remarkably flexible economic institution yet to come along.

None of this implies that this transition by corporations and governments has been or will be a smooth process. Third World bargaining power parallels the international business cycle, fortified in the upswing and weakened by recessionary downturns. There are numerous country examples in which both sides have exercised overkill or unpredictable behavior. And there still are cases in which multinationals and the ruling elites of Third World societies corrupt each other. Iran is a vivid example. Not only was there corruption; there was a headlong plunge into massive but uncontrolled industrialization. Together, each for its own reasons, the government and the multinationals tried to do too much too fast and much more than a developing society could absorb either politically or economically.

Despite the many changes that have occurred, it is difficult to measure the true extent and ultimate significance of the transition.

But clearly a new pattern has emerged in Third World relations with multinationals, one in which the former adversaries have become in many instances more like collaborators. And the transition has revealed another policy lag: no one knows the exact quantitative dimensions of the pattern because conventional statistical reporting requirements were designed and legislated at a time when such "new forms" of post-market interactions were unimaginable. Thus, the measurement and analysis of what has occurred over the past decade must rest on the firsthand observations of those involved—in governments and corporations, as well as in the new cadre of international experts and consultants who busy themselves with either studying or promoting such corporate-government relations.

Both their observations and the theoretical notions about them would seem to confirm that what has happened in oil—the marriage of multinationals with OPEC—is also happening in other minerals and in manufacturing. The new power of the poor nations "is the result," as Jack Baranson has written, "of evolutionary trends in the world economy that are changing many corporate viewpoints on foreign involvements and have altered the relative bargaining positions of suppliers and purchasers of 'operative technology.' "

Nevertheless, these new "micro" relationships were based on an expectation that the industrial democracies would continue to function as the engine of the world economy, just as they had through the 1960s. Instead, the motor sputtered into stagflation. Moreover, no one anticipated all the consequences that would flow from this new relationship. One of them was a massive increase in Third World imports in the industrial world, what one commissioner of the European Community termed "a veritable hemorrhage of labor and capital-intensive imports into the developed nations." The persistence of stagflation and the growing protectionism in the North are now eroding the very foundations on which global expansion and industrial development in the Third World have been built—free trade and free flows of money. And without those two conditions the globe's newest growth engines—symbolized by the creation of Third World multinationals, the dynamics of Brazil's export strategy and Mexico's controlled use of foreign investment—will stall. These disorders have further complicated efforts to build new political relationships between nations of the North and South and to develop joint institutional reforms based on the realities of a transformed global economy.

What has developed instead at the end of the stagflation decade are new economic and political schisms, not only between the North and South, but among nations in each group. These schisms have come about not because of renewed clashes between the global corporations and the governments of the Third World. Rather, stagflation has hobbled efforts by the industrial democracies to adjust quickly to the new international division of labor brought about by Third World pioneering by governments and corporations.

This instability is producing further fragmentation in a world economy no longer under the "old order" of Bretton Woods and smoothly functioning trade rules but not yet under a new order of governing economic principles and institutions. Confronted with continued instability, rich and poor nations alike are trying to secure their positions and advantages, reverting to defensive mechanisms and regional and bilateral deals that tatter international accords on trade and monetary stability. The emerging schisms of disorder are no longer strictly between groups of non-Communist and Communist or between the haves and the have-nots. There are new divisions, alliances, and alignments with consequences barely visible for the world economy and world politics.

CHAPTER 5

Global Schisms

I

THE NATIONS of the industrialized world, when they deal with the underdeveloped nations of the South, resemble a rich uncle who is putting a poor relative into business. When the relative's business starts thriving and taking customers from the old firm, family jealousies and fights erupt.

That is just about what is happening in the world economy today. The efforts of the industrial nations in foreign aid and development and corporate expansion are finally bearing fruit. A new class of nations is emerging—the newly industrializing nations of the Third World. Along with the OPEC nations, they constitute a new source of wealth in the world. But their riches have not been evenly distributed, either in their own societies or within the Third World.

The emergence of this new class of nations has produced new divisions in the world order. No longer are the nations of the world simply lined up into camps of North and South, rich versus poor, which was the dialectic of global economic rhetoric in the last decade. The industrial nations, even as they all imposed trade barriers on the Third World, were developing divergent policies, flowing from their different levels of dependency on the resources and export markets of the South. The old solidarity of the industrial nations, rooted in both the Cold War and the postwar boom, began splintering as the Cold War seemed to wane, as Europe and Japan began to challenge American economic hegemony, and as the United States provided increasingly uncertain political and economic leadership. The tensions created between the U.S. and Western Europe during the 1973 Middle East war showed how quickly the old solidarity could be replaced by economic national self-interest and dependency on a vital Third World resource. As the 1970s wore on, this pursuit of economic self-interest was demonstrated in the proliferation of competitive bilateral deals for oil and other resources between the industrial nations and the producer nations. The divergence of interests between the United States and the Western European nations has grown even sharper in the months since the Iranian and Afghanistan crises of 1979–80. For President Carter, seeing a potential Soviet challenge in the Persian Gulf, these events represented the greatest threat to peace since the end of World War II. Yet the European allies, whose dependence on Middle Eastern oil is even greater than ours, refused to see the threat in those terms and hedged their responses accordingly.

In three decades the world has gone from the simple bipolar division between Communist and non-Communist nations into a highly fragmented world. The East-West polarity has been replaced by serious divisions within the socialist camp—most recently shown in a war between two socialist nations in Asia. The solidarity of the West also has been eroding, although not so dramatically. In the South the breakdown of solidarity is also apparent. The desire of many Third World leaders to create a unified Southern bloc to confront the Western industrial world has virtually vanished. The New International Economic Order proclaimed less than a decade ago by the South against the North has become a sand castle of UN paperwork. The Third World is dividing into its own classes of haves and have-nots. These divisions are further complicated as regional blocs of nations begin bargaining with one another. Most notably, the European Common Market, dealing as a bloc with blocs of Third World nations, has become a principal vehicle for Europe's economic penetration of Third World markets.

China's reversal of Maoist isolation and its pursuit of industrial development with outside help has created more confusion in global alignments. Japan has been diverted from a budding relationship with the ASEAN nations of Southeast Asia by the lure of technology, trade, and energy deals with China. American businesses are dazzled by China's market of nearly 900 million people, but our European allies are worried that a too ardent courtship of the Chinese will create new problems with the Soviet Union. And China's entry into the development derby will put new pressures on global financial markets and increase competition among Third World nations for investment capital, which is already in short supply for them.

"Economic growth is one of the most cruel phenomena invented by mankind," said the noted Mexican economist Miguel Wionczek.

Nowhere does this appear truer than in the Third World, where some have-nots are becoming haves, while the others fall into even more abysmal poverty. The success stories of the Third World are highly visible, especially through their exports. Brazil, South Korea, the Philippines, Malaysia, Taiwan, and Singapore, among others, are firmly established in the class of newly industrializing nations that are becoming leading exporters. But their success has done little for Bangladesh, Pakistan, Chad, Paraguay, and Peru.

The monolith of the South no longer exists, and this is certainly evident in the alphabet-soup realm of the United Nations. *LDCs* used to mean "less developed countries." Now it means "least developed countries," referring to those nations that have slipped from the ranks of the Third World into something called the Fourth World, the poorest of the poor. The richest of the once-poor are now referred to as either "Middle-Income Developing Countries" (MIDCs) or "Newly Industrializing Countries" (NICs). Finally, there are the no-longer-poor, known as OPEC, and a few other resource-rich giants, such as Brazil and Mexico.

In the Third World nations that have achieved real and statistical economic success, the benefits flow in very uneven patterns. In Brazil, one of the fastest-growing nations of the world, the poorest half of the population has actually suffered a drop in living standards and consumption in the last decade. The richest 20 percent of the Brazilian population meanwhile has increased its share of the national income from 30 to 40 percent. Brazil is not an isolated example. Similar patterns have emerged in Mexico and even in democratic Venezuela. Only a few countries, South Korea and Taiwan, for example, have been able to mitigate the Law of

Uneven Development. And of all the Third World nations to come into new wealth, only Venezuela has been able to maintain both a democratic and a stable political system. The new wealth of such nations as the Philippines and Brazil was accompanied by ruthless political repression that fell especially hard on the struggling poor.

Rapid growth combined with repressive politics creates new powder kegs around the world. This is especially true when the industrial nations depend on the kegs for tapping strategic resources. Iran has become the textbook example of the destabilizing aspects of new wealth in a poor land. As events there have proved, a sudden flow of new riches can create massive social dislocation and even revolution.

The combination of repression and uneven development creates instability, even though many argue that Third World growth is impossible without authoritarian government. The instability, moreover, has far more than local or regional implications. It is creating new diplomatic tensions in the industrial world as Western dependency on Third World resources and markets continues to increase. France is resuming an old role as African gendarme as upheavals in Zaire threaten European interests.

The chaos of the 1978–79 Iranian revolution, where Western stakes were so vital, seemed to many to beg for intervention. The United States, which had put the Shah back on his throne in 1953, could not keep him there twenty-six years later. But when the Soviets drew closer to the Persian Gulf with the invasion of Afghanistan, the U.S. began to assume the burden of protector of the region, abandoned more than a decade earlier by Britain. Rather than diminishing, the temptations for intervention clearly have been growing as nations compete for fewer resources. And over oil, the most vital resource, looms the risk of confrontation between the two nuclear superpowers. Doubling the risk is that a confrontation could come in an area, the Third World, for which the superpowers have no established "rules of the game," as they do for Europe.

The decade of stagflation has produced the conditions for a new set of global schisms. If stagflation persists, these schisms will become more pronounced and will create new tensions and risks of conflict in the world. And the existence of these schisms continues to undermine the interdependent world economy, contributing even further to the persistence of stagflation.

For the global economy of the 1980s, the persistence of these schisms means spreading disarray in all areas of international economic relations, from trade and finance to the sale of nuclear power and conventional arms to the Third World. The persistence of these schisms means an increase in tensions around the world. The objective for the 1980s is to reduce the sources of tension through medium-term efforts to end the cycle of stagflation. The medium-term objectives of the 1980s are at once both modest and immense—to cut the cycle of stagflation and strike at the tensions existing in a world divided into many competing camps.

II

The success of the newly industrializing countries—the very success that the industrial nations have been promoting for a variety of reasons for the last three decades—has created in its wake crises of global gluts and shortages, rising protectionism, and financial debt owed to the industrialized North by the developing South. Success, as we have seen, means competition and exports. But with those exports came a brutal lesson: that Western economies can no longer sustain at economic levels a variety of basic and high-employment industries. The success of the South means severe structural adjustment problems for the North, initially in such labor-intensive industries as shoes, textiles, and electrical appliances, then later in more basic industries such as steel, petrochemicals, and shipbuilding. The initial reaction—especially under pressure from the threatened industries and unions—is imposition of trade restrictions, tariffs, quotas or "orderly marketing agreements" which limit the exporting nations and hurt their growth prospects. These restraints also result in higher prices for consumers in the industrial world, even further contributing to stagflation. (A Brookings study found that if the U.S. reduced its tariffs on Third World imports by 60 percent, U.S. shoppers would experience a one-quarter percent decline in the consumer price index.)

How did the new industries of the Third World—textiles, for example—manage to get such a jump on their competitors in the industrial world? There was a booming demand for textiles in the industrial world in the 1960s, but the American firms were trying to meet it with antiquated technology and products appealing only to local tastes. The development planners of such nations as South Korea, India, Brazil, and Hong Kong saw a potential breakthrough. The initial phase of their strategy was to capitalize on their large and low-cost labor forces. Their wage rates were as much as 80 percent cheaper than those in the industrial world. By means of the bargaining arrangements with multinational corporations outlined earlier and export rebates, subsidies, and cheap credit and technical assistance to manufacturers, the Third World nations built a production base and rapidly achieved astonishing growth rates in their worldwide sales of clothing and cloth. Between 1970 and 1975, South Korea's exports of textiles increased by 436 percent, Taiwan's by 347 percent, and Hong Kong's by 191 percent. At the same time, the nations of the European Economic Community went from net exporters of clothing to net importers, exchanging a $540 million surplus for a $1.5 billion deficit.

Similar success stories followed in other industries. Taiwan and Korea alone put 300 million more pairs of shoes on world markets in 1976 than in 1972. It was the "perfect example," concluded an EEC Report, "of massive Japanese and American investments" in export industries of another country. The growth of the Brazilian and Spanish footwear industry was also "made possible by massive foreign investments," the report found. These investments, which are now haunting the industrial world, originally were encouraged by a variety of subsidies and tax breaks of Western governments. A now-familiar pattern has developed. In textiles, shoes, and other industries, the exports of the newly industrializing countries start with high-labor-content products. Then, with the success of the industry assured, further foreign investment and experience bring "the final blow." In this second phase of their development strategy, the newly industrializing nations move into "areas of the highest value-added per worker"—namely, the most modern and capital-intensive operations.

The United States, Japan, and Europe, suffering the stagflation slowdown in demand, were already "finding it increasingly difficult to absorb Third World exports of textiles, shoes, transistor radios, hand-tools, and the like," in the words of another Common Market report. But now, a *Wall Street Journal* survey in March of 1979 noted, "These [Third World] nations are developing their own steel, chemical and auto industries, and preparing a more advanced stage of manufactured goods." For example, Third World exporters are rapidly expanding their steel mills. In 1975 the developing world had the capacity to produce 37.7 million tons of steel; by 1985, the UN estimates, Third World steel capacity will rise to 146.8 million tons—more than tripling production in ten years and creating an aggregate steel capacity greater than Europe's, the U.S.'s, or Japan's.

As the case of steel illustrates, there is an ironic twist to this export revolution. Invariably, such capital-intensive export goods are produced by state-owned enterprises, either in partnership or in technology transfer arrangements with multinationals from the United States or other home nations. For example, Japan moved to replace lost export revenue from its declining steel sales by selling its advanced technology abroad. Sometimes it acted in partnership with other multinationals, as it did in building huge steel complexes for Brazil. The irony was particularly brutal for the ailing U.S. steel industry when Taiwan received $121 million in U.S. EximBank steel loans for its local mills. A few years later, Taiwan became one of the first "dumping" cases to be investigated under the United States 1978 "trigger price" antidumping regulation. In all, since 1945, a U.S. congressional report found, the U.S. had lent $4.5 billion for Third World steel production. What in boom times was considered a virtuous aid loan became, in the stagflation decade, a scapegoat candidate for the "Golden Fleece Award."

The nations of the industrial world had become victims of innovative supply economics applied to systematic development strategies that included intimate cooperation between government and business to expand production. In a short time, the combination of multinationals and host-government Third World planners had brought about a basic change in the division of international labor across a score of major industries.

During the booming sixties, the industrial nations might have had sufficient breathing space to adjust calmly to such a shift in production and imports. They certainly could not during the stagflation decade. Third World exports were exacerbating structural problems in the industrial world, problems that, in the words of a 1978 Common Market study, "had earlier been masked by steady and unprecedented growth in demand." A new pattern of protectionist response and counterresponse developed. Even during the tariff wars of the Great Depression, protectionism was a simple bilateral affair. If one nation raised its tariffs, others retaliated directly against it. The new postwar links among nations led to more complex protectionist intrusions into world trade.

The global protectionist crisis started with textiles. President Nixon came into office on the shoulders of the "New South" and such politicians as South Carolina's Strom Thurmond, who were clamoring for limits on Asian textile imports. The Nixon Administration moved to keep its southern promises by negotiating orderly marketing, or import restricting, textile agreements with the Asians. With the large U.S. market cut off, the Asian textile manufacturers began pouring their exports into the still open markets of Western Europe. The result was massive unemployment not only in the European textile industry but also in the petrochemical factories that supplied the dyes. The Common Market was forced to negotiate the Multifiber Agreement with Asian textile manufacturers. And burned once by the Americans, the Europeans made sure they would take the first crack at bat against any new exporter who threatened to disrupt a vital industry. By the mid-1970s, steel imports started pouring into Europe from Asia and Brazil, and the Common Market quickly imposed curbs on them. The overflow then moved to the United States, which in turn had to impose its own trade restrictions to pacify the domestic companies and unions.

The nations of the industrial world were reverting to the disastrous "beggar-thy-neighbor" responses of the 1930s, which then only helped worsen the Depression. But there was more involved than merely failing to learn the lessons of history. The industrial nations were also in danger of cutting off one key avenue of future growth, and a path out of the stagflation cycle. Through the markets of some increasingly prosperous Third World nations, U.S. and European companies were able to find outlets for their goods during the deep recession of 1974–75. According to the Senate Budget Committee, that recession would have been far worse without those relatively new Third World markets. But now the industrial nations are faced with their own supply crises of productivity, technology, and modernization, reflected in the inability of their industries to compete with the modern technologies, cheaper labor, and higher productivity of many Third World nations. The response of the industrial world has often been to tell the Third World to revert to an earlier standard of poverty, even though the expanding Third World wealth offers the industrial world one of its best hopes of breaking the grip of stagflation.

Schisms are developing not only between trading nations but between borrowers and lenders. With the oil price rises of 1974, many Third World nations on the margin of solvency went deeply into debt to pay their fuel import bills. As the global money pool expanded, many of these nations—Zaire, Turkey, and, later, Peru being three of the more prominent examples—borrowed from Western multinational banks to continue their development and industrialization programs. Much of the bank money was recycled cash from the vastly expanded oil payments of the Western nations to the OPEC nations, which they deposited in Western banks. From 1974 to 1977, the borrowed money did enable the non-oil Third World nations to keep on buying Western products and reduced the impact of the recession in the West. It also drew those nations deeply into debts that they had little prospect of paying off.

Between 1974 and 1976, the U.S. multinational banks were happy to ply the Third World nations with loans, because the recession at home had dried up their domestic business. Yet most of the money was offered in short-term loans, based on the expectation of a revival of world economic growth and trade which would enable the Third World nations to pay the money back on time. But the recovery from the recession has been limited, and protectionism has intensified. By 1979 it was clear that many Third World nations were over their heads in massive debts and would be for some time.

Several Western banks experienced a brief panic in 1975 and 1976, but the economies of the Third World nations grew robust enough to allow them to maintain some sort of repayment schedule. But by 1980 a newly menacing situation had developed. A combination of higher oil prices and global stagflation had triggered a new debt explosion. The total debt load of Third World countries had climbed above $350 billion, compared with $201 billion only two years earlier. The situation can only grow worse if Western protectionism, exacerbated by a new global recession, further cuts into Third World export and foreign exchange earnings. And Third World nations faced payoff demands, both principal and interest, of $45 billion by the end of 1979, double what they were two years earlier.

Despite the debts and service charges, Western banks have been competing for Third World business. Until the end of 1979 they had money to lend. Third World nations were happier to go to banks, which, when flush with excess funds, sought their business with few strings attached, rather than to the International Monetary Fund, which often demanded politically unpopular austerity in return.

As *The Wall Street Journal*'s Richard F. Janssen reported from the IMF meeting of late 1979, "to some analysts, the possibility that defaults on those debts could topple the world into depression ranks right along with sudden oil scarcity as one of the most nightmarish threats to an already troubled world economy."

Janssen quoted one banker as saying big banks and poor countries had become "so interdependent that you do not know whether the banks will eventually bring about the collapse of the countries or if the countries will trigger off the collapse of the banks."

Already the list of countries falling behind on their payments is lengthening. Many non-oil developing nations are spending more than 20 percent of their export earnings to cover current debt service.* Increasingly, they are asking for help or falling behind on their payments. If this struggle with debt becomes more than a temporary problem, Western governments face an ugly choice: either more chaos in international financial markets or a bail-out of their multinational banks with infusions of rescue monies that will force-feed inflation.

The scramble for money is increasingly coming to resemble the scramble for markets and trade, except now the competitors are the Third World nations and not the rich industrial barons. Ideology plays no more of a part than geography, and this has been dramatized by China's sudden entry into the world's capital markets. With the Third World nations already competing for a limited supply of capital, the arrival of China means even more intense

* Brazil, the largest Third World borrower, will by 1981 face the growth-stifling situation of using some 60 percent or more of its export earnings to pay off old debts.

competition, and the likelihood that less money will be available for the needs of other nations. China will need, after deducting for export revenues, something like three to five billion dollars a year to finance its modernization policy. This is 20 percent of the estimated total loan capital available to the Third World from international sources. China's vast potential market makes it a prize competitor for Western capital as well as management assistance. The thinly stretched resources available to the Third World will become all the more thinly stretched as the nation that once carried the banner of self-reliance and socialist development succumbs to the lure of modernization with the help of its new capitalist friends.

III

Between the late 1960s and mid-1970s, most of the nations of the Third World had rallied to the banner of what they called the "New International Economic Order." Its theories and premises were advanced by such leading thinkers of the South as Venezuela's Manuel Perez Guerrero, Pakistan's Muhbul Ul-Haq, and Argentina's Raoul Prebisch, and they were led diplomatically by such ideologically diverse politicians as Venezuela's former President Carlos Andrés Perez, Tanzania's Julius Nyerere, Algeria's late Prime Minister Houari Boumedienne, and the Philippines' Ferdinand Marcos. Its objective was to bring about greater equity in the distribution of world income, to give the Third World greater participation in international organizations, and thereby to promote, through greater global efficiency, greater world growth.

Behind the call for the New International Economic Order was the assertion that traditional "market forces" and their laws of uneven development had created a world economy in which two-thirds of the world's population consumed only one-third of the world's resources. The very economic success of the rich nations was blamed for the poverty of the others.

The philosophy was summed up by a former Egyptian planning minister, who wrote:

> From the gold of Peru to the oil of the Middle East, the natural resources of the Third World fed the unprecedented growth in the North.

After the OPEC price increases of 1973–74, this truism became more obvious to the North, and the principles of the New International Economic Order gained a wider following in the industrial world. The new arguments of interdependence and self-interest, combined with guilt, gave the old arguments added clout among academics and politicians in the industrial world.

Through the 1970s the concept had been woven into the United Nations bureaucracy, with more than 2,000 meetings taking place every year under UN auspices to discuss North-South relations. To some, these meetings constituted a "dialogue," to others, a "confrontation." The topics for these meetings were commodity price stabilization, trade, development assistance, relief of Third World debt, technology transfers, codes of conduct for multinational corporations, and Third World participation in exploitation of seabed resources. (The overall aim of the South was to parlay the desire of the North for a steady supply of commodities and open markets for investment and trade into needed wealth and power for themselves.)

There were some successful conferences, especially the UN meeting in September of 1975. But disillusionment was already setting in, especially as bickering increased over the issue of oil prices.

Before 1973 the South had spoken with one voice, while the North was scattered. But the issue of oil prices and OPEC concentrated the minds of the North on one issue. Through think tanks, through such private organizations as David Rockefeller's Trilateral Commission, and through such governmental organizations as the OECD and its International Energy Agency, the approach of the industrial world toward the Third World began to focus on energy and oil prices. But this was a fragile and elusive unity that ignored issues important to the South, such as international curbs on multinational corporations and new voting rules for the IMF and the World Bank that would reflect the "new power of the poor."

The collapse of the North-South dialogue came at the 1977 Conference on International Economic Cooperation and Development in Paris. The nations of the South arrived with high expectations and left bitterly disappointed because the North offered few real concessions. There was a promise to create a billion dollar fund to help the poorest nations struggle with their debt problem. But there were only vague promises on the vital question of commodity price stabilization; what started as a $6 billion commodity stabilization fund then dwindled to $300 million by the time the promises were to be put into action. And there was no progress on obtaining pledges from the rich nations to increase their development assistance to the poor nations; over the 1970s, development aid had actually declined as a percentage of gross national product, to 0.4 percent for all the OECD nations, and an even lower 0.21 percent for the United States. The attitude of the South was summed up by Venezuela's Manuel Pérez Guerrero, a key spokesman in Paris and long active in Third World economic and development issues. As a result of the Paris meetings, he said in a private interview, the future of a North-South dialogue "was uncertain, at the least, if not finished, at the worst."

With the collapse of the North-South dialogue came the collapse of the relative solidarity among nations on both sides. In March 1979 a reporter writing for the United Nations Association summed up the North-South dialogue of the prior ten years as a "frustrating experience for both sides. The North is accused of lacking a political will to get something accomplished, and the South is said to fall apart as soon as the talks get down to the nitty-gritty specifics."

IV

In the atmosphere of collapsing solidarity that followed the Paris conference, one reality remained strikingly clear—that the nations of the globe more than ever before lived in an interdependent world. Whether rich or poor, they all were vulnerable to some extent to events outside their borders. If groups of nations could not devise unified strategies within alliances to cope with these vulnerabilities, then they would strike out on their own. The vulnerabilities remained after Paris. What changed was the way nations tried to deal with them.

The Europeans and Japanese, with more dependency than the U.S., have been pushing far more vigorously than the Americans to develop new forms of trade-investment-aid links with the South.

The Europeans, like the Americans, are facing protectionist demands from companies and workers threatened by Third World imports. But they are more willing and ready than the Americans to promote and profit from a bigger Third World role in the global economy. The European Commission in Brussels concluded that restructuring was essential to "adapt to a new international division of labor . . ." because labor-intensive, and now, "to a growing degree, capital-intensive industries, have burgeoned in regions outside the three leading industrial powers." Recognizing that "such a development is certainly acceptable and, indeed, desirable," the commissioners saw clearly what U.S. leadership has not: that "the impoverished two-thirds of humanity" have a crucial role in "creating new markets that will help provide, towards the end of the century, the main sources of economic growth for the whole planet."

The response of Europe and Japan has been the "pioneering" of bilateral and regional deals with the Third World, first with OPEC and other resource-rich countries, and more recently with groups of newly industrializing nations. The economic fragmentation of the industrial bloc is most pronounced in energy as the Europeans and Japanese try to cover their vulnerability in Third World deals negotiated with hardly a by-your-leave to the United States. In the Third World, some nations gain through these arrangements, and others who are not included fall further behind in their war against underdevelopment.

This splintering process represents one of the most dangerous, if least visible, failures of America's world leadership. The U.S. Government continues to preach the doctrine of free trade and free markets, but its failure to pull its own and the world economy out of stagflation puts the practice of free trade in ever deeper jeopardy. The fragmentation flows from the opposite reality—the post-market collaboration of business and government in economic and political strategies that often make free trade and free markets a mockery.

The energy deals being pursued by industrial nations are the most noticeable example of this fragmentation. One dramatic case was Japan's 1979 *coup de théâtre,* its energy deal with Mexico. In exchange for Mexican oil and gas, Japan provided technology and long-term loans. This deal shocked the U.S. Government, which was still quibbling with Mexico over gas prices, dealing with that country as if it were still on the U.S. umbilical cord. The Mexicans are being courted ardently by the Europeans as well as the Japanese. France, for one, signed a ten-year pact for 100,000 barrels of crude oil a day, and offered a series of joint trade and investment incentives with Mexico to sweeten the deal. (French Industry Minister Giraud exclaimed enthusiastically that the accord was "unlike any other," in that it offered terms and agreements for a stable and permanent bilateral tie between the two countries.)

Mexico is not the only nation being pursued by the Japanese. Similar swaps of oil for money and technology have been made with Peru and two OPEC nations, Saudi Arabia and Nigeria. And these arrangements are not being made only in energy. The Japanese again have pioneered deals for vital minerals, such as copper and bauxite, in Latin America, Asia, and Africa. Nor are these swaps made only for the means of production. Increasingly, the swaps are also made for the means of destruction—arms, sophisticated weaponry, and military technology—in exchange for the natural resources of the Third World.

The French led the parade of European nations to the Middle East and Persian Gulf after the 1973 crisis, working out trades of energy for either technology or weaponry with several nations. More surprisingly, the West Germans followed, making energy deals with Saudi Arabia and other Middle East nations.

Even more sweeping are the arrangements being made by regional blocs, most notably the European Common Market. Beyond the pursuit of natural resources, the principal aim of these deals is to grab as big a share as possible of the growing Third World market for technology and capital goods. The most prominent example of such an arrangement is the Lomé Agreement, first signed in 1974 between the Common Market and the former European colonies, particularly in Africa. The Europeans have now expanded this into a Lomé II agreement with fifty-eight nations in Africa, the Caribbean, and the Pacific.

Lomé is a trade-investment-aid package between regions, and it is also the opening wedge of the effort by the Europeans to guarantee both growing shares of the big Third World market and stable sources of vital commodities. The Europeans have granted participating countries preferential access for their exports into the

Common Market. There is also a commodity price stabilizing scheme known as STABEX, which goes part of the way to answering demands of the developing countries for assured prices for their raw materials. And the European Community's Development Fund is being tailored to the needs of the fifty-eight Lomé nations. Lomé also set a pattern for other industrial nations, especially Japan, which in 1977 accelerated negotiations for similar arrangements with countries in Southeast Asia.

But the opening of China as a market in 1978 brought a quick shift by Japan away from the ASEAN group. Japan had espoused a "doctrine" that the ASEAN group had a special place under the rising sun, but there was no significant follow-up in trade or aid. As Japan directed more attention to China in 1978, the EEC countries started an intensive effort to fill the ASEAN vacuum with their own offers of a trade-investment-aid package.

Until November 1978, the EEC nations dealt with ASEAN on a bilateral, nation-to-nation basis. A meeting in Brussels began an accelerated process of creating an EEC-bloc-to-ASEAN-bloc relationship. *Far Eastern Economic Review,* noting that the meeting had more than political significance, observed that "it also put before [ASEAN] the tempting prospect of more European investment in their countries, trade benefits, transfer of technology and aid for the region—in fact, just what the ASEAN countries have been seeking from Japan." Indonesia's Mochtar Kusumaatmaja, ASEAN's spokesman, said, "This is all welcome if you project it against what is happening as a consequence of the Japan-China treaty."

These arrangements, useful as they may be for the participants, represent a second stage of post-market forces. As we have already seen, bargaining between Third World governments and multinational corporations has displaced classical market forces of short-run supply and demand. In the second stage, there is bargaining between governments or regional blocs, in consultation with their major industries and corporations. The essential elements of the bargaining remain the same: technology, finance, and marketing. So are the results: the supplanting of competitive market forces.

Industrial nations have a supply of technology and finance which is in demand by Third World nations. The industrial nations need access to Third World countries to sell their excess supplies of technology, capital goods, and intermediate products such as spare parts. The Third World nations need access to the markets of the industrial nations to sell their commodities, both raw and processed, as well as their manufactured goods.

For some Third World nations, the export markets are helpful in pushing them toward new levels of wealth and development. For others, exports are vital just to stay even. World Bank President Robert McNamara is fond of quoting these statistics to dramatize the situation: If Third World exports could expand from $35 billion in 1975 to $114 billion by 1985, the poorest countries would increase their growth by only 2 percent. The middle-income nations would increase annual growth by only 4 percent. For all the Western fears about Third World exports, these sales would do little in many cases to narrow the vast differences in national wealth between the world's rich and poor nations.

There is one more wrinkle in the question of global supply and demand. While Third World nations need the markets of the industrial world for their commodities, they have gained new power and leverage in deciding to which nations to sell. Their power rests in the relative vulnerability of the industrial democracies and their different degrees of dependence on strategic raw materials of the Third World. For example, the European Community nations rely 100 percent on imports for five of the thirteen standard categories of strategic materials, and these do not include oil. Japan is totally dependent in seven of the thirteen categories. In contrast, the vulnerability of the United States ranges from 20 percent in iron ore to 98 percent in manganese.

Europe and Japan have had a historic vulnerability and a dependence upon Third World resources. In the immediate postwar period, some of the dependence shifted toward the United States. The postwar economic dominance of the United States rested, in part, on the dependency of Europe and Japan on American, Australian, and Canadian raw materials, and on U.S. finance. The economic surge of prosperity and consumption of Europe and Japan has now once more intensified their dependence on Third World resources. This has been complemented by a diminished reliance on American finance and technology. And since 1975, the Third World has replaced the United States as the principal export market for Japan and Western Europe. These shifts in dependence, in differing degrees in different industrial countries, are a major cause of the schisms in the industrial world.

There are indications that a more serious economic *realpolitik* is in the making. Economists working in the glass skyscraper that houses the European Economic Community headquarters call it "maximizing complementarity," or "targeting." It really is a parceling out of markets and manufacturing between two trading partners or blocs. Its implications for the global economy in the 1980s are dramatic.

For example, the Europeans are turning to joint production ventures of auto vehicles and parts in the ASEAN countries. ASEAN is pushing for the realization of an all-ASEAN vehicle, and the Europeans are attempting to offer a most attractive choice of finance and know-how to these governments. If successful, the lucrative ASEAN vehicle market will become a virtual EEC–ASEAN joint-venture monopoly. In addition, ASEAN wants to assign to each of its five member nations a "specialty"—giving, say, to Thailand a monopoly on the production of body parts and to Malaysia a monopoly in power train units and electrical systems.

"Fierce competition" was the theme of a 1978 strategy paper of the European Economic Community. The community officials predicted there would be "immense needs" in the Third World countries for capital goods for industry, energy, transport, communications, and urban housing and construction. Rushing to fill these needs would be the industrial nations, the Eastern bloc countries, and, increasingly, the Third World nations themselves. The paper advocated a "growth strategy" that would make a reality of "the potential additional demand represented by the developing countries . . . through joint measures whose implementation is favored by the special links of the community and these countries" —in other words, take advantage of the historic colonial and postcolonial ties and build on them. The paper advocated "more support for research into the needs of, and the most appropriate technology for developing countries." The second element of the strategy was "mastery of the art of mobilizing and organizing, in partnership with the developing countries, the entire array of supplies, services, and finance needed. . . .

"This ability to integrate and administer all the elements of the project can be a trump card in the hands of Community suppliers competing for a stake in the development process," the report asserted. In other words, package deals organized between European governments and European companies are penetrating the Third World behind the wedge of historic relationships. The report did not need to say that these "trump cards"—either the historic bonds or organized business-government relations—were absent from the hands of American competitors.

The package deals between industrial nations or blocs and the Third World serve a variety of diplomatic and political as well as economic objectives. In the present atmosphere of stagflation and unemployment, the industrial nations can no longer proclaim their borders open to the free trade of Third World imports. The industrial nations and their potential Third World trading partners are caught in a descending spiral. The bilateral deals offer a way out, dressed up as they sometimes are in the cloak of "orderly marketing arrangements." For instance, in the negotiations between Japan and the Southeast Asian nations, there also was talk of targeting, or setting specific objectives for trade-investment-aid packages.

Aid that goes to the supply sector of a Third World nation—a shoe factory, for example—would be set to achieve a specific level of production. During the start-up time, the industrial nations such as Japan would have a chance to make structural adjustments in their home industries likely to be affected by the new Third World imports. The Japanese shoe industry could be diverted to producing high-quality handbags or, over a longer period, be converted with new machinery into an industry not in competition with the newly industrializing countries'.

Obviously, "targeting" and other package deals are a final admission that the "automatic adjustment" of supply and demand through "free" markets and "free" trade can no longer be trusted. Ironically, such deals end up achieving the same results the proponents of free trade have historically advocated: a poorer country is selling what it has to offer—lower cost, abundant labor, or natural resources. A developed country is selling what it has to offer—technology, capital, and management expertise. But instead of being based on classical market forces between companies or corporations exclusively, the deals now involve the heavy intervention of governments. The governments of at least some Third World countries now have a new leverage—the dependency of the richer country on their raw materials. And government intervention guarantees the poorer country what it could not obtain in straight deals with the corporations in the 1950s and 1960s—an adequate rate of return for its labor.

V

The possible consequence of this bloc-to-bloc negotiating is the development of regional spheres of economic, and perhaps political, influence. Present global leanings and alignments could become institutionalized, first by economic arrangements and later through political collaboration. The emergence of competitive blocs with their spheres of influence resembles the competition among the giant multinationals a decade or more ago. Their existence and competition were a stabilizing influence for a time, but soon price wars and other rivalries tended to develop. Nations within such arrangements will inevitably feel the temptation to leave the sphere and to stretch their bargaining power, perhaps with members of a rival bloc. Unless the role of regional arrangements is clearly delineated and coordinated internationally, the potential for rivalry and conflict abounds.

For example, there is a geographic logic for Indonesia to enter into a regional economic bloc with Japan and other Southeast Asian nations. Yet, within a few years, Indonesia's level of economic and industrial development and the structure of its industry and agriculture could make it a more likely trading partner for Europe or North America. Conversely, Japan may find (as it has in China) a more attractive partner elsewhere. Once in a bloc, a country would be under great pressure not to desert its partners. A Hobson's choice of either economic inefficiency and stagnation or bloc instability and tension would be the likely result.

The Americans have a direct interest in these developments, which are taking place under the free trade rules of GATT while violating their very spirit. It will be American exports that start running into protectionist walls if these trade deals continue to expand. American multinationals will be trying to compete with foreign corporations that have the weight of their governments or regional trade blocs behind them in negotiations with Third World governments. Even an active export promotion policy by the American Government would be a limited weapon against these trade deals. The best American weapon is the reassertion of American economic leadership. As detailed in the next chapter, it should pursue globally coordinated growth programs involving the effective and equitable participation of industrial, OPEC, and Third World nations. This would attack a root cause of the shift toward regional blocs. Lifting the economies of the industrial democracies from stagflation is the counterforce to the pressures for protectionism. The renewal of U.S.–led economic growth would at least slow the race toward Third World trade deals.

There can be two principal losers in regional-bloc arrangements. The first are the very poor countries that have no resources to offer the industrial nations or whose markets are too small to attract sales of technology or capital. The second is the United States, whose government has always stood aloof from export promotion and systematic business-government cooperation in pursuit of foreign trade deals. *Systematic,* as it is used here, means an overall policy of package deals and trade promotion. In the past there have been obvious examples of U.S. Government–business collaboration in the Third World. (After World War II, the most noticeable were the intimate arrangements between the State Department and the major oil companies in the Arabian peninsula which writers Anthony Sampson and John Blair so clearly detailed in their studies of the oil giants.) Other examples include pre–World War II collaborations with U.S. fruit and mineral companies in Latin America. Later, these were rationalized by Cold War national security objectives, with the economic goals a convenient by-product for the corporations. More importantly, they were consummated in the absence of competitive opposition from other industrial nations and at a time when Third World governments had little bargaining power.

Curiously, the best ally of the U.S., should it resume its leadership role in pursuing an international approach toward world trade and financial problems, might be certain newly industrializing nations—even though it is their recent export surge that has created so much of the protectionist pressure. For all their exporting strength, such nations as South Korea, Hong Kong, Thailand, Malaysia, Kenya, and Singapore are resource-poor. The resource-dependent nations of Western Europe and Japan will be increasingly compelled to make trade-investment-aid package deals with resource-rich nations in the Third World and less so with the resource-poor exporters. Why should a country such as France, already under corporate and union pressure because of such product imports as Pierre Cardin imitations, make a deal with a country such as South Korea, which is only going to provide more of those imports? France, or any other industrial democracy, is far more likely to look for the same kind of deal with a resource-rich country such as Nigeria, which will also provide much wanted oil rather than unwanted textiles or shoes.

A common interest in revising global growth approaches should emerge among the resource-poor newly industrializing nations and the United States, Canada, and Australia, the least dependent of the industrial nations on foreign resources. Yet such potential common interest will be for naught if the U.S. fails to cooperate and lead in a global effort to revive world economic growth.

The U.S. can take much of the blame for the movement toward regional deals as well as trade, investment, and aid swaps. A major lag in its foreign policy has been an unwillingness to admit to the problems of GATT, particularly as stagflation has intensified and resource shortages have become more marked. There is a proper role for regional trade and for the use of swaps. The problem today is the absence of any formalized rules of the game which assure a common ground on which to compete. Even the U.S. treatment of its neighbor, Mexico, has failed to heed the lessons of the European Community with southern Europe. Mexico, like the latter, has surplus labor and a high demand for technology. Yet, in contrast to Europe's our policy focuses only on trade and refuses to see the link to a new arrangement governing legalized labor migration. Not surprisingly, Mexico is reluctant to negotiate formal commitments on oil when we shrink from talking about formal technology swaps and labor outlets. Similarly, during the seventies, the U.S. took for granted the rest of Latin America, failing to respond to proposals for new regional forms of cooperation.

This blind spot in U.S. foreign policy has not gone unheeded either in Latin America or among our industrial partners. In the absence of a U.S. focus on the new problems, which are not being addressed by existing multilateral institutions, they have proceeded on their own. When, for example, Mexico raised the price of its oil in late 1979 to the level of $32 per barrel, the U.S. sent an angry protest. But a few weeks later, the American Government at a public auction sold off oil at some $41 a barrel! This incident renewed the Mexican Government's interest in oil-for-technology swaps with other industrial nations and reinforced its decision not to join GATT despite U.S. pressure.

The U.S., like other nations, does have an interest in developing regional relations and, inevitably, will have to achieve a new bilateral arrangement with Mexico. Increasingly, American business and labor will also want to gain the advantages afforded by barter and swap trade. These as well as the inherent instability of arrangements not governed by a set of internationally accepted rules, should suggest a U.S. initiative in this direction. That this will come at a timely juncture is not at all assured, given the history of U.S. foreign economic policy during the past decade.

VI
Where Economic Rivalries End

History, as historians are fond of saying, does not repeat itself. But as the eminent historian Wilhelm Dilthey once wrote, there are patterns and meanings in history. Without being unduly alarmist and without predicting the start of another war, we might note that economic rivalries and economic upheavals have preceded political upheavals twice in this century. Europe's race for resource markets and colonies preceded the political tensions that erupted into World War I. Hitler came to power in the economic chaos of post–World War I Germany and then went on to gobble up a Europe whose political will and military strength had been sapped (in large measure) by the first war and the Depression.

In each of these prior historical periods, the industrial powers were at similar levels in three of four basic indices of economic power. Each had arrived at about the same point in technology, finance, and consumption. The cutting difference between them was their different degrees of dependence on strategic raw materials and markets; albeit in the 1930s all were suffering slower growth, relatively higher unemployment, and greater protectionist strangulation than at the end of the 1970s.

Economic rivalries can stimulate more intense political rivalries, even among nations that have been friendly trading partners. The current drift to bilateral and regional trading arrangements can only cause a shrinking of total world markets. Sustained protectionism always causes a slower rate of growth of total world production and consumption. For every Third World nation that benefits from a specific trade deal, there will be others left out and falling deeper into poverty and misery. There is also the question of whether the Soviet Union and the Eastern bloc will be satisfied with the slim pickings left over from these regional trade deals or whether they will try to enter the competition directly. Since the Soviet bloc has little to offer the up-and-coming nations of the Third World in technology or finance, its best card might well be to play on the discontent of the left-outs of the Third World. And this at a time when the two superpowers have now formalized "rules of the game" in the Third World.

Above all, the economic and political leadership of the United States would be eroded still further by the splintering and polarization of the industrial democracies. In the immediate post–World War II era, the United States responded to the economic errors of the pre-war period by promoting order through international organizations that helped smooth the way for the growth of world trade and finance. Now the global revolution has overtaken some of these institutions, and new forms of instability have arisen. The decade of global stagflation has produced new institutional gaps. New and modified institutions are not a substitute for new policies, but along with new policies, they can create a new basis for global economic stability that in part will have to be based on the Third World as the planet's newest growth frontier.

The 1980s are a transition period in which the paramount goal of rejuvenating economic growth in the North, and therefore in the South, must be pursued. Nevertheless, establishing economic growth as a priority does not diminish the need to create a new international order. Whatever policies are followed to achieve growth in the 1980s, they must, at a minimum, set the stage for the creation of a new institutional order to sustain the more complex growth and development goals of the 1990s. It is to this twofold exploration that we now turn.

CHAPTER 6

Toward a New Order: The Next Frontier

I

THE OBSTACLES TO CREATING a new global economic order are staggering, but no more staggering than the consequences of failure. The alternative to reform, for rich and poor nations alike, is economic regression, social disorder, and, for many nations, political authoritarianism. In this book we have talked about the global economic revolution, and it is that revolution that offers the prospect either of reform, which the U.S. can help lead and direct, or of further revolution, over which this country will have little or no control. Political reform is a more difficult task than political revolution. The luxury of revolution is its annihilation of existing institutional structures and power centers, of the very historical circumstances that created it in the first place.

Reform, in contrast, must accept all the stresses and contradictions that created need for change and carry them several steps forward. International economic reform means taking what we have—the existing international institutions such as the World Bank, IMF, and GATT, the economies of the industrial and oil nations—and directing them to the most pressing condition—namely, the nations of the Third World and their suffering and poverty and their potential to become a major motor of world economic growth in the coming decades. Successful reform usually means small but innovative efforts, frequently falling short of the ultimate hopes of those calling for them, but capable of being put

NOTE: The author gratefully acknowledges the collaboration of David H. Moore in the research, design, and drafting of this chapter.

into effect. Unlike panaceas, they do not necessarily promise to solve problems but begin to make them more manageable.

The object of the reforms we will be discussing is to achieve for the American and world economy a certain period of "breathing space," allowing us during that time to start making the necessary and fundamental long-term adjustments and adaptations to the global economic revolution and new global economic order. In chapter 3 we described a "vicious circle" existing in the American economy. There is an even larger vicious circle existing in the world economy. For a decade there was no growth, or slow growth, especially in the industrial world. Without growth it is impossible or nearly impossible to achieve reforms, which are necessary to create more growth. For example, the response of governments to stagflation has been regression to protectionism. In contrast, the fundamental necessity for growth and reform is structural adjustment, adapting old industries and creating new ones to meet the new global competition and international divisions of labor. Protectionism makes adjustment more difficult and less likely to occur. As stagflation persists, the vicious circle becomes ever more difficult to break: Without growth, no reform; but without reform, no growth.

Until the last decade, the industrial world could look upon the Third World as a problem, an area of potential conflicts and even an occasional source of guilt, but not as a realm whose economic fate would be pivotally tied to ours. In the last decade the Third World has been drawn into the links of global interdependence with the industrial world, in part because of and in part despite the great differences in wealth and standards of living. For all the gains of the OPEC and newly industrializing nations, and the improved conditions for millions, the basic statistics for human life remain grim. Today, of the 4.2 billion persons living in the world, nearly two-thirds live out their lives in the worst kind of poverty. In the forty-five nations of the so-called Fourth World, which includes 1.5 billion people, the average life expectancy is less than fifty years. The chances are one in three that these people will be able to read and one in ten that their children will survive the first year of life. Half of those surviving will suffer permanent brain damage because of childhood malnutrition.

Yet, despite these grim figures, there has been real improvement. Life expectancy in the next-to-poorest countries of the Third World has gone up by ten years since 1969; it took the Western nations nearly a century to make the same improvement. Adult literacy in the Third World has increased from one-third to one-half in thirty years, and per capita income has increased an average of 3 percent per year. Per capita income is a coldly misleading statistic for measuring the condition of people in the Third World, but even so, their hopes for a better life depend on a dynamic and growing world economy. The Third World's recent economic growth cannot be sustained without a return to stable growth in the industrial world. Developing nations continued to grow between 1974 and 1978, despite global stagflation. This created, in the words of David Hausego of the *Financial Times,* "a delusion that has gained surprisingly wide currency"—that the Third World nations will continue to grow at a rapid clip even if slow growth persists in the industrial nations.

This condition, this position of dependence, is hardly new for the Third World. What is new are the forms of dependence that have arisen in the industrial world. The industrial world not only needs the resources and labor of the Third World nations; it now needs their more rapidly growing markets to lift the Western economies out of stagflation and to new levels of growth. This is the fundamentally new link of global interdependence. To succeed, global economic reform needs both to recognize and to exploit this new interdependence.

The elements of global economic reform are the same as those underlying domestic economic reform. There is the need for better global efficiency to restore economic growth, more global equity to ensure better distribution of that growth, and more global political participation to accommodate the new centers of power. These are not mutually exclusive goals; more participation, for example, will help achieve more equity. But, achieving these objectives will not be easy. Reform is frequently accompanied by political conflict, by the grudging giving up of some power to new competitors.

The primary objectives of global reform also resemble those of the domestic economy—to break the bottlenecks in demand, supply, and finance. As one Swedish minister said, the world economy needs "a globalization of the Keynesian maxim of demand stimulation." But as the 1970s have shown, demand stimulation by itself is not enough. Equally crucial are measures to rationalize and expand supply, to handle the crucial problems of adjustment. The objectives and goals have to be realized within living institutions and programs. The aim of the proposed reforms is to modify institutions and programs, not to create wholly new ones. Essentially, this means expanding the IMF–World Bank complex to give it some characteristics of a central bank. Its primary responsibility would be to promote global monetary stability, essential for ensuring investment growth and for balancing global supply and demand. But to do this would require supplementing the reserve role of the dollar. Global growth will have to be triggered by coordinated programs that also promote the SDR into the role of the international reserve currency. Within the IMF–World Bank or elsewhere, such programs are needed to channel investment to the "new growth frontier" of the Third World. It is in developing nations that tremendous potential demand exists, and it is there that many conventional industries such as steel can operate more productively and at higher rates of return than in the industrial world. Equally important, global economic management also requires a limited effort at supply coordination, breaking production bottlenecks in energy, food, and mineral resources. Unless these bottlenecks of global shortages are broken, the industrial world is threatened with persistent inflation throughout the 1980s.

It was the OPEC price increases of 1973 and 1974 that drove home the new nature of global interdependence to the average driver of a car. The OPEC action also gave new professional credence and currency to the concept of vicious circles. Until then the concept of vicious circles, once found only in the theoretical work of development economics, had been largely ignored by both Keynesians and Chicago monetarists in the mainstream of free market economics. Now it is a theme at least picked up in the press. The process of reform starts by identifying where incisions can be made within the vicious circles to convert those circles into a virtuous spiral of growth. This process will also start with the recognition and agreement of governments that these incisions—in global finance, demand stimulation, and supply shortages and gluts—cannot be created through an exclusive reliance on the automatic workings of the laws of short-run supply and demand.

II

In the late 1940s the United States assumed, partly by default, the position of global economic and political leadership. It confronted a Europe devastated by World War II and becoming divided by the Cold War. The American economy, undamaged and preeminent after the war, needed new and bigger markets to sustain growth and to avoid slipping back into a depression. The response of the American leadership and political elite was the Marshall Plan. Its imagination and ingenuity were greater than even its scope, a relatively small $13 billion in grants and loans to Western European nations. The Marshall Plan has gone down in history as one of the great successes of American foreign policy, an act of enlightened self-interest that fulfilled its political objectives of maintaining democratic stability in Western Europe and preventing the western expansion of Soviet power and influence. It also more than fulfilled its economic expectations, creating in Europe not only a vast new market for American goods but a realm of activity for expansion of American multinational corporations and banks.

In the 1980s a similar situation exists. The industrial nations of the West are suffering stagflation and are in search of new export outlets to promote growth. The nations of the Third World, all anxious to achieve economic development, offer a vast new source of immense potential for Western goods and technology. What is new is, first, the existence of several hundred billion dollars of idle investment funds held largely in the Eurocurrency market; and, second, the fact that, as opposed to the forties, when the United States was at least in a position to succeed Britain in the world leadership role, there is today no heir apparent among individual nations or groups of nations, such as the Common Market. The United States, to the degree it chooses to exercise leadership, is more first among equals. Leadership now means multilateral leadership, more trying and frustrating, especially to the neoconservatives, who think we can resolve our economic problems with a return to protectionism and outright military supremacy on a globe spending almost $400 billion per year on weapons.

During the 1950s and 1960s, the industrial North was the globe's leading engine of growth. Today, there is a growing recognition, at least in Europe and Japan, that the planet's major growth motor in the 1990s will have to be the developing South. But to bring the South on line as the globe's major growth center in the nineties means it will have to be explicitly treated as the new growth frontier of the eighties. Pioneering this frontier requires more than "simple Keynesianism." Demand stimulation must be targeted globally so as to overcome two other bottlenecks. Simply building pyramids to stimulate demand will not break the blockages in international capital markets and the blockages to global supply expansion in energy and other resource areas. In the North, this will require adjustments to declining industries on which the more competitive South's future growth is dependent and which currently is stalled by the rise of protectionism.

It is the very existence of a curious anomaly that now offers hope in the global crisis of confidence now crippling the world economy. The anomaly is that investors are holding a global liquidity pool approaching one trillion dollars which they are apprehensive about committing, even though there is a deep need for new fixed investment in the United States and in the Third World. The United States needs new plant and equipment to create jobs, as we detailed in chapter 3. The Third World needs capital goods and technology to overcome poverty. For example, there is an estimated $25 billion to $30 billion in feasible mining and energy projects in the Third World for which no financing is currently available.

It is up to the United States to take the initiative and seize it, as other nations have been urging us to do in a variety of international economic and political forums. The irony of massive idle investment funds existing side by side with massive unmet needs suggests an approach that would move this money to areas where it is needed. That is what the Marshall Plan did, with far less cash and a lower return thirty years ago, and what a new global Marshall Plan could put into motion now. An infusion of now often idle wealth of the Eurocurrency pool into developing nations would allow large segments of the Third World to import from us the capital goods and technology we produce. This would have an obvious circular effect, stimulating our economy and the economies of the Third World, helping poorer nations overcome their mounting short-term debt problems, which have curtailed their ability to buy our exports.

After 1976, there was a flurry of proposals from leaders in both North and South for a global Marshall Plan approach to the contradictions of global interdependence. Behind the many proposals was the intrinsic idea of "targeting" the Third World as a new growth frontier to break the blockages of the supply and demand sides of the world economy. West Germany's Helmut Schmidt raised the issue in a significant speech before the International Institute for Strategic Studies.

"Today," said Schmidt in 1977, "like the situation after the Second World War, the economic and military aspects of our security policy are again on a par with each other. . . . The task [of the original Marshall Plan] presents itself anew today under different conditions."

Two other European leaders have also pointed to the need for new markets to help lift the industrial democracies out of the recession. Claude Cheysson, the European Community's development commissioner, proposed a Marshall Plan approach to the Third World specifically as a countercyclical device—to pump up world demand and renew growth. Independently of Cheysson, Austrian chancellor Bruno Kreisky said the industrial nations needed to exploit the lessons of the original Marshall Plan.

Kreisky told a trade union convention in October 1978 that a "political incentive" was required to overcome the international economic crisis and that a plan similar to the Marshall Plan "would be an enormous step forward in the development of the countries of the Third World and the Western industrial nations." Without such a plan, he said, the Third World remains a market only in theory and lacking the means to pay for the goods it needs.

"Of course this idea requires consideration of how this could all be financed," Kreisky said, "but I am of the very simple, almost banal point of view that if thousands of millions can be raised for armaments, it must be possible to raise a fraction of this in order to bring about a new economic relationship between the modern industrial nations and the countries of the Third World, and, if you like, the Third and Fourth Worlds—to be more exact."

This interest was not limited to the Western world. In April 1977, Venezuelan President Carlos Andres Pérez asked me to draft a memo on a number of issues he wanted to discuss on a forthcoming trip to the Persian Gulf.

"Would it be possible," Pérez asked, "to design a mechanism that would promote world growth in the mutual interest of OPEC, of the industrial nations of OECD, and of non-OPEC Third World countries yet could, in fact, be feasible and politically acceptable to all three sides?"

Three major issues had to be addressed. The first was the existence of the billions in the Eurocurrency cash pool, symbolic of the global inefficiency and sitting idle while rich and poor nations both were suffering a capital formation crisis and desperately needing new and productive investment. And, of course, a big part of that cash pool, somewhere between 25 percent and 35 percent, was OPEC petrodollar surpluses, unspent money from their oil exports. That cash pool, and the OPEC surpluses, large as they are, are expected to expand.

The second issue was how to alleviate the growing problem of Third World debt, even given a commitment to a global Marshall Plan. And, finally, there was the question of how much a global Marshall Plan would contribute to promoting growth in the poorest of the poor, in such Fourth World countries as Bangladesh and Chad. And, as a part of that question, what would be the role of OPEC and other Third World nations in such a program—would they be genuine participants in the decision making? These questions, raised in a variety of bilateral meetings and at the ill-fated North-South conference in Paris in 1977, remain fundamental as various nations and advocates grope toward creating a global Marshall Plan.

In fact, they were raised that same year in official visits to the White House by the leaders of both Venezuela and Saudi Arabia. The response then was one of polite interest but was never followed up very far within the Washington bureaucracies. The predominant official feeling then, a reflection of mainstream economic thought, was that the 1974–75 recession was a "transitory anomaly" and that growth policies by the industrial nations, as advocated at the 1977 London economic summit, would set the world economy on an upward and noninflationary course. As that assumption became untenable in the stagflation of 1978–79, new interest did percolate in Washington.

The study of a Marshall Plan by the Venezuelan Government

picked up press and academic attention. There was also more interest in Congress. In 1978, forty senators and congressmen offered resolutions suggesting the creation of a global capital pool, money that could be loaned to Third World nations to buy capital machinery, technology, and technical services from industrial nations. "Thirty years ago," stated Representative Michael D. Barnes (D., Maryland), "the United States adopted the Marshall Plan to rebuild a world devastated by war, hunger and disease. We should consider a similar approach today." The flaw in many of the congressional plans, however, was that they would help the newly industrializing Third World nations but offer little to the poorest Fourth World nations.

The global Marshall Plan, with various themes and variations, was gradually gaining more credence in international forums. In April 1978 the Secretary General of the OECD proposed a "stepped-up investment plan for the Third World." Rather than relying upon a centralized financial mechanism at the World Bank, the OECD plan discussed a variety of "co-financing" arrangements between private banks, OPEC countries, and multilateral banks. By the end of the year, Sweden and ten other European nations proposed resolutions at the United Nations suggesting further study and implementation of some kind of global stimulation program. Other proposals were made, one by the Mexican Government.

And at about the same time in 1978 that the OECD secretariat in Paris and officials in Mexico City were making their separate proposals for "global stimulation," another was forthcoming from Japan. It emanated from Masaki Nakajima, head of the think tank of one of Japan's largest and most influential industry groups, the twenty-six corporation Mitsubishi Combine. "To overcome the worldwide recession, there is no way but to stimulate private business activity in the major industrialized nations." Noting that "we are faced today with the urgent task of evolving means to absorb the prevailing excessive international liquidity," and that inflationary pressures and Proposition 13 politics mean that "all the conventional types of public investment have their limits in terms of needs and capability when looked at solely in light of each national economy," the Mitsubishi group proposed a "global New Deal." It focused on massive multinational public works projects in the

Third World—the Greening of the Deserts, Collection Stations for Solar Heat, Electric Power Stations Using Sea Currents, Himalayan and African Hydroelectric Projects. The research institute, which does much of its work for the Japanese Government, said: "[We] believe that in order to allow the existing world economic system to follow a peaceful and steady course without excessive dependence on military expenditures, a type of public investment would be strategically effective [by] removing restraints on resources . . . to eliminate latent factors causing inflation." The group's proposal called for a $13 billion annual expenditure with $5 billion from other industrial nations, that would have a multiplier effect of increasing global income by $25 billion a year.

In the face of these proposals, the U.S. Government has maintained silence, offering not even a hint of whether it thinks kindly or ill of them. In this instance, however, the Europeans and Japanese are not waiting for the U.S. leadership. As we have detailed earlier, their governments have embarked on a variety of regional and bilateral programs to stimulate Third World economies and to create markets for their own exports. Lacking a clear plan of its own, the United States may find itself backing into a Marshall Program, at least in the Middle East. It is picking up the check for the Israeli-Egyptian peace treaty. Now all of Egypt's development schemes hinge primarily on private and public American aid since its richer Arab brethren have severed economic as well as diplomatic relations. Whether the Egyptian programs become the groundwork for a Marshall Plan or merely a salvage operation for President Sadat remains to be seen.*

The idea of a global Marshall Plan has not met with universal acclaim. The principal opposition springs from two very different camps. One, curiously, consists of certain elements of the "devel-

* Despite the massive American political and financial stake in Egypt, Europeans are jumping with more speed into the most lucrative business deals there. While their governments give only grudging assent to the Egypt-Israeli peace, for fear of upsetting other Arabs, German and French companies are pulling off financial coups in Cairo. A contract for rebuilding the country's collapsing telephone system was not won, as expected, by a consortium of American firms, but by a combination of German, Austrian, and French. This consortium was headed by Siemens of West Germany, a firm with long experience in the area. Beyond a $1.8 billion plan for fixing the phones, there will be a $1.2 billion package that includes modernization of the railways, developing coal mining and power generating in Sinai, and a joint venture company to transfer technical expertise from Europe.

opment bureaucracy" of the international and bilateral assistance agencies. The other camp comprises the Marxist theorists. The view of the development bureaucracy, caught up in the day-to-day struggle with development programs, was summed up in a 1979 conversation I had with a high official. He told me that only "the charitable inclinations of the rich nations, rather than their own immediate interests, dictate stepped-up investment in the Third World." Like all bureaucracies, the development people have their own vested interests and live in their own cocoons. As one member of the World Bank's board of directors lamented, "the bank's leadership is too often paralyzed by its dependency on technical expertise that hasn't been updated for many years."

The Marxist argument, stated by Paul Baran more than twenty years ago, remains intact. "What is decisive," Baran wrote then, "is that the economic development of underdeveloped countries is profoundly inimical to the dominant interests in the advanced capitalist countries."

What this argument ignores, of course, is the demonstrated flexibility of industrial capitalism and its ability to expand wealth and also the capacity of Third World economic development to further rather than hinder industrial capitalism's basic interests and its driving force for new markets.

To make this argument does not suggest that industrial capitalism has risen to the task of alleviating Third World poverty—far from it. If anything, the individual governments of the industrial democracies (except for the Netherlands and Scandinavia) are giving proportionally less in traditional aid programs than in the past. The UN target of 0.7 percent of GNP in development aid from each industrial nation has never been met. In fact, it has slipped to something like 0.3 percent. And whatever relative or marginal improvements there are in the standard of living in the Third World, the overwhelming condition of poverty and misery intractably exists.

As Malaysia's governor on the World Bank board once said, the nations of the North have failed to pull the world out of persistent slow growth. At the same time, their traditional aid to the South is shrinking.

Given these parallel failures, proposals for international economic and financial policy reform increasingly must center on the multilateral approach. A variety of North to South transfer programs could fulfill the objective of what otherwise could be a global Marshall Plan, or what some call a "world development fund." They are all multilateral in approach and aimed at avoiding the schisms created by some of the regional and bilateral trade and aid deals we discussed earlier. Some have primarily economic motivations, such as the World Bank's special petroleum development program, and others have a mix of economic and national security motives such as the proposal for a development plan to cement the Egyptian-Israeli peace treaty, under joint financing by the U.S., Japan, and Europe.

Styled for the 1980s, Marshall Plan initiatives represent a catch-up, an overcoming of the policy lags in international economic relations brought about by the speed and depth of post-market changes of the global economic revolution this book has been tracking. Such initiatives are a form of pioneering, of experimentation in working out processes of decision making, as much as they are a new type of policy tool. They are as much "process" as they are "content." Such experimentation, in one sense, is a parallel—at the grand "macro" level of multination decision-making—to the experiments in new bargaining power and decision processes pioneered by Third World governments and multinational corporations at the "micro" level of global interdependence.

In another sense, a Marshall Plan attacks the poverty and debt of the Third World in the mutual interest of the industrial states' growth. This form of global stimulation is a "globalization of Keynesianism," *but* with an important modification. While these transfers to the Third World increase the South's demand for the output of the North, they are not, as has been the case with national applications of Keynesian tools, an indiscriminate stimulus of the globe's aggregate level of demand in disregard of the supply side. Surely, in a book that has as one of its main theses the emergence of a post-market global economy, these initiatives could not place sole reliance on the workings of competitive markets and "invisible-hand" economics to assure "automatically" which sectors of production will expand and contract in response to this new tool of global demand management.

Instead, a Marshall Plan stimulus applies the development

economics principle of targeting. Funds are allocated by policy decision into strategic sectors to overcome global shortages that, if left untouched, would be a key source of worldwide inflation by the mid-1980s. In these cases—the extraction and processing of energy and minerals, the production of food, and basic infrastructure—the econopolitics of imperfect and nonexistent market forces have to be dealt with by post-market policy remedies that recognize their existence. Similarly, in the first round of a Marshall Plan stimulus, the industry targets in the South should not be shoes, textiles, petrochemicals, or others that are symbols in the North of global supply gluts and adjustment failures. These Third World industries must await a second-round stimulus, affording a "breathing space" within which higher growth allows the industrial democracies the political circumstances to launch their own national structural adjustment efforts on the supply sides of their domestic economies. Indeed, a multilaterally financed and managed global stimulation program is as much a medium-term growth tool of supply expansion as it is a Keynesian device to overcome insufficient demand.

Finally, North-South Marshall Plan experimentation should have, by design, in its decision-making process, "checks and balances" to guard against both understandable and less understandable fears that emanate from both sides of the globe. Various ideological camps must be persuaded that this will be a feasible exercise in international econopolitics. It is here where perhaps the most telling of policy lags is encountered. The "tripolar" decision-making of the OECD group of industrial democracies, the OPEC group, and the Third World recipient nations is a double "check." One is on the South's fear of reigniting international economic forces that perpetuate the North's historic dominance —a fear of persisting global inequality shared equally by the Right and the Left in the South. A second is a check on the North's fear, particularly among its elected officials, of having to argue for increased aid budgets only out of moral concern at a time when the majority of their electorates have seen their real incomes wracked by inflation and eroded by slow growth and intractable unemployment. A global ethic still lags far behind the global economic links that have already made the planet, in a material sense, a global community.

That there are "balances" in this global stimulation experiment comes out of the message of the microcosms of change surveyed in chapter 4. In a Marshall Plan attack on the "development war" of the South and the "stagflation disease" of the North, there are roles for both private enterprise and nation-state government. The financing of this assault is either through a bond mechanism or cofinancing schemes, and must involve both private and public financial institutions. The actual projects in the Third World will have to involve both private multinational and state enterprises, as they already have for so many years. A 1980s North-South Marshall Plan will be as much of an experiment in business-government cooperation as its original predecessor was.

III

The mechanics of a global Marshall Plan are basically simple, and certainly the proposals offered in the last two years fall within the realm of the possible. They could be fitted easily into existing international institutions. They would stretch rather than dramatically change existing patterns of finance, investment, and development.

For example, securing OPEC participation is vital because the other holders of the uninvested hundreds of billions of dollars in the Eurocurrency market cannot make commitments without knowing what OPEC will do. One approach envisages a series of "OPEC Development Bonds" to be issued in U.S. and foreign capital markets. OPEC itself would buy 25 percent of the bonds and guarantee them with a Triple A rating, giving them the best available combination of interest rates and security. The other 75 percent would be offered to banks, insurance companies, pension funds, and other private investors, especially in the Eurocurrency market.

The money raised in selling these bonds would go into a special fund trust with its own directors, an existing device used for extraordinary but temporary purposes by the World Bank and its affiliates. This would give OPEC and the other bond-offering nations a vehicle for participation without getting involved in creating new organizations or rewriting the World Bank charter. Within the

World Bank, the United States and other industrial nations could provide a second guarantee for the bonds and could as well make their own direct contributions to a newly established "world development fund."

Financing raised by the bond issues could be supplemented by contributions from industrial nations to a World Bank "special window." Of the total fund, between 20 percent and 25 percent would go to the least-developed countries in the Fourth World. The rest would go, via the World Bank, to projects in other developing nations which could generate a rate of return required for a Triple A bond, and which would mature over twelve to twenty years. Through the special window, there would be an annual transfer to the Third World of $10 billion to $12.5 billion. At least $8 billion of this would represent a net increase in financing for non-OPEC developing nations. The money would be available to finance more port, irrigation, food production and storage, mining and processing, hydroelectric, and other basic development projects in the Third World. Much of the equipment and technology purchased under such arrangements would come, as it does now, from the United States and other industrial nations.

The investments would be targeted to such areas, rather than into such glut industries as steel, shipbuilding, and textiles. A coordinated investment program offers the opportunity of cooperation between industrial nations coping with their ailing industries and the Third World nations trying to build an industrial base. In the past, uncoordinated aid and investment programs have contributed to the gluts. This kind of supply-side coordination is necessary to gain the cooperation of the industrial democracies now confronting protectionist pressures.

The bond issue would serve as a credit mobilizer of idle liquid funds. It is estimated that for each dollar of bonds purchased by OPEC, another three to five dollars would be purchased by private investors. This feature also helps to limit any potential inflationary factor, mopping up excess liquidity rather than generating new money.

As in the original Marshall Plan, and a key to its success, decisions would be made with the participation of the recipients. One of the most dramatic aspects of the first Marshall Plan was the requirement that the European nations develop programs and priorities for the American aid. With a special trust fund arrangement at the World Bank, nations of OPEC, the OECD, and the Third World would all participate in the crucial decisions on allocation. This would give OPEC the larger voice it has sought in international organizations without the politically cumbersome and time-consuming effort to rewrite the Bank's constitution. It would also give the Third World nations a more important role in determining how best to use the aid money. In fact, such a mechanism is similar to the original Marshall Plan, although there was only one donor—the United States. Once the Europeans reached agreement among themselves on programs and priorities, they went for approval to the small group of Americans running the European recovery program to set the plans in motion by providing the money.

A global Marshall Plan, functioning primarily within the existing World Bank organization, or regional plans with such institutions as the Asian, African, or Inter-American Development Banks, would not require a vast new bureaucracy. It could be carried out by these institutions' operational staffs. In fact, global and regional Marshall Plan funds could be allocated to existing programs of international development banks, for example, the energy and minerals programs of the World Bank, which OPEC countries have already approved. In many ways, therefore, a global Marshall Plan program represents a major new initiative in international decision-making at a political level for economic purposes. But it does not require new organizations and bureaucracies. Indeed, this is one of the appeals of the idea.

Three-way decision-making—among the industrial nations, OPEC nations, and Third World recipients—would not be easy, but it would offer a unique way to overcome some existing policy lags, via a new form of checks and balances. The OPEC and developing nations would have checks on what they might fear as an attempt by the North to reassert its historic dominance. The industrial nations would have checks on their persistent fear of waste and inefficiency. They would also be able to justify such a program to their skeptical electorates not as a matter of charity but as an investment that would help pull them out of stagflation.

The experience of the World Bank's current oil exploration program offers a precedent and an illustration of how a Marshall

Plan program might work. The $3 billion fund for the program was created because the major oil companies had failed to explore in many areas of the Third World, even though all preliminary evidence points to a 10–1 advantage in barrels of oil in non-OPEC developing nations over the United States and Western Europe. As William Lane of the U.S. Energy Department's Office of Competition put it, there was "a significant market failure; the *laissez faire* system the oil companies operate under has simply broken down."

Even within the World Bank there was initial opposition. Some officials argued—in the face of evidence showing no great increase in exploration despite the great price hikes of 1973–74—that a fund was unnecessary, because higher prices would provide adequate incentives to the majors. There was also opposition from the majors. According to the Washington *Post,* Exxon Board Chairman Clifton Garvin went to Treasury Secretary Blumenthal (the U.S. representative on the Bank board) to urge the U.S. to oppose the fund. Garvin argued that investment in Third World countries was too risky politically and that the market mechanism should be left alone.

The industry's fundamental opposition to new supply sources was best described by the late John Blair, in his most respected and final work, *The Control of Oil.* In an interview before his death he summarized what he believed to be one of his basic findings: "OPEC and the companies have a system that works to both of their benefits. Certainly from the company point of view, expanded supply would only complicate their very profitable and existing relationship with OPEC."

The Bank's U.S. representative did manage to resist the Exxon blandishments, and the fund was created with American support. But the need for such an energy fund and the struggle to create it illustrate the role a global Marshall Plan could play in supply as well as demand economics. The funds could be directed, as much as possible, at supply bottlenecks that have developed in the post-market world economy. The more coordinated such programs are, the less likely the world is to swing between gluts and shortages, which have characterized the economy in the past decade.

Three major issues have to be addressed in any discussion of global and regional Marshall Plans. First, would the financing contribute to international monetary and financial stability? Second, would it set an example and establish the Third World as a new growth frontier? Finally, could it lead to a loose form of global supply management if it incorporated sector targets for supply sources along with early-warning systems and programs for structural adjustment?

There is little disagreement that Third World nations would benefit from a combination of more grant aid and commercial investment. But there is also the question of how much they can absorb without triggering inflation or social dislocation. This is a principal argument of many in the international development bureaucracies. After Iran, certain OPEC leaders are worried about too much modernization too fast. Obviously, absorption is a valid argument for developing nations with an abundant inflow of foreign exchange, but this is hardly the case for most Third World countries.

More often than not, the absorption argument is a political bogey. "Be it a penny or a billion dollars," one development official said, "absorption will always be raised when any discussion of increasing the flow of financial resources to developing countries comes to the fore." Interviews with staff in the multilateral regional development banks invariably raised the fact, summed up by one vice-president, "that when it comes to special trust funds or increasing funding for other agencies, World Bank staff cry absorption constraints in recipient countries." Even discounting this for possible interagency rivalry, there appears to be a grain of truth. "Isn't it curious," adds another official, "that absorption hasn't stopped the World Bank from asking for a large increase in its own funding levels?" Not surprisingly, in scores of interviews with development officials around the world, the absorption issue was almost always raised by those from industrial nations and not by representatives of the Third World. As we have seen in chapters 4 and 5, many Third World governments are improving their capability of controlling development inflows of either grant aid financed by international institutions or commercial investments from multinational corporations. And Third World nations in combination with improved international technical assistance efforts are making real headway in overcoming absorption problems.

Absorption is a minor problem compared with the debts confronting many Third World nations. These are bound to grow even more steeply in the 1980s, threatening Western financial markets and banks, unless global growth is accelerated. Since the 1973 oil price increases, the debt of non-oil Third World nations has risen dramatically, and they have been forced to shift a larger proportion of their borrowings from public international sources to private multinational banks—a fourfold increase, to $26.4 billion. The ability of private banks to take over a good part of this lending role from the international institutions (from 27 percent to 45 percent of Third World debt between 1973 and 1977) showed great flexibility in the system but could lead to major problems in the 1980s. Many of these private bank loans were based on the assumption that old levels of world growth would return, giving the Third World nations outlets for exports and money to pay back the loans. What is happening instead is slow growth in investment and protectionism that limits export earnings. The resulting crunch has forced Third World nations since the mid-1970s to take on mostly short-term private loans.

According to *Euromoney* magazine in 1979, the non-oil Third World nations were spending 27 percent of their foreign exchange funds to refinance maturing debts. This will increase to 65 percent by 1986. These projections have already become reality in some countries. Brazil's debt-to-export-earning ratio has already reached a historic 47 percent and could rise above a staggering 60 percent by 1981. Peru, Zaire, and Turkey are already reeling under heavy debt.

By early 1980, big borrowers like Brazil faced "in the days ahead" what David Rockefeller, head of Chase Manhattan Bank, likened to "treacherous economic seas and gale force financial winds, strong enough to capsize even large and well-manned ships —unless sails are reefed early, and all hands are ready at their stations when the gale hits."

One major concern about private loans is where the money goes. Sometimes, understandably, it finances current consumption of food and essential machinery. In other instances it goes to armaments. As Alan Greenspan noted, "there is disturbing evidence that in some LDCs weapons may become a larger segment of budgets." The evidence is more than disturbing. Consider the 1980

Brandt Commission finding that "one-half of one percent of one year's military expenditures would pay for all the farm equipment needed to increase food production and approach self-sufficiency in food deficit low income countries by 1990." * How much of this perverse spending pattern was made possible by multinational bank loans is unknown. The uncertainty would disappear if the debt-financing work were done by public international programs. "Why doesn't the IMF borrow from the private banks and relend to the governments?" asked a lone voice at the Fund. "That way we'd know more the hell about what that money is used for."

Once set in motion, the financing of armament sales to Third World governments politically becomes self-perpetuating. Observes Solon Barraclough, director of the UN Research Institute for Social Development, "These military-industrial complexes have become social forces in their own right, often crucially influencing government policies towards objectives of their own that diverge sharply from those on the international consensus on development goals." But to date neither the U.S. nor any other arms exporter has initiated a coordinated action to stem the sale of weapons. Instead, each directly or indirectly fosters the trade to bolster its own balance of payments.

The pressures on Third World nations to increase exports to pay off the debts have another perverse effect. For example, many Latin American nations stepped up beef production, but for export, not for home consumption. One result, according to economist James Bass, was a 66 percent increase in child malnutrition over the past decade.

Another major problem of private bank lending to governments is perhaps the most corrosive: governments overborrowing to win elections and private banks increasing their exposure beyond prudent levels. Then the countries get into trouble paying their debts. The global oligopoly competition of the banks inevitably creates an explosive situation in one country or another. In Turkey, for example, the private banks competed with each other for loan business despite the high risks. Then, having gone too far, the banks forced a political crisis by shutting off the credit. This

* In 1976, developing countries spent 32.2 percent of their domestic government budgets (excluding grants and aid loans) on military expenditures, compared to 17.7 percent on health and education.

zwas followed by demands from the IMF for austerity measures that risked a deeper recession, more unemployment, and political chaos. The upshot, in the words of *The Wall Street Journal,* is that Turkey's "future as a western-style democracy may be in jeopardy."

The question of prudent Eurobanking loans goes beyond just Third World recipients. Concern about an eventual meltdown of the Eurocurrency market is definitely growing even though the bankers retain a discreet silence. The central banks of Holland and West Germany have said a reserve requirement is necessary to stabilize the Eurocurrency market. By early 1980 the Japanese Ministry of Finance had imposed a "ban" on further Japanese Bank lending in the Eurodollar market. In the previous year these banks had increased lending activity by 40 percent. Only in 1979 did the U.S. break its silence on the subject.

The late 1979 U.S. freeze of Iranian assets in U.S. multinational banks dramatized the most worrisome problem of private bank lending: the potential instability and political vulnerability of Eurobank loans as a reliable source to finance Third World debt. Whatever the reasons for the U.S. act, it has created tremendous additional uncertainties for the international financial system. Bank loans are based on their holdings of deposits, a large proportion of which, in the Eurocurrency market, are owned by OPEC governments. When the U.S. attempted to extend its freeze to the offshore branch offices of American banks in the Euromarket, it created fears among all OPEC deposit holders. For the first time, the long-held fear of OPEC seemed real. Petrodollars "could be seized by a foreign government for whatever reason," an oil official told me. "Where will the U.S., or for that matter, the English, Germans, or any other home government of the banks hold the line? Eurobanks are no longer an assured safe haven for our deposits," he added.

What this episode indicates is that a Euromarket meltdown can come either from the default side by a major borrower or from the deposit side by a major withdrawal. Since there are no established rules among governments about the treatment of Eurobanking, its future as a reliable source of Third World debt financing is in greater jeopardy than ever. On the one hand, the private banks themselves increasingly doubt they can alone be relied upon to meet the new debt needs from higher oil prices that in 1980 and 1981 will reach staggering proportions. On the other hand, the banks are more vulnerable than ever to the vagaries of future international politics. By the spring of 1980 the international financial system was indeed poised on the edge of an abyss.

The needs and benefits of a Marshall Plan approach thus become clear. It would help both Third World and industrial nations resurrect a platform for financial stability. It would provide long-term finance oriented to real investment and capital formation. Repayment would be spread over the gestation period of the investments in contrast to the "quick fix, forget about tomorrow" loans issued in the mid-1970s. Also, through a focus on investment in food, minerals, and energy, as the Venezuelan and OECD proposals suggest, the program would help to check inflation in the industrial world and slow the major draining of foreign exchange from the Third World.

Financial stability would also be enhanced by drawing OPEC money into productive investments and out of the volatile liquid balances of the Eurocurrency market, where they rest as potential financial dynamite. An investment program would offer the OPEC nations one route out of their present dilemma. They now hold most of their reserves in dollars of diminishing value which are made less valuable with every OPEC price hike, even though these price hikes are imposed partly to make up for the diminished value of their dollar holdings. The OPEC nations want to expand worldwide economic growth, but not with cheap oil as they did in the 1950s and 1960s. A multilateral investment guarantee or insurance scheme would give them an avenue to productive investment without the risk of seizure or major erosion in the purchasing power of their assets.

The annual OPEC surplus was $25 billion at the beginning of 1979, down from its record levels in the early years after the big price increases of 1973–74. It began to bulge again with the post-Iranian revolution price increases and by the end of 1980 is expected to approach the record $37 billion of 1976. Most of this surplus, according to the Bank of International Settlements, is held in short-term investments, such as commercial paper, which can be converted quickly to cash.

Before the 1979 price increases, many analysts were reaching the conclusion that the OPEC surpluses were not depressing world growth. After all, they argued, none of the prophecies of disaster which greeted the original accumulation of surpluses had come true. The private banks, in the words of the analysts, had done a "masterful job" of recycling the money. Nevertheless, little of this money has gone to productive investment, and the surpluses are building again, and will be an ever larger pressure on the world economy in the 1980s. Even before Iran and the price increases, a Rand Corporation study by Arthur Smithies estimated that the accumulated surplus of Saudi Arabia, Kuwait, and Iran alone would reach between $225 billion and $286 billion by 1985.

Without new institutional investment mechanisms, the surplus OPEC nations appear to be in a dilemma. On the one hand, they have been prudent in not using their unspent petrodollars in ways different from other cash rich global investors. "Exceedingly cautious and conservative," is a finding by a 1979 study by First National Bank of Chicago economist Dr. Odeh Aburdene. "They have not engaged in the financial maneuvers to upset the economies of those nations where their oil is sold," finds the study, "nor have they bought the major companies of the world as was predicted in 1974."

A major question raised since the 1973–74 price hikes is why OPEC has not spread this new wealth around, especially to those Third World nations with which it proclaims fraternal or religious bonds, and which have been hit even harder than the industrial nations by the higher price of imported energy. Many Third World nations criticize the OPEC aid performance. The *Financial Times* reported from the 1979 UNCTAD meetings in Manila that Third World representatives accused the Arabs of seeing "aid as a charity rather than . . . a sensible way to improve prospects for their own economies by boosting world economic growth."

In fact, many OPEC surplus nations are giving in excess of 2 percent of their GNP, a far higher percentage than the industrial nations, in aid. They have created their own development institutions, such as the OPEC Special Fund in Vienna, but these institutions still lack sufficient technical resources and expertise to channel a large volume of loans. From my own work with OPEC financial managers, it is clear they are interested in new development approaches, such as a global Marshall Plan, particularly because of their frustration with existing institutions and channels for current development programs. The development institutions created in the postwar period, such as the World Bank and the OECD Development Committee, still do not give the OPEC countries voting participation equal to their new economic power. The appeal to OPEC investors of the Marshall Plan approach is that it would be housed in special trust departments in the World Bank or regional banks. The OPEC members would have voting rights equal to their contributions on boards of these special funds.

The total effect of a global stimulus program on the United States and the industrial nations would be positive in terms of net employment, income, and balance-of-payment gains. There is an abundance of figures showing direct links between the economic performance of Third World nations and growth in the industrial world. One UN study estimated that a 3 percent GNP growth for non-oil developing countries can result in a one percent increase in the growth rates of industrial countries. Over a five-year period, this could mean a Third World contribution of $250 billion to growth in the industrial world. A U.S. Treasury study indicates that between $1.2 and $1.8 billion of U.S. exports are the result of multilateral development bank lending. For each dollar the U.S. pays into international development assistance, it receives at least $2.50 in economic growth or, measured otherwise, its annual contribution creates 50,000 jobs. Even more jobs, as many as 2 million in U.S. export industries, or one-third the number of the currently unemployed, could be created if Third World countries maintained growth rates achieved in the late 1960s and early 1970s. What has happened instead in the years since the 1974–75 recession has been mounting Third World debt cutting into the ability of those countries to buy more American exports. For example, before its oil revenues began flowing, Mexico's purchase of U.S. goods fell from $5.1 billion to $4.8 billion between 1975 and 1977. As Brazil sputtered, that country's imports from the U.S. dropped by half a billion dollars. Taking into account inflation, the volume decline was even greater. According to the OECD, more than a third ($15 billion) of the deterioration of U.S. exports relative to imports can be attributed to the inability of Third World nations to buy American goods because of their debt problems.

A second issue is whether such a program will stimulate inflation. That would be a valid fear if there were tight capital markets. But, as we demonstrated in considerable detail in chapter 3, the world economy is suffering from a savings gap in developing nations and idle savings surpluses in industrial and OPEC countries. Owing largely to investor uncertainty, potential global investment capital has gone into short-term holdings in the Eurocurrency market, corporate acquisitions, real estate, and gold. There is a significant pool of idle balances in private capital markets. A global stimulus program could draw on them without creating inflation, and it would be the first effort especially designed to woo "stateless" monies—an effort that to date has escaped nation-state programs operating in isolation from one another.

While private capital would make up the bulk of global or regional Marshall Plan funding, there would be some increased spending directly by governments. But even the most ambitious proposals call for only an additional $10 billion to $15 billion over four years from the industrial nations, less than 10 percent of their current overseas development spending. If the present Proposition 13 anti-spending drift continues in industrial nations and no new public money is forthcoming, there are other devices to bring in government funds. A small portion of existing development funds could be temporarily shifted to Marshall Plan windows at the World Bank and the regional banks to provide backing for a development bond issue having a multiplier effect on attracting idle savings that current programs do not enjoy. Part of the OECD portion of the financing is to be provided on a "callable capital" basis. Simply put, this is a guarantee from donor nations to back the plan's loans. But although requiring legislative appropriation, callable capital is not an actual budget expenditure. And in some thirty-five years of World Bank experience, these callable reserves have, in fact, never been called upon. Another proposal would collect the OECD contributions, both public and private, in dollars and other hard national currencies and then convert them to loans in Special Drawing Rights through the IMF–World Bank complex. This would be a novel step toward reducing global dependence on the dollar and would establish precedents for long-term finance programs for developing countries. We will discuss these proposals for international financial reform later in this chapter, but it shows the dual role of a concerted growth program: to demonstrate both the political and financial feasibility of power sharing among OECD, OPEC, and Third World nations.

There have been some attempts to measure the multiplier effect of a global stimulus program on the growth of the industrial nations. One detailed study projected a 5 percent growth in exports with special benefits going to such excess capacity industries as steel.

If there is fault to be found in these estimates, it is that they are too low. They fail to capture what could be a most important mutual benefit of a global Marshall Plan: a revitalization of investor confidence, or what Keynes called the "animal spirits," that help generate investment. The effect of the psychological phenomenon was summed up by former Presidential economic advisor Marina Whitman: "If the present state of confidence has a significant impact on the levels and growth rates of economic variables (and there is considerable and mounting evidence that it does) then the present sense of uncertainty must inevitably be manifesting itself negatively—and in global levels and growth rates of income, investment, employment and economic activity."

Confidence is tied to leadership. The latter tends to inspire the former. A Third World Marshall Plan, symbolizing the ability of American leadership to be exercised in the new multipolar rather than the old bipolar world, could be a major incision into the vicious circles of the current global crisis in investor confidence.

The original Marshall Plan reversed not only the fortunes but the confidence of a Europe wrecked by war. It broke through the immediate postwar drift to vicious circles that threatened only more privation, despair, and an incipient threat of renewed political disorder. It provided scarce foreign exchange, and turned out to be the catalyst not only of Europe's economic recovery but of the greatest sustained worldwide economic boom in history. The vision, the ingenuity, and the practical generosity inspired by the wreckage of the Ruhr await a rekindling in the misery of the Ganges or the Nile. Now, as then, the benefits would flow in more than one direction.

IV

Unfortunately, global policy reform cannot stop short with a global stimulation program. Monetary order is also essential if there is to be an expansion of growth and world trade. Just as bank failures bring a run on savings and a retreat from investment at home, so does international currency instability diminish savings and investment globally.

Even for professional economists, the world of international money, monetary systems, and monetary order is something of a mystery. The last decade of crises in the system has been even more of a mystery, although some of its causes are fairly obvious. Yet behind the maze of domestic and international *haute finance,* many of the fundamentals are much the same as they are for, what economists call, the "real side" of the economy—the human, technological, and natural resource capabilities that are the tangible ingredients for the production and generation of income for consumption.

The question is: Does money matter? It is one of the important questions that have divided the conservative monetarists and liberal Keynesians in the mainstream economic debate of the last decade. Nationally and globally, production and consumption levels can change because of real changes in technology, resources, and human achievements. Without improvements in these real forces, increased production and consumption will not take place for an extended period.

But for successive short-run periods money does matter, although how much is a debatable question. Over time, an expansion of the money supply that exceeds the growth in real output will lead to inflation. Yet both industrial and Third World nations have improved production for short-run periods by a rapid expansion of the money supply that made financing growth easier and that gave the public an impression of confidence and buying power. The question is: When and by how much must the growth of the money supply be tuned downward to prevent galloping inflation? At some point, money supply and demand must match. Too little money can depress the economy just as too much can create inflationary pressures that frighten investors, which in turn leads to recession. This problem of "fine-tuning," of how much and when to expand and shrink the money supply, has never been easy for central bankers or politicians. It reached nightmarish proportions during the stagflation decade.

International monetary systems must reflect the economic and political power of individual nations. What has happened, however, at least twice in this century, is that the trappings and perception of dominance by one power have outlasted the realities of that power, contributing to instability in the international system. For example, the sterling system was based on British preeminence. By the end of World War I that preeminence was lost, but the monetary system remained unaltered into the 1930s. Similarly, the dollar has been the pillar of the international system since World War II, although in the last decade the American economy has lost its preeminence.

The dollar system was created at Bretton Woods in 1944, although the British pound also won status as a reserve currency. Given the relative standings of the postwar American and British economies, the dollar quickly became the principal reserve currency with the pound diminishing to a much lesser role. For three decades the dollar system and the outflow of dollars to the world provided the lubricant for global economic growth, banking, and trade. But the massive spread of dollars around the world eventually led to problems for both the American economy and the international monetary system.

As Benjamin Cohen pointed out in his recent book *Organizing the World's Money,* the dollar standard represented a bargain between the United States and the war-torn economies of the rest of the world. It was a bargain cemented by noninflationary growth. The United States was free to run large balance-of-payments deficits and, by doing so, promoted the expansion of American trade, investment corporations, and banks around the world, as well as its diplomatic interests through NATO. As long as there was little inflation, it did not need to worry about restricting domestic growth or running of balance-of-payments deficits, even as it was financing European and Japanese imports to this country. On balance, the world economy reaped the benefits. There was no repeat of the 1930s practice of competitive, beggar-thy-neighbor devaluations by nations seeking to improve their trade positions.

By the 1960s a dollar glut was developing. As other economies, including Japan's and some in Western Europe, gained strength, there was less need or tolerance abroad for the growing U.S. payments deficits. By the late 1960s our allies were worrying that we were exporting our budding inflation to them via the dollar surpluses. Balance was lost, the checks of the Bretton Woods system came into effect; the European and Japanese dollar holders exercised their option to convert their dollars to gold. As Cohen described it, "the post-war bargain became unstuck." The formal break with the past was President Nixon's decision in 1971 to detach the dollar from gold and commence what would become a series of dollar devaluations.

By the late 1960s, in the midst of a series of currency crises in Europe, it became clear that significant reform of the global monetary system was necessary. In the years since then there has been a series of *ad hoc* steps in this direction, but nothing like a new Bretton Woods, which would effectively replace the dollar with a multilateral system that accurately reflected the varied sources of economic power in the world. Monetary reform, rather than patch-up efforts, remains a principal item on the economic agenda for the 1980s. What has taken place up to now is a series of crisis-abating measures such as the creation of the two-tier gold market, creation of a European Monetary System and, most recently, the November 1978 and October 1979 salvage operations for the dollar.

The surprising but temporary success of the November 1978 effort to bolster the dollar illustrates why true monetary reform comes so slowly. Starting in 1977, and notwithstanding a disastrous slide throughout 1978, the dollar has gained 9 percent against the West German mark and 20 percent against the Japanese yen—most of it in the first five months after the November emergency actions. Banks and corporations began to shift their holdings from foreign currencies back into dollars, strengthening the dollar even further. "The framers of the November 1 rescue package," wrote financial columnist Hobart Rowan, "admit in their wildest dreams they didn't visualize such a scenario . . . of spectacular success." Yet, despite that short-run success, the outlook quickly became gloomy. The root cause of the problem has not been removed, and the dollar continues as the principal reserve currency.

In May 1979, Assistant Secretary of Commerce Frank Weil warned that the trade deficit would persist and could be $40 billion by 1990 because of higher energy costs, protectionism, and the continued competitive decline of U.S. exports. With such persistent deficits and continued U.S. inflation, the revival of the dollar could not be long sustained. By October 1979 yet another set of "emergency" measures had to be enacted. Facing such circumstances, and to promote a return to sustained growth in the 1980s, the United States has to take the lead in pushing for permanent monetary reform and an orderly replacement of the dollar as the world's principal trading and banking currency by the SDR in a modified form, permitting its use in private and business transactions.

The major problem in a monetary reform is converting the billions of dollars scattered around the globe into the new reserve unit. As *Euromoney* magazine stated: ". . . the dollar is in a structural long-term decline, and its reserve asset role is going to have to be complemented if not replaced by something else." The debate concerns that something else—as if the SDR had not yet been established through international agreement.

And "that something else" is not immediately and readily available. Whatever its signs of terminal rot, the dollar remains the major reserve currency. Even if central banks have been bailing out of dollars, most of their reserves are still in that currency. The dollar continues to dominate world trade and investment. While the Common Market nations have created the European Monetary System (EMS) and a new European Currency Unit (the ECU), they are a long way from replacing the dollar system. The EMS is basically a protective measure against the fluctuations of the dollar. As weak as the dollar has become, a move out of it to a new reserve currency requires political will on the part of the industrial nations to let the SDR evolve as a genuine international currency and reserve unit.

The problem of getting out of dollars is very difficult, but there are no real alternatives to doing so. Given the large overhang of dollar holdings, any move to a new reserve needs to be gradual and steady to avoid prompting a panic of people trying to get rid of the dollars they hold. This would jeopardize the reform. The problem has been experienced to a much lesser degree by central banks, which in recent years have tried to diversify their holdings out of dollars. According to an IMF study of twenty-one unnamed countries, the central banks reduced their dollar holdings by 12 percent between 1976 and 1977. As Bank of America President A. W. Clausen observed in a *Euromoney* survey, "As major dollar holders, the central banks are confronted with a classic dilemma. On the one hand it's appropriate for them to diversify their foreign exchange holdings further. On the other hand a massive shift of dollars will lead to further depreciation of the dollar and thereby erode the value of their remaining assets."

Any shift out of dollars to a new reserve will have to be gradual and incremental and should be tied to programs of global economic management such as a global Marshall Plan. In fact, a multilateral growth stimulus program offers a logical vehicle for participation of SDRs in providing reserve and liquidity assets. The value of the Special Drawing Rights rests on a basket of twelve major national currencies. In September 1979 the U.S. Treasury finally overcame domestic lobby groups and agreed to start negotiations for a partial substitution of dollar reserves by SDRs. But instead of going decisively ahead with this action, at the 1979 Belgrade annual meeting of the IMF the U.S. only agreed to back further studies of this project to be discussed at some future date, presumably during the first half of 1980. In the meantime, the SDR is still inching into the world monetary system at a glacial pace, partly because it has not been attached to existing programs to stimulate growth. Third World nations have long asked that SDRs be created and used to help finance their development. But their demands, in the views of the industrial world, have been too sweeping, too much of an all-or-nothing approach, and too threatening, to gain acceptance among bankers or treasury ministers of the industrial nations.

But less-sweeping responses are being designed and considered, tied to programs to stimulate Third World growth. For example, Sir Richard King, executive secretary of the Joint IMF–World Bank Development Committee noted in an interview "the need to study seriously the idea of using SDRs to finance Marshall Plans and other specific programs of growth stimulation in the Third World." Similarly, Eduardo Mayobre, Venezuelan executive director at the World Bank, has written about the need to develop ways to put SDRs into use in the world economy through development financing. For example, in a global Marshall Plan, the IMF would hold the initial dollars and credit a developing country with an SDR equivalent in import purchasing power. Purchases, say of machinery, would be made by the Third World buyer transferring SDRs from its central bank to the central bank of the exporting industrial nation. In turn, that bank would pay the machinery manufacturer in local currency. The volume of SDRs as reserve assets would be expanded. A precedent would also have been established, combining monetary reform based on wider participation with a global program of economic stimulation.

Such institutional experimentation would require a redirection of the IMF–World Bank complex toward a more Keynesian role in the world economy—but not so Keynesian as to ignore the supply side. Lord Keynes did argue at the Bretton Woods conference in 1944 for an IMF to take a more active role in global stimulation. The U.S. delegation, led by Harry Dexter White, argued successfully for a more limited facility. Ironically, it was the United States that ended up playing the role of world banker that Keynes had advocated for the IMF. Then, as now, world growth depended upon the expansion of economies whose needs for imports were greater than their ability to export. Then it was Europe and Japan. Now it is the Third World. Keynes's arguments anticipated the original Marshall Plan. But beyond the similarities, there has evolved, as anticipated all along, a greater need for the IMF to be involved as both a holder and issuer of reserves and a manager of international liquidity. Its policies also need more emphasis on supply economics than originally envisioned by Keynes. If it were allowed the appropriate role in the creation of an expansion of SDRs, it would be far more greatly involved in the creation of global liquidity than it is now. This would create for the IMF the same problems facing any central bank: how much and when to expand the money supply. But it would at least offer a balance to its role as a "whipping boy" for nations falling into hock. Yet the IMF is more a scapegoat than a villain. Under Bretton Woods, it must push every Third World and even occasional Western governments into practices of austerity, regardless of ensuing political upheavals, from bread riots in Egypt to street fighting in Turkey. Giving the IMF more of a central bank role would finally allow it to offer carrots as well as sticks and thereby make it more effective.

Naturally, moves to replace the dollar with Special Drawing Rights and to expand the scope of the IMF have met with resistance, especially from the financial and corporate interests whose overseas expansion was floated on dollars. National sovereignty was and is the rationale for not dethroning the dollar. The argument grew increasingly thin as U.S. balance-of-payments problems through the 1960s and 1970s mounted and as the U.S. Government had to take steps to protect the dollar, which threatened the prosperity of Americans at home. The dollar rescue packages of November 1, 1978, and October 6, 1979, with their higher interest rates and explicit risk of recession, were dramatic indications of how little national economic sovereignty meant when the dollar was under attack in the international money market.

In the 1930s, nations learned of the folly of trying to protect their industries in isolation. In the 1970s, nations learned through increasingly bitter experience the folly of trying to protect their currencies in isolation. Just as free trade became a necessity rather than an intellectual luxury after the Depression, international monetary reform has now become a prerequisite to stability and growth.

But for engineering both global "growth" and "monetary" reforms in the 1980s, leadership remains the crucial uncertainty. And the testimony of the twentieth century regarding the leadership role in shaping a new order is bittersweet. As good a way as any to characterize the disastrous worldwide depression of the 1930s is Charles Kindleberger's statement about leadership: "In 1929, the British couldn't and the U.S. wouldn't." At this last critical juncture in the transformation between two stages of development, the similarity of the thirties with our contemporary transition is striking. Britain had provided the world with stable economic leadership from the 1870s through the First World War. As London's financial strength began to wane, the United States was in a position to fill the leadership vacuum but consistently refused to do so, until after the Second World War.

What is apparent today is that no unilateral heir is apparent—including the Europeans. Rather, the course of responsibility today is for the United States, the European Community, and Japan to push for the SDR as an effective multilateral replacement of the dollar.

V

If the purpose of global reform is to provide breathing space in which the industrial nations can adjust to new global competition, then a primary feature of reform must be limited global management of supply. It is on the supply side of the economy that the "grand vicious circle" is most evident. Global gluts in such industries as steel, shipbuilding, and petrochemicals lead to protectionism. This has happened because of dramatic changes in the world economy which few have been able to comprehend much less manage. The answer to the problem of both supply gluts and bottlenecks is economic growth, but growth will not come without reform, and reform will not come without growth. The next two decades will require major structural adjustment of the industrial base of the North as more basic manufacturing—steel, ships, cars —moves from the North to the South. Global supply-side reforms would ease the transition and allow growth to occur and limit the damage of politically induced protectionism.

This movement of manufacturing from North to South is just beginning, and it has already sent severe protectionist waves through the political systems of most industrial nations. Several studies, such as one by University of Sussex professor Constantine Vaitsos, found that less than 5 percent and perhaps as little as 3 percent of European unemployment was caused by Third World imports. Even so, the Third World has become a scapegoat for unemployment in the industrial world. At the same time, there has been little recognition that allowing Third World imports—relatively free trade rather than protectionism—has prevented inflation from growing even worse.

The beneficiaries of low-cost Third World imports are widely dispersed—namely, all consumers. Not only governments and multinational organizations but also consumer organizations like Ralph Nader's evince policy lags. They have chosen to concentrate on the more popular lobbying fights against domestic big business, failing to educate their members on the already significant cost savings afforded by Third World imports, and the potentially larger ones in the future. They rarely devote their resources to lobbying on behalf of free trade. In contrast, those who bear the immediate cost of more globally efficient production from the Third World are concentrated and politically powerful groups that neither party in the U.S. Congress can stand up against. Affected unions and industry manufacturing associations, as in steel and textiles, are the tightest of allies in mounting a two-prong attack that in one sweep garners both Democratic and Republican votes. Recall Mr. Nixon's timely 1971 restrictions on textile imports, the starting link in the global protectionist chain, which won for him many a vote in 1972 in the southern United States. Politics make import competition from developing countries a villain totally out of proportion to its economic significance as a cause of unemployment. In Europe it is no different. "Advocacy of protectionist measures against low cost imports is an almost instinctive reaction in times of recession," lamented a group of adjustment experts of the European Community in early 1979.

"Whatever the protectionists may say, the developed world is not being 'flooded by cheap goods,'" observed World Bank President Robert McNamara at the Manila 1979 UN Conference on Trade and Development (UNCTAD) meetings. "Developing countries today supply only a miniscule portion of the manufactured goods consumed in the developed countries: less than 2 percent . . . even in the most successful [case]—textiles and clothing—this share is still low: 5 percent, for example, in the U.S." Mr. McNamara, like scores of other international officials, can also point to the crucial lack of "correctly administered adjustment policies" of industrial nations that are "required both for efficiency and equity." Yet, despite their validity, such statements do little, if anything, to reverse protectionist econopolitics in industrial democracies as long as stagflation persists.

The international organizations best prepared to cope with trade and adjustment problems are, as we mentioned in chapter 5, torn by multiple new schisms induced by global stagflation. These are now added to a traditional division: the South does not trust GATT, nor does the North trust UNCTAD.

"In GATT we have no power, it's a rich man's trade club that's made a mockery of Mr. Schmidt and Mr. Carter's calls to help the Third World," a Third World ambassador said to me in 1978. "Not only has UNCTAD become a sham," remarked a State Department economist, "but the industrial nations will never accept it as the organizing vehicle for a new trade organization." As to the United Nations Industrial Development Organization (UNIDO) and its program in industrial redeployment, "Until recently, it was the industrial nations' reaction to UNCTAD within the UN family," concluded a professor who had spent time studying UNIDO. "Many in the Third World saw it as a lay-away station for retired AID and State Department officials from Washington and Bonn." These and scores of similar views reflect the rampant distrust between the North and South.

The point was just as much conceded by Mr. McNamara to his 1979 UNCTAD audience at Manila, when he observed about the GATT Tokyo Round that "developing countries were often only marginal participants in these negotiations." Yet *New York Times* correspondent James Sterba, looking out over the same audience, just as correctly wrote: "In fact, the old Third World today looks more like a collection of fragments held together more by political rhetoric than by mutual economic concerns." In evaluating UNCTAD's progress over the seventies, Ferdinand Marcos chose in his keynote address to use the word "impotent" four times. And so it is that entering the 1980s, the global community must rely on a GATT and an UNCTAD as the chief mechanisms for restoring free trade, without which its growth and efficiency, and certainly equity, cannot be assured. "The old economic order has been replaced by not a new order," wrote Sterba, "but by a new disorder." GATT and UNCTAD have become less than effective as forums in which are formulated truly interdependent policy approaches: those that yield "positive sum" outcomes of mutual gain for North and South.

Even so, from some political head-knocking in these organizations or the creation of new offices in the World Bank, arrangements need to be made to help countries adjust to rapidly changing trade patterns. The first principal reform needed is a surveillance and monitoring system to determine who is violating the international trade rules and to recommend appropriate penalties. The second reform is an "early warning system" to alert governments as to which industries are likely to face sudden new trade competition.

Because of the distrust they engender on one side or the other, GATT and UNCTAD could probably not be given the surveillance function logically suited to them. The latest Tokyo Round trade agreement did create innovative mechanisms for settling disputes, including countermeasures by injured countries. But for these remedies to be effective, countries involved in the dispute will have to trust the information. They will also have to trust the surveillance capability of the monitoring organization; otherwise, they will continue the practices that have been gaining such favor recently, making temporary and emergency trade barriers permanent to protect weak industries. At some point, participation in GATT will have to be overhauled and its decision making and staffing revised to take Third World economic power into account. Until this happens, a technical staff that is "least mistrusted" by either side will have to be established within another international organization, probably the World Bank. Third World countries still object to the division of power on the Bank's board and in its voting procedures, but they generally trust the objectivity and experience of the Bank's staff.

"Nevertheless, we still have some of our best people working in the Bank and they do have some influence on analysis and information," said another Third World ambassador in Washington. "Their staff and lending biases are still skewed," a trade minister in Latin America told me, "but compared to the early 1960s, the Bank's penchant for free market approaches has been significantly tempered by its experience with Third World realities." This "tempering" also has come about because of particular checks and balances at work on the Bank more so than on other international agencies. Its very concentrated visibility in one location, and its concentrated lending—the largest of any single multilateral organization—subjects it to a public exposure worldwide that is more focused than is possible for the diffused and sprawling programs of the UN or the lesser-known activities of the regional development banks like the Asian, African, or Inter-American Development Banks.

In the late 1960s, British journalist Teresa Hayter's *Aid as Imperialism,* an exposé on development assistance, included a focus on the IMF and the Bank. It was a Washington joke at the time that locally most copies were bought by Bank and Fund staff members, judiciously kept out of sight under lock and key in desk drawers. While many officials branded it as "muckraking," many academic economists took the work seriously, and its message was not totally lost. McNamara, in contrast to prior presidents, has carefully included among his top advisors a sprinkling of well-known development economists from both North and South who are sympathetic to Third World views—a healthy innovation where the staff directors were once predominantly conventional mainstream economists and financial experts.

The World Bank is a likely choice to provide the information and analysis for surveillance evaluations of trade practices that will be used by the new GATT dispute mechanisms. This is in keeping with this book's thesis that as long as the global economy is choking on stagflation the movement toward a new global order will have to start with the best we have today—and cannot afford to await a major reform that will be longer in coming. The data collection and analysis for surveillance purposes should, however, also be combined with other information to develop an "early-warning signaling system" of future North-South structural adjustment gluts.

The European Common Market has already initiated an early-warning system. Its purpose is to anticipate major shifts in manufacturing and get a jump on starting "dynamic adjustment" programs for European nations. These changes in the international division of labor, if left to market forces, would bring even more gluts and create more unemployment. The Japanese, through their finance ministry and their trade and industry ministry, have taken similar steps. The United States has not moved at all, but if and when it does, the monitoring systems of the industrial nations could be patched into a global early-warning system of the World Bank.

Both the evaluation of North-South trade practices for the GATT surveillance disputes and the early-warning system would extend, at the global "macro" level of government to government, the "honest broker" role the World Bank has been increasingly playing in the "micro" interactions between the multinational corporations of the industrial nations and the governments of the Third World. For example, the International Financial Corporation, an agency of the Bank, often intermediates the management and "turn-key" contracts of governments to multinationals for large-scale minerals and basic infrastructure projects. Without the management and technology services of the multinationals, many of these nations would have difficulty in efficiently absorbing these funds—and without the "honest broker," they would be afraid of negotiating inadequate contracts. Thus the "honest broker" role could be a catalyst to make developing nations receptive to Marshall Plan approaches for overcoming the resource shortages of the supply side of the global economy.

VI

If the reforms suggested seem unduly pragmatic, it is because they are offered in the hope and expectation that they can and will be adopted. A proposal for a modest reform does not necessarily mean the problems are of a modest dimension. Far from it. In the next five years, as hard as it is to make projections, a combination of domestic and global stimulation, matching the massive need for new investments, could point the way to new levels of growth. Whatever the levels of growth, the shift of basic industry from North to South will continue, creating adjustment problems for the old industries of the North. The higher the growth, the easier the adjustment. The reforms offered here are aimed both at prompting the growth and at easing the problems of adjustment. But these new mechanisms are intended to move the global economy toward the efficiency goal common to the needs of both North and South. They are also aimed at initiating progress toward greater equity and toward greater participation and eliminating the old deadlocks. Without growth and without the reforms that will give growth a chance to take root, the world faces severe problems of structural adjustment and intense new protectionist pressures which threaten political and economic stability in many countries.

In 1975, Henry Kissinger spoke of "an extraordinary opportunity to form for the first time in history a truly global society, carried by the principle of interdependence.

"And if we act wisely and with vision," Kissinger said, "I think we can look back to all this turmoil as the birth pangs of a more creative and better system. If we miss the opportunity, I think there is going to be chaos."

Five years after Kissinger and many others of both conservative and liberal persuasions have made such calls, the world totters ever more precariously between these alternatives. So far it has managed to avoid sliding into chaos, but it has taken few firm steps toward implementing the rhetoric of a global society and interdependence that has come from scores of politicians and diplomats.

PART III

Critical Juncture

CHAPTER 7

Pioneering at Home

I

IN THE MIDST of great transformations it is always difficult for those directly involved to understand what is taking place and why. In a storm, one seeks shelter rather than an ideal perspective for viewing events. Clinging to conventional wisdom and comfortable ideas is more commonplace than seeking new visions, philosophies, or policies. "When the world is messy," observed Daniel Bell, "you fall back on either ideology or technique."

This phenomenon was very much on the minds of the pioneering economists during the last transformation in the 1930s. "We have made virtually no preparation for economic disasters," economist Marriner Eccles wrote in 1937. "Stable prosperity can be obtained only if we are aware of the problem and if we are willing to tackle it vigorously."

Alvin Hansen, the American pioneer of Keynesian economics in the 1930s, voiced a similar frustration. "We are living in a period of transition; yet, in this period, men's thinking is still dominated by frozen patterns of the past into which people try to mold the facts of the present."

As the postwar transformation approaches the critical juncture of the 1980s, there has been cause for the same kind of frustration.

At the highest levels of government, the President is accused by a former speechwriter of lacking a "central philosophy." The

NOTE: The author gratefully acknowledges the collaboration of William M. Castner in the research, design, and drafting of this chapter.

absence of such a philosophy can be seen in the promulgation of inconsistent economic policies. But the problem really goes beyond Presidential personality. "There is a link between the frequent contradictions in the Carter administration and the void left by those with a reputation for elevated thoughts on high policy," notes Bernard D. Nossiter. "Why, I don't know what I would have done," admits Harvard sociologist Nathan Glazer. "The cupboard of ideas is bare. If Carter had task forces, I wouldn't read their papers. Now there is nothing. No new departures." Claims economist Robert Lekachman: "Any sensible politician knows better than to listen to [the heavily credentialed economists in government]. The economists are in substantial disarray. I can understand why Carter listens to Jody Powell instead."

Surrounded by monuments of failure, a decade of stagflation, the conventional economics debate continues pretty much as it has done for the last generation, focusing almost entirely on demand management. At the edges of this debate are two alternatives. The thrust of one is a return to a "hands off" policy, Adam Smith's *laissez-faire,* or what Kenneth Boulding called the "cowboy economy." The other is heavier and more direct government involvement in the economy, from wage and price controls to nationalization of industries.

Amid the failures of the stagflation decade, these alternatives are unattractive or simply impossible. Doing nothing, or returning to a cowboy economy, is more a pipe dream than a serious alternative. Concerning the second alternative—massive direct controls and nationalization—one only needs to look to Britain to see its inherent futility.

Between these two alternatives is an array of issues that have consumed the debate among conventional economists. It is a debate that is becoming increasingly fruitless and increasingly burdened by the weight of conventional wisdom when transformation calls for more than that. Static wisdom can hardly exist in such a time of rapid change: when a South Korea can become a major shipbuilder, at a rate of thirty ships a year, just four years after building its first; when an Iran can dissolve within weeks as a "safe" source of critical oil supplies; and when our economic policy choices, once measured by the Phillips Curve trade-off between inflation and unemployment, become choices between inflation, stagnation or depression.

The economy grows not only more globally interdependent but technologically interdependent. Stoppages or rising costs in one area, such as steel, have a ripple effect all the way to auto showrooms and appliance stores. The problems of oil supply filter all the way down to racks of plastic wrapping in the local supermarket. Government, which ceased fifty years ago to be a mere bystander in the economy, is becoming an increasingly active mediator, not only between competing demands but among the competing forces of old and new holders of economic power. The role of government as mediator is slowly replacing its earlier role as adversary of business and labor in the Galbraithean vision of three countervailing centers of power.

As economist Robert Heilbroner asserted: "To the extent that we no longer let the game of economics proceed unhindered to its natural outcome, we are going beyond the [Keynesian] economic revolution. . . . We are leaving behind us a world in which our futures were shaped, at least in the large, by the pressures of economic action. We are proceeding into a world where economic forces play an important but no longer predominant role."

Although the ground under the economic debate is shifting dramatically, its outer limits and ultimate goals in a U.S.–style democracy remain the same: the pursuit of efficiency, equity, and participation. In the debate among the conventional economists there are areas of agreement and disagreement and areas most tend to ignore. The principal division in the establishment of mainstream economics, as we have cited before, is between the liberally oriented "fiscalists" and the conservatively oriented "monetarists." They are always horrified to be lumped together, but in practice they both end up relying on demand management as their ultimate policy tool.

By the end of the 1970s, the debate of the fiscalists and monetarists over the most appropriate short-run demand management approach, "over how few of Keynes' ideas need [still] to be taken seriously," in the words of economist Alfred S. Eichner, began to appear even to themselves as inappropriate to the reality of the stagflation problem. Yet with the exception of a humble preface that no "quick fix" of the economy was possible, the mainstream economic advisors of both camps still offered a policy mix of their old economic demand management chestnuts as the solution.

The response of the monetarists to inflation is to recommend a stringent monetary and budget policy to drain excess money from the system. The high social and economic costs of such a recession-inducing policy is thought an unfortunate but necessary evil. The existence of large firms in concentrated markets, which interferes with their romance for a free and competitive market, is dealt with by various suggestions for antitrust policy. "The obvious and economical solution," stated venerable monetarist George J. Stigler, "is to break up the giant companies. This, I would emphasize, is the minimum program, and it is essentially a conservative program." While profiting from the institutional support of big business, the monetarists have been able only to provide the intellectual rationalization for the public posturing of business leaders. As Milton Friedman, the monetarist "Godfather," is quick to bemoan: "[The businessman] is all in favor of free enterprise and free markets. But when it comes down to practice, it turns out he's in favor of free enterprise and free markets for everybody else but not for himself. Oh, no. He's a special case. His business requires special government protection." The end result, claims Friedman, is that businessmen are "the most insidious and effective enemies of free enterprise."

The fiscalists have attempted their own formulations of demand restraint to attempt the elimination of inflation without triggering a recession. This "soft landing" for the economy is an impressive testament to the keeping of the Keynesian faith in "fine-tuning" the economy. However, as the late Keynesian Arthur Okun of the Brookings Institution explained, "Those imaginative strategies have been tried, and have been proven false. It is time to face the realities of the new disease of chronic inflation and to focus on the prescriptions that are appropriate for curing it." What Okun and many other fiscalists have advocated is a return to the use of an incomes policy. While this suggestion will be considered in chapter 10, the advocacy of control devices for wages and prices is an admission, as Okun did not blush to concede, that stagflation is "a new and different phenomenon that cannot be diagnosed correctly with old theories or treated effectively with old prescriptions."

Yet, for all their debates in the past decade or more, both monetarists and fiscalists have ignored forces in the post-market economy which have made many of their arguments irrelevant.

The reality of global interdependence, if not ignored, has not been blended into demand management. The tapping of Third World demand, as noted in the last chapter, offers a noninflationary vehicle to stimulate demand at home, but it has been systematically ignored. There has been a tendency to concentrate on aggregate demand rather than on targeted demand. And finally, there has been almost a complete absence of supply-side policies other than the neoconservatives' sweeping, across-the-board, "cowboy" insistence on less government.

Both mainstream Keynesian fiscalists and conservative monetarists still cling to the notion of a free market, and their policy tools rely on the market to maintain stability. But this is a failing faith, and there are economists, classified as "institutionalists" or post- or neo-Keynesians, who acknowledge the demise of the market. The role of the multinational conglomerates in negating the price system and in fostering the inequality of income distribution is acknowledged by these economists, including Galbraith, Heilbroner, and Robert Lekachman. To spread equity and participation these economists and their colleagues advocate more public ownership and regulation and more taxation aimed at redistributing wealth. Whatever beneficial effect their proposals might have on equity and participation, there is growing evidence that global interdependence makes such strategies less realistic and less efficient. If anything, the experience of public corporations—British Steel and British Petroleum, for example—offers little hope or expectation that government ownership or direct control of production necessarily adds either to efficiency or to a greater public spirit of equity and participation. (That there is a new role for government, however, particularly in energy, we shall leave until chapter 9.)

Far more than economics is involved in these choices among equity, efficiency, and participation. The massive debts of British Steel and the massive devastation of the South Bronx are not economic failures but political failures. As Heilbroner said, ". . . the success or failure of any particular nation seems more likely to reflect its political genius, its traditions, its ideology, than its underlying economic structure."

The economic tools—changing the composition of industrial output, balancing economic demands with those of ecology, assuring jobs—are all part of political management. And they carry price tags. Each involves economic, political, and social costs as well as benefits.

New institutions and philosophies emerged from previous critical junctures—the Federal Reserve in the early 1900s and the New Deal agencies after the Depression. The present critical juncture offers the same opening to innovation, to the adaptation of the old vision to a new central philosophy, and new concepts and pioneering. These innovations, this emergence of a new pioneering, will not occur in a single instance. The movement is already occurring in small ways. But, at its core, it requires a new definition of private enterprise and a new definition of the role of government in the economy. It must acknowledge global interdependence and post-market competition: in short, a new definition of our economic system.

In the remainder of this chapter we describe three kinds of pioneering now taking place in this country. They are not offered as panaceas but as microcosm examples of the pioneering philosophy needed to take us out of the stagflation decade. The examples involve the humanization of work, government regulation, and the adjustment of industry to new patterns of world trade and international divisions of labor. In this pioneering, there is a new definition of private enterprise. The corporation, as an employer and buyer and seller, is becoming a social institution and not an isolated free agent. Government is no longer only in an adversary position. It is becoming a participant and mediator. For better or worse, government is a principal actor locked into the center of the new bargaining power relationships that are replacing the Adam Smithian market mechanism as the major force behind the price system of a post-market era.

"Through our subsidiaries around the world, we are learning some novel approaches to business, government and labor relations," reflected Questor Corporation's CEO, P. M. Grieve. "Slowly some of us (in the U.S. business community) are learning to adopt those approaches here at home."

Learning from others may seem as basic as growing up. As we have already noted, Third World governments actively pursue the lessons gained from other governments in dealing with multinational corporations. But this learning, this spread of the "demonstration effect," eluded U.S. political-economic pioneering in the 1970s. Even in this period of stagflation, business, government, and labor leaders have been reluctant to acknowledge that new tools are needed in a post-market world. For every innovation that does take place, no matter how slowly, there must also be an explicit weighing of costs and trade-offs between efficiency, equity, and participation. Failures as well as successes must be studied. The examples of innovation in this chapter demonstrate that new forms of participation can yield new results in efficiency and equity.

These examples are not offered with the idea that their general implementation will sweep away stagflation or the rest of our economic problems. They are offered as successful examples of pragmatic measures that have resulted from looking at current problems in new and innovative ways. They manifest the quality of all good ideas: that they appropriately address the new forces pressing against the status quo. As an economy evolves and matures, it gives a good idea a certain evolutionary aspect; for example, the standardization of parts introduced by Henry Colt set the stage for the evolution of mass production by Henry Ford. The quest for a new vision in the 1980s demands that today's pioneers build on each previous advance and gain in knowledge.

"Today we have no choice but to go forward," wrote Russell W. Peterson, director of the U.S. Office of Technology Assessment. "We can no longer simply muddle through, concentrating only on the problem immediately before us. We must broaden our perception to include a holistic [policy] perspective." But more is required than just the recognition that things must be seen in a new integrated way for the 1980s.

The postwar global revolution reflects transformed impulses stemming from the new attitudes of workers and consumers, the new forms of corporate organization, and new roles for government worldwide. Stagflation is the synergistic outcome of these transformed microeconomic interactions, an emerging post-market economy blunting with the policy tools of an anachronistic marketplace vision. Thus, the micro innovations outlined here mirror some of the important impulses that at one and the same time are the challenges and part of the ingredients of a revised policy vision for the 1980s.

The essential condition placed by the global revolution on the reshaping of old and the casting of new policy efforts is that the hierarchical—from the top down—approach will prove by itself increasingly inadequate. The experience of development economics in battling stagflation is that effective policy must begin with a frank recognition of the impulses of people at the bottom. Albert Waterston, the eminent former World Bank development economist, lists as the central lesson of his field studies of the successes and failures of policy approaches in European and Third World countries—regardless of political ideologies—that "top-down" visions were never fruitful unless they were at heart reflections of the impulses from the "bottom-up."

II

As we said in chapter 3, the drop in the rate of U.S. productivity growth has become the subject of alarm. It has a variety of causes, so many that the Carter Administration's search for remedies ended up looking in vain for special causes behind the alarming drops of 1978 and 1979. The Administration came up with no clear answers. The same trend is starting to catch up with other countries. Industrial world governments are under pressure to increase output and benefits. Unless productivity increases, these efforts will lead only to further inflation. As also noted earlier, the causes of declining productivity create a vicious circle—low investment, declining research and development, government regulations, and finally worker alienation.

While the other causes of productivity decline require longer-term answers, the problem of worker alienation can be tackled immediately and with immediate benefits to productivity. Efforts to humanize work and to make workers feel more valuable and useful have been made in a variety of circumstances by different corporations and companies in both Europe and the U.S. The most successful of these experiments has had as a primary aim an increase in job satisfaction. Where this has been attained, a by-product has generally been an increase in immediate productivity benefits. Nevertheless, these gains hold up over the long term only if they are followed by new investment and technology.

The complaint that "people don't work as hard as they used to" has been heard throughout history. Even in *The Iliad,* Homer often complained that soldiers of Greece could do only one-hundredth the work of their forefathers. What has occurred in the 1970s, precipitating in part the decline in productivity growth, is increased worker education and the attitudinal revolution of rising expectations clashing with the grim realities of old factories and outdated supervisory techniques. A Yankelovich poll in 1978 showed fewer than 25 percent of U.S. workers finding satisfaction or importance in their jobs.

Throughout the industrial world, and especially in the United States, all workers are reaching higher levels of education. An auto assembly worker today may well have some college training, while the older generation in the plants was lucky to have finished high school. And this older generation is still close enough to the Depression to be satisfied with having a job. The current generation does not live with that memory. It is the first generation raised on television, fed from infancy on advertiser images of the good life and aware from childhood that they could always fall back on unemployment compensation. Modern industrial societies are paying in worker alienation for their past investments in education and for their promises of plenty.

The Opinion Research Corporation, in a survey completed in 1979, listed technology, automation, the increasing impersonalization of work, and large organizations and the instability of old values as major causes behind the growing worker alienation.

"This is not a myth; it is an emerging reality. . . . The impact of these forces on the working world is not yet visible as was the dissent in colleges during the late 1960s, but discontent among hourly and clerical employees is every bit as pervasive and seems to be growing."

In most instances, workers' values have been changing faster than the personnel management of corporations. But there have been some notable pioneering efforts by a diverse array of corporations, including among others General Motors, Corning Glass, the Eaton Corporation, Gaines Pet Food, Cummins Industries, Nabisco, and several smaller companies such as Donnelly Mirrors. Experiments by all these companies have increased productivity by decreasing job dissatisfaction and absenteeism.

Despite the successes, the "demonstration effect" of these programs has been limited. According to Jerome Rosow of Work in America, Inc., a principal reason is that companies do not want to help competitors by publicizing the results and contents of their programs. Unions have generally resisted such programs, at least initially, viewing them as management-imposed efforts to gain more work for the same dollar and time.

But there are even notable examples of pioneering by unions in cooperation with management. One of the most interesting is the project at a Bolivar, Tennessee, auto mirror plant of Harman Industries. The innovator and technical advisor on the project has been Dr. Michael Maccoby of the Harvard Center on Work, Technology and Character. As Maccoby said, business has been losing millions of dollars because of labor-management distrust reflected in everything from wildcat strikes to control systems over the workers.

The Harvard Center has long been involved in programs with other blue collar workers. But more recently, Maccoby has increasingly been initiating projects with white collar worker companies like CBS and AT&T, and for good reason. "We are people, not machines," was the rally cry of a 1979 nationwide campaign launched by the 500,000-member Communications Workers of America, a major AFL–CIO union. Their protests were not over the traditional bread and butter issues of wages and "job security" in the face of increased automation, but rather over controls and computerized scheduling so rigid that they result in what a union report called "timed potty breaks." The CWA's campaign was aimed at both its blue collar and a rising proportion of white collar members, many at the giant AT&T. Similarly, the Labor Department in a national survey found a dramatic decline in job satisfaction particularly among white collar workers. "Although white collar workers are likely to work in cleaner surroundings than their coworkers in factories," wrote CWA President Glenn Watts, "they often find themselves reduced by automation to tasks that are just as monotonous." What the union was asking for, summarized labor journalist Helen Dewar, was "more worker involvement in decisions affecting how their jobs are done, more use of flexible work periods, and 'human impact studies.' "

Several features distinguish the Bolivar project from earlier efforts. First, the program was begun with full union participation, explicitly to overcome the too often justifiable suspicion of "job enrichment programs" as a new anti-union device. Second, it started with the principal objective of maximizing the "human development and growth potential of the individual worker and manager, rather than aiming only at improving productivity." Third, it developed what Maccoby calls a "humanization of work by workers" program in an existing plant rather than in a newly designed factory, a significant characteristic for the national policy programs discussed in the next three chapters.

From the beginning, the Bolivar project was a joint effort by labor and management, as the most successful of subsequent work improvement programs have been. The development of this kind of cooperative program shows how the concentrated power centers of the post-market economy have to adapt to cooperation rather than confrontation in relations between management and labor and business and government. In other words, just as the multinationals have done with governments in the Third World. After generations of antagonism and conflict, such trust will be hard to build, but the place to start, says Maccoby, is in such projects as Bolivar and with leaders of character, competence, and principle. The economic benefits of trust can be seen in a country such as Japan. The lessons of pervasive distrust can be seen in an economy such as Britain's.

A key figure in the Bolivar project, which began in 1973, was United Auto Workers International Vice President Irving Bluestone. Under Bluestone's influence, quality-of-life programs have expanded in the auto industry, first at General Motors and later at Ford. Bluestone and company President Sidney Harman together initiated the Bolivar project. Maccoby and his team were independent third parties.

Also setting the Bolivar project apart from other quality-of-work experiments was the decision to implement it throughout the entire plant, not just in one section. And this project was conducted in a workplace filled with dust, chemicals, emissions, unbearable heat, and many boring jobs. The workers were independent-minded rural Tennesseans, many of whom would have preferred to be full-time farmers.

Even the fundamental principles of the Bolivar project were

different from the normal goals of improving jobs or morale or productivity. At Bolivar, a union-management committee established four principles: security, equity, democracy, and what Maccoby calls "individuation." The first two are standard objectives for a union. The second set can be frightening to both management and union leaders used to typical hierarchical arrangements. Democracy meant giving workers effective say in decisions affecting their work life. Individuation meant "that no one should be treated as a standardized mechanized part and that workers should have the right to develop their skills and their lives and that each person in the factory has different needs and wants."

Putting these principles into practice meant overcoming resistance both of managers and of workers. Middle management and floor foremen were, not surprisingly, the most skeptical. Partly to overcome their skepticism, the factory had to adapt its management to a more democratic environment. But the changes that have taken place are not as dramatic as the results. The program's shift to a more collegial style of decision making gave the company not only much more effective management but higher productivity and profits.

Workers from the beginning were suspicious that the program was an attempt to induce more work for the same amount of pay. These suspicions were only slowly overcome as workers decided in small groups among themselves how to improve their work. The important principle here was relying on the experience of the workers. In most work improvement and productivity schemes, the ideas came from management. To draw out worker ideas, a joint union-management committee was established.

At first, this committee dealt with obvious issues, such as improving ventilation, improving parking and ending congestion at the parking lot and on the time clock line, and finally establishing a credit union. But this did not address the issue of worker democracy. The project called in Einar Thorsrud, director of the Norwegian Industrial Democracy Project. After a week of seminars, the work committee developed the strategy of inviting volunteer groups of workers to decide and experiment with changes in the assembly and buff-and-polish departments of the plant. In some instances, these worker groups developed changes typical of job enrichment programs, such as job rotation and more flexible work periods. But for Maccoby, the crucial element is that the workers decide which changes to make. After an initial nine-month experiment, the project was expanded to include all divisions and workers in the plant.

An outsider coming into the Bolivar plant would not notice many surface differences from a normal auto parts factory. It would appear just about as noisy and grimy, and the workers would not appear as characters in some utopian vision. The changes have been more subtle, the most important being that workers have effective channels beyond standard union-management confrontations to seek changes and to voice complaints. The mechanized and routinized work is still there, but it does not continue on the standard shift basis. Production goals are established, a certain number of mirrors per day, and workers can end their day whenever the goal is met. For many workers, this means they can leave several hours before the three-thirty plant closing. Many go home, to their families or farms. Growing numbers are participating in classes and seminars ranging from welding to black studies to courses in management.

The results and benefits of such programs and experiments are incremental, not revolutionary. There is increased worker satisfaction, though it is hard to measure. Some workers, pursuing increased satisfaction, follow that pursuit to a logical conclusion—another and more satisfying job. The Bolivar plant negotiated contracts with the UAW, far in advance of the contract deadline, and the workers received earlier salary boosts.

For the union and the big automakers, Bolivar has been a beacon in an industry beset by worker alienation. The industry was abruptly confronted with this phenomenon at the General Motors Plant in Lordstown, Ohio, in the early 1970s. Lordstown was one of the most modern and sophisticated auto plants in the world, but both the quality of production and productivity kept declining as a young work-force expressed its dissatisfaction through high absenteeism and poor production. GM's experiences at Lordstown, plus a desire to improve productivity, pushed the auto giant into quality-of-work experiments. One experiment that has produced notable results is the joint GM–UAW program at Tarrytown, New York. The glass assembly plant once had such a poor production record that GM was threatening to close it down. Now it has one of the best records in the GM system. The Lordstown story is more complicated. The changes have been coming more slowly; worker alienation is still high. There has been less open rebelliousness, but largely because recessions and heavy layoffs have pushed workers to worry more about job security and less about work quality.

Despite the mixed record, GM insists it has revised its priorities. Its work improvement programs, initiated at the beginning of the 1970s, were aimed primarily at improving productivity. Work quality was considered a bonus benefit. GM Vice President George Morris says the corporation has now reversed those objectives.

"We feel that by concentrating on the quality of work life and wisely managing the systems that lead to greater job satisfaction and feelings of self-worth, that improvements in the effectiveness of organization will follow."

The Bolivar project also forced new thinking by unions. The floor-level leaders of the union were initially skeptical of the work committees, especially since they were not pitted against management in the normal confrontation atmosphere. Such confrontation is more than just an old basis for the power of union leaders at that level. It comes from more than a century of experience. An American management elite steadfastly, and at times violently, resisted what for an industrial democracy was the inevitable, from the legislation of unions to the broadening of their bargaining rights. Against this tradition, changing plant-level attitudes of shop stewards has been as hard as changing the views of management. America's labor-management legacy also explains why national union leaders, even while participating, have to overcome skepticism that such projects are not merely a device to draw more work for the same rate of pay. The International Association of Machinists and Aerospace Workers (IAM) has negotiated twenty-two productivity and quality-of-working-life programs, the second largest of any U.S. union. But by the end of the stagflation decade, productivity slumps, slow growth, and rocketing investment costs had triggered a new management response that threatened these programs. Some firms were regressing to an old employer phenomenon in contract bargaining, the "takeaways" of removing standard provisions like rest periods, sick leave, and severance pay. "Management can't have it both ways. It can't ask for improved productivity and launch a 'takeaway' attack," noted IAM President William Winpisinger. " 'Takeaway' demands strike at the very essence of the quality of working life."

Yet, in the face of old attitudes and realistic fears, delicately negotiated trade-offs can make quality-of-working-life programs successful for workers with the secondary, albeit important, effect of raising productivity. The UAW, which pioneered in productivity deals with automakers, is adapting and promoting quality-of-work programs in more and more GM plants. The other two big automakers are moving more cautiously. What management and the union can both point to, as indicators of increased job satisfaction, is a dramatic drop in absenteeism, job turnover, and reduced scrap and repair costs. Perhaps the best indicator is the rate of grievances at assembly plants, the normal hotbed of daily union-management confrontation. Between 1973 and 1976, grievances dropped from 55,000 to 12,000. UAW's Bluestone concludes from his experiences that there are at least three essential criteria for successful work humanization programs: Unions and management must have "co-equal status in designing and implementing the program" to eliminate fears such as the use of speed-up techniques. To this he adds that the programs should be voluntary and fashioned by the workers "from 'the bottom up' rather than 'the top down.' " Finally, workers should share in the benefits from rising productivity gained in a quality-of-working-life program.

In 1974 a group of workers from Bolivar visited the famous trend-setting Volvo plant in Kalmar, Sweden, and another project in Norway. There they studied Kalmar's "lessons of experience" —both the successes and failures of the Swedish innovation. They returned home convinced that they would have to develop their own model of industrial democracy, far different, but profiting from what they had seen. The conclusions of the Bolivar workers show a curious phenomenon that has emerged in an economic world generally characterized by increasing similarity and interdependence. The budding American and the more fully evolving European practices of industrial democracy may share the common goal of restoring human satisfaction and dignity to the workplace, but they need not and are not taking similar routes in getting there.

Largely because of the political strength of their unions and social-democratic parties, European nations have pushed industrial democracy to frontiers unimagined even a decade ago. Staunchly capitalist West Germany enacted "codetermination" legislation in the fifties, and strengthened it in the sixties and seventies, giving union representatives 50 percent of the seats on some corporate boards. In other European countries, work councils have gained real strength since their postwar inception and have pushed for better working conditions, company performance, and other demands beyond standard wage and hour bargaining. In Italy, which has no industrial democracy legislation, unions are bargaining directly with corporations for more social benefits and decisions in management.

Where these various European approaches will end up is still anyone's guess. As Edwin S. (Ted) Mills pointed out in the *Harvard Business Review,* the true cost of the array of European worker benefits is difficult to assess. On the one hand, the combination of high wages, high prices, and high taxes and sagging economic performance is forcing a rightward political drift even in Scandinavia. Efforts to share profits are running into the stagflation phenomenon of shrinking profits, witnessed most recently in the breakdown of Sweden's labor-management consensus in a national strike.

On the other hand, "it is clear that the number of humanization experiments in Western Europe is growing," observed State's Harry Pollak in late 1978. The Dutch Government financed some of Europe's first projects in the sixties, but after a decade they waned. Now, through its Productivity Committee, it has targeted five new programs with essential differences, adapted in part from the latecomer experiments in the U.S. Unlike the earlier programs, the new ones involve workers from the start, and the projects come under joint union-management supervision.

The West German Government has just completed a three year $70-million job enrichment and work-restructuring effort, including projects at such giants as Volkswagen and Bosch. Other projects are linking job satisfaction with technological innovations like robots. They are probing through actual programs at the effects of automation on humans in the workplace. CWA President Watts asked in 1979 that at least this should be studied in the U.S. It is too early for final results to have been evaluated. Initial union and management reactions have been mixed; there are successes and problems. But the German Government seems to reflect a pragmatic attitude that this is what first-round pioneering is all about. It has commenced a second round of funding, and as one ministry official said, "We have already achieved something if we have made people more aware of the problems, both human and organizational, of new works processes and technologies." It is a consistent decision of a nation that has long promoted work humanization and democratization even as it has been a leader in productivity growth and global competitiveness.

In any event, American labor and business are pursuing their own path, just as Samuel Gompers decreed when he enforced a nonpolitical, nonsocialist direction for the labor establishment at the end of the century. The Gompers tradition remains alive and well in the ruling circles of American labor—that is, it did until recently. Present-day labor leaders, particularly at the top of the AFL–CIO, have long been criticized in some quarters as being forces of institutionalized conservatism. For their part, these union leaders believe that their views on participation and industrial democracy reflect the traditional feelings of their membership. Old-line labor leadership has never wanted to become involved in corporate management. But they are being pushed by the guarded experiments of major AFL–CIO unions like the American Federation of State, County, and Municipal Employees; Winpisinger's Machinists and Aerospace Workers; Watts's CWA; and more recently the United States Steel Workers, which have brought quality-of-work-life into the collective bargaining package.

Certain critics point to an apparent contradiction between a cooperative union-management work-life program and the UAW's basically adversarial relationship with management to promote wage and hour demands. The track record, observes Irving Bluestone about the Bolivar, GM, and other UAW projects, is that "experience indicates that normal collective bargaining and the introduction of quality of work life can exist and succeed side by side." As long as the necessary checks and balances earlier mentioned are in place, the coexistence of both cooperative and adversarial relationships is understandable. Successful programs with a primary emphasis on increasing dignity and job satisfaction through worker participation generally accomplish a rise in productivity, the minimum common goal of both union and management. Common goals can be pursued cooperatively even if the distribution of benefits of the attained goal of increased productivity among workers, management, and shareholders is settled by an adversarial relationship.

While European labor becomes increasingly involved in corporate decision-making, U.S. labor and corporations are just beginning to experiment with quality-of-life programs that in turn produce new labor-management relationships. Meanwhile, worker alienation and the quality of work become bigger and bigger problems for the U.S. economy. The growing magnitude of these problems was summarized by the findings of a major survey undertaken by the Opinion Research Corporation in early 1979: "The changes reported here are ubiquitous, pervasive, and nontransient; any reversal is unlikely in the foreseeable future. The goal for management is to be aware of and prepared for new and surfacing employee needs, before it is forced to take reactive, ignorant, and resistive postures." Even the University of Michigan's Survey Research Center, whose previous studies of worker satisfaction showed "the sky was not falling as everyone else asserted it was," found in their 1979 report: "The findings of [our latest] survey surprised us. The sky has finally fallen." These findings parallel those in Europe and explain why there business, labor, and government have strengthened their efforts to adapt to changing human values and technology by overcoming outmoded labor-management relations in the workplace.

In the U.S. the response to the intensifying alienation-productivity blues syndrome is still largely "characterized by redoubling efforts to use traditional solutions such as pay raises and human relations training for supervisors," notes the Opinion Research report. "Although management practices and personnel policies have been evolving," adds the report, "employees' values and expectations have been evolving at an even faster pace." Management's race to catch up was not helped any by a 1977 decision of the U.S. Government to dismantle its National Center of Productivity and Quality of Working Life and reduce other funding programs. The decision reflected more than just another policy lag of a Washington economic power center still preoccupied with "fine-tuning" the demand side of the economy. This retreat from a supply-side attack on stagflation flew in the face of mounting evidence that declining productivity is significantly interrelated with growing worker alienation. In all the many experiments to increase worker participation and job satisfaction, observed by Edwin S. (Ted) Mills, director of the American Quality of Work Center, "there has never been an instance in which improvements in the quality of work have failed to increase productivity substantially."

The problems of worker alienation and quality of work life coupled with declining productivity constitute a major item on the nation's development agenda for the 1980s. But like other items, they will require solution through consultation and cooperation rather than through confrontation alone.

III

The futility of confrontation in economic policy-making is most notable in the regulatory struggle over clean air, clean water, and open spaces, and the safety of the workplace. The intensity of the struggle, as it has developed in the last decade, is all the more curious because it revolves around the issues of participation and efficiency rather than equity. Yet, in their own way, the environmental battles have been class struggles—essentially the upper middle class trying to protect, enhance, and expand its way of life and employing the tactics and techniques of 1960s confrontation politics to issues that are essentially scientific and economic. After a decade of battles, both sides have become locked into their rhetorical positions. Yet even in this emotional fight, a few pioneers have emerged. Their efforts point the way to new policies and, more importantly, to a new process for deciding policies that protect the environment without damaging the economy.

As we have already pointed out, government regulations on the environment and health and safety have clearly added to business costs and contributed to declining productivity growth. There is increasing evidence that the costs of these new regulations are being passed on to customers and contributing to inflation. At the same time, as we have also stated, there is a government policy-lag, a failure to develop measuring and statistical techniques that can count the economic benefits of clean water and air and improved health and safety.

Government regulation will become an even larger target for

reform as the struggle against inflation grows more desperate and as the drop in productivity continues and becomes more alarming. The issue in the politics of the 1980s is whether regulations will be modified to protect both environmental and economic interests or whether they will be more severely crippled in a return to cowboy economics. The answer depends not only on the corporate and political forces pushing to avoid or cripple these regulations but also on the regulators and environmentalists who have viewed any attempt at economic rationality as a sellout to the polluters. It finally will depend on whether a new regulatory process can be created that will take these issues out of the arena of confrontation and into a realm where jobs and efficiency can be better balanced with clean air and worker safety.

The various costs of regulation have only recently become apparent. A Business Roundtable study of forty-eight companies found that federal regulations cost them an annual $2.6 billion, representing 10 percent of their capital expenditures. This money was diverted from other investments and the costs were passed on to consumers. The investment required for pollution control between 1970 and 1985 will be at least $187 billion, with most of the costs coming in the 1980s. The proposed ban on saccharin would have cost food companies $110 million a year. A proposed blanket ban on industrial use of benzene, according to Harvard physicist Richard Wilson, would have prevented one leukemia death every two or three years at a cost of $500 million annually. The balancing question arises in various forms. Achieving better gas mileage is clearly a national priority, but is the regulatory device of fleet averages for the auto companies the most effective way to achieve it? Are the mileage and pollution control regulations in direct conflict, and what is the cost of trying to achieve both simultaneously? How far can the United States go in imposing regulations on home-based companies when their international competitors operate more freely? At what point do the regulations chase plants and jobs overseas where there are few if any such laws to worry about?

"They've done 95 percent of what there is to do in pollution," said one automotive executive whose company has long favored environmental controls. "Now we are going to spend an inordinate amount of money on the last three and a half or four percent. It probably won't affect clean air at all."

The executive said the pollution levels of individual cars in some instances had been reduced as much as 90 percent but the fleet average was only about 80 percent.

"They've got about ten percent more to go. So from where they've come from, we ought to be standing up and cheering their public responsibility. But we're bitching about it because they haven't reached the last ten, which probably should have never been required in the first place.

"If we could somehow get the policy back to being based on facts, and say, 'what are the facts of that last ten percent and what is it costing us in inflation and productivity?'—I think we would elect publicly not to do it. But we're arguing about that last ten percent as if it is theology."

The debate on health regulation is being complicated by the so-called "threshold" issue. Most health regulations are based on the assumption that there is a threshold of exposure to dangerous substances and set standards below that point, usually without regard to cost. But more scientists are now questioning the threshold concept. Instead, they argue that health hazards gradually diminish to zero. Since few substances can or will be completely barred from use, the setting of any level of exposure requires a balance between health and economic costs.

Achieving flexibility is difficult, especially if Congress and the regulators are emotionally swayed by the cause of cancer prevention. The Delaney Amendment bans the use of any food additive if it is found to have caused cancer in animals. The costs of this inflexibility have been revealed in the saccharin fight. The Occupational Safety and Health Administration is trying to impose a similar ban on any substance in the workplace that is proved to have caused animal or human cancer. That could require the replacement of 250 industrial substances at a cost of at least $1 billion.

The regulatory pioneer will have to emerge from the wreckage of past battles and from the rigidity and zealotry on both sides. In government, hundreds of officials of the Environmental Protection Agency threatened to resign if the Administration went ahead with a plan for economic review of environmental regulations. The credibility of business is similarly exhausted. The auto companies, for example, fought so long against any pollution controls that no one takes their current complaints seriously.

Replacing conflict with some kind of consensus is crucial to the new regulatory pioneering. Two examples of pioneering show that a new consensus can be achieved among government, industry, and environmentalists in Washington and between industry and environmentalists in corporate boardrooms.

In 1975, as Congress was revising the Clean Air Act, a member of the House Commerce Committee added an amendment requiring an 80 percent reduction in emissions of hydrocarbons, carbon monoxide, and nitrogen from heavy-duty truck engines. An indication of its legislative clarity was that the amendment made the same requirements for motorcycle engines. While even committee staff members considered the standards impossible, the amendment looked as if it were headed for passage. The heavy-duty truck lobby assembled its lobbying force, mainly to push conservative congressmen, to kill the measure.

Officials from Cummins Industries, a company already noted for its environmental commitment, broke ranks with the industry and tried a different approach. It went to committee liberals as well as conservatives with a substitute proposal that hinged on the determination by the Environmental Protection Agency of the effects of heavy-duty-engine air pollution on public health. The crucial question was not what standard would be set (75 percent versus 80 percent), but the *process* of setting standards. Based on the EPA study, Congress could set target goals for emission controls. The standards would be reviewed periodically to assess health, technology, and economic factors. A monitoring system would be established on the assembly line to test compliance. Financial penalties would be assessed on noncompliers to provide an incentive for compliance and to eliminate any competitive advantages for manufacturers of nonconforming engines.

The Cummins proposal was adopted unanimously in subcommittee and by the full committee, drawing equally enthusiastic support from conservatives and liberals. It could be described, at least by cynics, as a brilliant case study of corporate lobbying. But the effort involved far more than bringing in the heavy guns to blast out a narrow majority in an acrimoniously divided committee. As a Cummins vice-president told us, the important thing is to prevent strong battle lines from being formed so early that the issue becomes an either-or fight between environmentalists and corporate interests. Cummins officials admit even now that standards may be set that will be difficult to meet. What pleases them is that a regulatory process has been created with which they can live.

Another example of consensus building and pioneering was cited by the Pulitzer Prize–winning writer Robert Kahn. According to Kahn, a multinational minerals corporation, AMAX, has structured its corporate management to assure that capital spending projects are assessed for their environmental impact. AMAX's real pioneering effort came in 1969 when it opened a new molybdenum mine in the Rocky Mountains. From the beginning, the company worked with a small group of environmentalists to limit the damage that might be caused by the mine, which was in a national forest. The major effort was the construction of an 8.5-mile tunnel under the Continental Divide which made it possible to process the ore with a minimum of damage. Based on this experience, AMAX set up its Environmental Services Group, a corporate department that includes scientists, ecologists, and financial experts and is responsible for assessing the environmental impact of capital projects.

Such examples of pioneering are still relatively rare. In the evolution of corporate and multinational bureaucracy, accountants are rising to the top faster than innovative thinkers. Stagflation offers a seemingly permanent excuse for doing nothing that would rock the profits boat. The AMAX approach is one way of expanding participation in decision making. Just as corporations have begun including women and blacks on their boards of directors, they will have to include environmentalists. As we take up in the next chapter, this process can go beyond tokenism. If nothing else, such representatives can serve as early-warning systems, guiding businesses to pragmatic decisions that avoid confrontation with either environmental groups or government regulators.

Government regulation, whatever its impact at home, totally ignores the existence of the globally interdependent economy. In the process of slaying the national dragons of pollution but ignoring the global danger, the regulators are crippling the ability of many companies to compete in world markets against foreign competitors who are not burdened by the same laws and regulations. This is not an argument for pollution or for dangerous jobs, but an explicit recognition of a policy lag that needs correcting.

Partly because of climate and geography, our industrial competitors have not been awakened as abruptly to the dangers of pollution. Only in the last few years, as pollution chokes the Rhine and clutters the once-pristine Mediterranean, has an environmental movement grown in European politics, and this has taken its real inspiration from Europe's growing dependence upon nuclear power. With the exception of the battles over nuclear plant sitings, the Europeans have generally evolved more of a consensus and scientifically oriented program of pollution control. The most notable examples of successful pollution programs are the British efforts to clean rivers and urban air.

In the Third World, there is obviously less concern over pollution and job safety in the push to industrialization. Third World nations are now offering pollution abatement havens to multinational corporations. As one automotive executive told us, a Third World exporting nation can save, just in comparative cost differences in environmental rules, $200 per engine over an American-made competitor.

The way around this competitive problem is, first, to acknowledge that it does exist for American companies, with a potential loss of profits and jobs in this country. The second step is an active foreign policy that recognizes its interdependence with domestic industrial and regulatory policy and promotes harmonization of pollution regulations in the industrial world as a necessary goal if trade liberalization is to proceed. There was a sputtering attempt at environmental cooperation within NATO in the late 1960s, clearly the wrong forum.

With our industrial partners and the Third World, a carrot-and-stick approach would be in order. The 1979 GATT trade rules were aimed at eliminating a variety of hidden subsidies and incentives. Certainly the comparative disadvantage in environmental rules should come under that definition. With the right amount of cajoling and pressure, the industrial nations might follow harmonized pollution and job safety policies. If not, tariffs making up the cost differential could be considered. But for the Third World, these nations would not be able to meet such harmonized standards within the coming decade. Thereafter a tariff, announced well in advance and phased in over several years, should be imposed on their imports that benefit from an absence of pollution control or job safety costs. While this certainly raises the specter of more rather than less protectionism, a balance has to be struck here too between protecting the health and safety of our own citizens while maintaining our economic competitiveness.

IV

Americans have always liked to think that business in this country operates freely and independently of the government. If the business of America is business, as Calvin Coolidge once said, the myth has been that it has prospered without the heavy hand of government. Nurturing the myth are the examples of what has happened when business and government have been in each other's arms—most blatantly the corruption of the Grant and Nixon eras. The myth is fostered on the Left by examples of these kinds and on the Right by a vision of unfettered "free" enterprise.

Like most myths, it had in the past at best only a limited approximation to reality; today it is the most misunderstood and abused piece of rhetoric in the econopolitical debate of the country. The American Revolution and Constitution had economic as well as political roots, and there have been varying measures of business-government collaboration since then. American industry first grew under the protection of tariffs. Railroads spread with the economic blessings of government. But until the New Deal the collaboration was more benign than active, although at times collusive. There was, in addition, an adversarial relationship foreshadowed before the battles of the New Deal and lingering well beyond. In reality it was an arrangement that suited almost everyone as long as the American economy led a global economic boom.

All this has been changed by stagflation and rising competition from imports spurred on by the intensified post-market relations of foreign governments with their own and with U.S. multinationals. Leading industries, employing hundreds of thousands of people, are in varying degrees of trouble. Steel mills close in Youngstown, Ohio. Zenith, one of the few American multinational electronics manufacturers that tried to hold on in the U.S., is finally being forced to close more of its factories around the nation, and like other such manufacturers, wipes out entire towns in the process. Shipbuilders close down entire yards. The response of the industries and labor unions affected is to run to Washington for help, usually to throttle imports, and complain that competing foreign products are being sold here at unfair advantage because the sellers are receiving all kinds of help from foreign governments.

And to some degree their complaints are well founded, given America's earlier history of an economy less fettered by foreign dependence, and a corporate and union belief in the marketplace vision. But this economic and political tradition has made the U.S. the least prepared of all the democracies to tackle the global crisis of industrial adjustment. Today there exists in almost every country—in the industrial and Third World alike—a national industrial policy that includes programs for systematic government assistance to corporations. All are subject to potential abuse, especially the violation of efficiency by the subsidization of a sick industry merely to maintain employment through the next election. Nevertheless, they are based on a pragmatic acceptance of a post-market reality that world trading patterns and prices are undergoing significant upheavals, that productivity bottlenecks have developed, or that new export market opportunities are to be seized if action is taken quickly. In all cases, however, these industrial policies are based on a realistic, econopolitical perception that individual companies and their unions, particularly where they involve concentrated capital and labor, cannot always adjust to these changes on their own.

Yet in the U.S. "the greatest problem in business-government relations is that of perception," wrote Alfred C. Neal, the former president of the Committee for Economic Development. It is a failure to perceive "that the beneficent self-adjusting world of our earlier history and later nostalgia does not exist, that much of our intellectual capital and social philosophy is obsolescent, and that the institutions and skills needed to cope with the world as it is are not yet invented." For Neal, as for a growing number of intellectuals and a small but significant minority of public and private officials, the "first priority" for a revised econopolitical vision "is to create an understanding that a partnership of business and government is a necessary condition for achieving individual and social objectives." And this is not to the exclusion of labor. At all points in the modern historical experience among European industrial democracies, built into the evolving post-market interactions between government and corporations are explicit political and legal safeguards that assure equity protection and increasing participation to workers and unions.

Also, after World War II, every industrial nation except the United States was forced into industrial rebuilding programs that required new degrees of policy coordination, the establishment of economic priorities, and the forging of business-labor cooperation. The worse the wartime damage, the more intense the rebuilding and cooperation—in France more than England, in Germany and Japan more than France. West German government-business cooperation is built around tightly controlled and self-disciplined unions that act as a lid on inflation and a prop under productivity and represent labor on corporate boards. While West German corporate ownership and control remains largely private, there is sufficient government ownership in key industries and heavy investment (25 percent of 951 major corporations)—directly or through government-controlled banks. This is enough to push business gently in the direction government wants it to go. At the same time, the government can promote mergers and efficiencies and ease the problems of structural adjustment. Similarly, the popular cliché "Japan, Inc." reflects the difficulty of telling where business ends and government begins in the island nation. Through the Ministry of International Trade and Industry (MITI), the government can dispense tax breaks, offer real estate, provide credit, create cartels, encourage mergers and foreign investment, promote research and development and new technology, and direct the flow of imports and exports from selected industries.

Most Americans would probably recoil from such a vision of government-business cooperation or collusion. If nothing else, it raises the specter of a corporate loyalist and corporate-financed President riding to the White House on the wave of indiscriminate "bail-outs" of the Chryslers of the 1980s. But the global economic revolution is forcing new arrangements between government and business. These arrangements can be guided by either a national industrial policy, an explicit thinking through of industrial needs, benefits, costs, and available resources, or emerge scattershot and hodgepodge as they have in the past few years. Facing import competition, the steel industry ends up with $500 million in loan guarantees plus import quotas but gives no assurance it will modernize sufficiently to meet the new competition, or much thought as to what kind and how much of a steel industry is needed in the face of the global steel glut. The track record of the stagflation decade indicates that without an overall industrial policy we will have a *de facto* policy of handouts to every industry threatened by import competition and receive little real structural adjustment in return for the billions spent.

Once again, we turn to the microcosm example of the pioneer, not to suggest a panacea but to demonstrate that such pioneering is possible as well as desirable if cast in an American mold.

By January 1977, as the Carter Administration came into office, the American shoe industry was being driven out of business by imports. Employment had been cut from 230,000 to 165,000 jobs in less than a decade. Production had dropped from 640 million pairs of shoes to 400 million, while imports grew from 175 million to 370 million. Under intense business and union pressure, President Carter negotiated a compromise and approved an orderly marketing agreement to restrict shoe imports from Taiwan and South Korea, while rejecting demands for stiffer import controls. Helping to make this compromise possible was a "novel" Commerce Department plan to help the U.S. shoe industry put itself back on its feet.

One irony of the U.S. shoe travail was that it was caused, unknowingly, in part by the success of one government agency and in part by a failure of another. The pioneering of business-government cooperation discussed in chapter 5 helped make developing nations the world's dominant shoe producers within a decade. The Third World strategy of exporting labor-intensive manufactures was inspired by the prodding of well-intentioned development agencies, among them U.S. AID, in the early sixties. The U.S. Ex-Im Bank financed many of the technology transfers of shoemaking machinery, and the policy proved a boon in helping to absorb the 20 percent-plus unemployed of the labor force of the poor nations that followed the advice. The accelerating growth of Third World producers was well known to AID, World Bank, and other international entities. Yet by the mid-seventies the plight of the U.S. shoe industry seemed to take Commerce and Labor Department officials by surprise—crosstown information sometimes travels slowly in Washington. At the same time and in contrast to mounting efforts in Europe and Japan, officials in the U.S. steadfastly resisted the creation of an early-warning forecasting system for anticipating structural adjustment problems. Thus, what was legislated as structural adjustment assistance in Congress was passed long after an industry had begun a death march. Among businessmen and union leaders, assistance monies came to be known as "funeral expenses."

The Commerce Department shoe program, initiated by Undersecretary Sidney Harman, met, from its inception, resisting layers of traditional bureaucracy unaccustomed to what in Europe is called "dynamic adjustment policies." When the early resistance initially gave Harman doubts about his "radical" idea, it was a midnight phone call to an advisor that reassured him. The reason: European and Third World nations had been successfully conducting such assistance programs for years to break the "structural bottlenecks" of sick or underdeveloped industries, and, in many such cases, did so with the cooperation of subsidiaries of U.S. multinationals, like the Sears Roebuck program in Peru.

The program, coordinated also with the Labor Department, was more than just an effort to speed up standard adjustment assistance to a then dying industry. More important, it innovated assistance for the industry's "self-help" by improving the quality and volume of private technical expertise provided to companies. Domestic retailers and manufacturers were brought together to identify market trends and style changes. An export promotion program was developed. The Office of Science and Technology was directed to develop new technology, the first government-industry program to develop a new generation of technology in a nondefense industry.

Harman had to overcome not only his own bureau and fundamental opposition in the Executive branch but skepticism in the industry from management and unions. Manufacturers and labor wanted import quotas and were far less enthusiastic about trade adjustment assistance plans. When they became convinced, their active participation was an essential ingredient in designing the program.

"The plan hinged on the ability and willingness of shoe manufacturers to take advantage of cost-reducing innovations and to respond quickly to changes in style," Harman told us. "I had a strong belief that the domestic industry could compete effectively against foreign competition if it was modernized and restructured. But the firms would not, or could not, take the necessary steps on their own. So our first step was to go out and find ways that we could help them help themselves."

The program was showing signs of success within six months. Half of the 150 companies eligible for help were applying. Imports were dropping, even on products not covered by the marketing agreements. Employment and production began rising, and by 1978 some companies were reporting record sales and earnings. In a remarkable turnabout, the Commerce Department reported that American shoe exports had increased by 28 percent in 1978.

The shoe industry remains, however, a troubled one. More than a year after the departure of Harman and other staff involved in the pilot program, the Commerce Department's enthusiasm had significantly waned. The pilot shoe program had brought results—the revitalization of essentially sound firms and the conversion to other manufactures of the essentially uncompetitive firms. The pilot project achieved success in the bolstering of the good and the conversion of the weak. Today, however, U.S. firms are again facing a growing tide of imported shoes and an overall decline in employment of shoe workers. And by the New England primary season of election year 1980, there were new appeals—and new-found sympathy—for increasing the quotas on imported footwear.

"I am not saying that this is something government ought always to do," Harman said, "but I am saying it is an approach that may often have great value.

"I think it is ridiculous to continue to lose U.S. industries and jobs to free trade when a consistent national policy of industrial priorities could allow us to keep both."

This judgment had already been made by many of our advanced industrial trading partners. Germany, under Economics Minister Karl Schiller, reactivated the industrial policy measures of the 1950s when in the early seventies growth slowed in certain sectors and labor and marketing bottlenecks occurred in others. Schiller designed a fourfold framework to guide government assistance of private efforts for restructuring ailing industries: that the entire sector—and not just some companies—must be in difficulty; that the actual restructuring program chosen be the decision of the private firms; that the government's role be to trigger "self-help" efforts to restore the sector's global productive competitiveness; and, finally, that the aids had to be both temporary and result in competitive efficiency. In practice the German program has taken many forms, from "targeted" depreciation allowances to encourage industrial innovation in a specific sector, to the engineering of voluntary agreements among firms in a sector to provide "breathing space" for rationalizing production methods.

In Japan the tradition of business-government cooperation is of long standing. With the creation of MITI in 1950, Japan began a deliberate peacetime effort to marshal the talents, expertise, and financial assistance of the state with those of the private sector. It faced a major obstacle, private sector resistance, a fact long since forgotten by those who resort to today's popular view of a monolithic Japan. MITI's first attempt had to have a credible demonstration effect. It chose breaking production bottlenecks that linked coal and steel production by negotiating a strict bilateral barter arrangement. The vicious circle of less steel output curtailing coal output which led to less steel output was broken by MITI's efforts, and the restoration of steel and coal companies as self-sustaining and internationally competitive firms convinced skeptical Japanese businessmen in other sectors of the advantages of government cooperation.

Thus the Harman experiment with U.S. shoe firms is only novel according to U.S. standards. The advocacy of dynamic adjustment programs and other aspects of a national industrial policy for the U.S. economy, however, pitted Harman and a few other senior officials against the fragmented and helter-skelter arrangement of the Commerce and Labor departments' bureaucracies. The career bureaucrats were resistant to the idea of a "big picture" approach to assistance and revitalization efforts in behalf of industry and labor. It challenged the existing arrangement of diverse and separate regional and urban development programs institutionalized in the fifties and sixties. The fledgling idea of a national industrial policy was paralyzed by the lack of internal unity at Commerce and Labor as well as by their second-order ranking as supply management agencies by a White House and Congress dominated by liberal Keynesians and conservative monetarists engulfed in the pros and cons of the latest demand "fine-tuning" debate. Only in 1979 did at least one committee, the Joint Economic Committee of Congress, unanimously endorse the need for giving equal policy attention to the supply-side causes of stagflation.*

After Harman left the Commerce Department in 1978, he summarized his view in a valedictory of sorts, one that if not addressed by policy makers in this Administration will certainly confront those in the next:

"We need to coordinate our trade problems, our unemployment problems and our antitrust problems and sit down and ask ourselves: What gave birth to these assumptions? Are they still as valid today as when they were made? And has the world changed in a way that ought to generate some change in us?

"These are questions that the best firms ask themselves. And these are the questions that should be asked in a coherent and coordinated national way."

Other policy makers have indicated the need for a complementary, not competitive, policy framework for managing the economy's supply and production problems—even if they could not break through the ingrained tradition of Washington's reliance on demand management policies. For example, former Treasury Secretary Blumenthal, before gaining his post, observed at a 1974 seminar at UCLA that "new skepticism and disaffection have become rife throughout the population. This makes the issue of the proper roles of government and of private business—and of the relationship between the two—both timely and important. The context within which these issues need to be addressed evolves from the observation that our system has, in fact, been working less well in recent years." Blumenthal's idea for dealing with the problems at the time was a call both for "redefined business-government relationships" and to gain from the fact that "many of our problems are similar to those of other industrial societies; and no doubt much can be learned from studying how other countries have attempted to deal with them." The call for redefined relationships and a flow of comparative studies has yet to come from Treasury, perhaps understandably, since it is a major

* The advice seemed to have been ignored by President Carter when in June 1979 he eliminated the secretaries of Commerce and Labor—whose departments are the prime originators of supply policies—from the Economic Policy Group, the subdivision within the Cabinet responsible for all major economic policy.

Washington power broker and keeper of demand management policies of which there is less to learn abroad than from industrial policy.

In keeping with Blumenthal's intent to learn from others, a participant of that same 1974 seminar at UCLA quoted Keizai Doyukai from Japan, who made these observations of the dilemma of the U.S. economy:

> The relatively low growth rate of the U.S. economy, combined with inflation in recent years, sharpened the problems of unemployment, poverty, and inequitable income distribution that had existed all along in the postwar period. The dominant belief in individualism and individual responsibilities and the fear of government encroachment upon individuals' rights and of government intervention in private economic activity led to the lack of appropriate public policy on such national problems as lags in industrial adjustment, deteriorating balance of payments, urban decay, environmental disruption, and the like.
>
> A series of factors are responsible for this slow growth in productivity, but the single most important one is associated with the lack of the organizational imperative of modern technology in the United States. This imperative appears in some other developed countries in the form of indicative planning, close collaboration between the public and private sectors, and/or various forms of far-reaching collaboration within the private sector itself. What they provide, above all, is the assurance that necessary complementary investments and government support will be forthcoming.

In 1942, Joseph Schumpeter wrote his classic work *Capitalism, Socialism and Democracy*. He described with eloquence the ability of capitalism to transform economics from a science of scarcity to one concerned with the management of growth. And yet, in the end, he made the prophecy of capitalism's demise. The difficulty of capitalism in the spurring of growth would be the rise of large bureaucratic organizations, which, he felt, would bring about an end to the innovative spirit, the entrepreneurial risk-taking that was capitalism's source.

The small examples of pioneering here can be taken as evidence that Schumpeter's vision was wrong, that innovation still exists. But the frustration of pioneers in a globally bureaucratized world can be taken as evidence that Schumpeter ultimately will be shown right. Our preference is to draw with hope, but tempered with considerable reservation, the first conclusion.

The value of the pioneering experiments is not in their existence or even their results but in how they point the way to new processes of decision making, to new ways of approaching problems and trying to achieve results. To emerge from the stagflation decade and to make the 1980s a decade of growth requires not only new policies but new ways of thinking and achieving those policies. The challenge, as these experiments show, is less in the realm of technical economics; it rests squarely with the philosophy that shapes and the politics that decide how a democracy manages its economy.

CHAPTER 8

Quest for a New Vision: The 1980s

I

BY THE TIME of the 1980 elections, the only short lines in the United States may be those at the voting booths. As America approaches the 1980 Presidential election, our democracy is at a stalemate. The social contract that binds us to common aims and goals, if not to the policies for achieving them, is stretched. The economic machinery that was supposed to produce prosperity has stalled in stagflation, shortages, and gluts, sagging productivity and investment, soaring family debt, domestic and international financial instability. Our political machinery, responsible for producing economic remedies, is locked in conflict, overloaded with information of dubious credibility, empty of new ideas. Citizens, whether farmers, renters, truckers, or gas station operators, are looking for their own economic solutions. Their direct actions strain the contract further and lock the political machinery into even more seemingly endless arbitrations of conflicting demands. Meanwhile, our democracy's basic remedy, the vote, is increasingly ignored by its citizens. Fifty-four percent of the eligible population voted in the 1976 general election, far fewer in the 1978 congressional elections. By 1980 a turnout of half the electorate may be considered a triumph.

The lifeblood of the body politic in a democracy is information, credible information. While the postwar global economics revolution has stalled the American economy, the crisis of credibility has helped to freeze the nation's political machinery and thereby block a return to economic growth. Political paralysis and lack of consensus reflect an electorate and its political leaders who are bombarded by contradictory "facts," as well as ideas and opinions. We are in an era of "information overload," noted one observer, "becoming a nation of fast-fact junkies."

Energy is but the most glaring example. To the citizen it reveals a failure in vision, a failure to reform the processes of government and politics which block the search for economic remedies. Perhaps to no one was the political failure clearer than to the driver waiting in the gas lines during the summer of 1979. It is felt even more strongly by those millions of us who live near a nuclear power station. Our uncertainty and fear, after the 1979 near miss at the Three Mile Island nuclear plant in Pennsylvania, have been exacerbated by a maze of inconsistent information on everything from comparative safety to comparative cost effectiveness. For those patient enough to tread through the maze, there are other problems. As Meg Greenfield lamented, ". . . there will always be someone on your side of the argument who gets caught telling a lie or stealing the cash register, or not having the vaguest idea what he is talking about." And, she added, "You can absolutely *count* on the electrical utilities and the oil companies, for instance, to come through in this connection, and also on some agency of government meant to monitor them." If the suburbanite in New York or Los Angeles finds the wait in the gas line traumatic, he will find little sympathy from those long accustomed to waiting in lines—the unemployed steelworkers of Youngstown, Ohio, or young blacks in all the nation's cities. What we are beginning to share is frustration with our government's failure to address our problems, or even to provide us with believable answers to our questions.

The paralysis of American democracy resembles schizophrenia. The citizenry is aware of the problems. It is equally aware that much of the information it is offered is contradictory. The United States remains the richest land in natural resources and in human and technological resources. Compared with the other industrial democracies, it has done little to apply those resources and talents to the process of adjusting to thirty years of global economic revolution. It is pushed by its conservatives to cut back social, health, and welfare expenditures, while our less rich industrial partners sustained and expanded such programs through the stagflation decade. The liberal Left fails to innovate as its European counterparts sometimes have, preferring solutions from a now dated New Deal or seeking the refuge of neoconservatism.

The nation is aware that it faces a major conversion in the 1980s in order to adapt to the more intense challenges that will come by the end of the century. It must change its work and consumption habits and convert its industrial base and energy sources to survive, and then compete on an increasingly interdependent planet that is reaching its finite resource capacity. At the same time, the global community requires creation of new wealth and a better distribution of existing wealth for the poor of the Third and Fourth worlds. Yet, when consensus is needed, the nation is locked in paralysis and stalemate.

The challenge of the 1980s in domestic politics as in international politics is the same: to reignite growth and to gain "breathing space" for the longer-term adjustments and adaptations to the global economic revolution, and to a global order that the resource limitations and social demands of the 1990s will require. Already we have tasted the consequences of failure—new social tensions at home which have deepened the spiral of political stalemate, and new tensions and schisms worldwide which could lead to local wars for food, energy, and resources. The American response must come in new ideas and new ways of thinking, a return to innovation and experimentation.

As we have proposed global institutional reform to help reignite economic growth, we propose domestic institutional reform —a revision of the national policy framework—to reignite growth at home and to give government a firmer grasp on the management of the economy. The new machinery would create new ways to approach decisions and to generate more believable information. Supplementing old institutions with new ones is needed to create and carry through a new energy and resource policy, a national industrial development policy for the supply side of the economy, and an updated demand management policy to fight inflation. Reform starts with the admission that our institutions and policies helped create the present paralysis. As Greenfield observed, "You have to begin with a concession that the basic structure of our government is spectacularly unsuited for the kind of organized drive that is required."

Our present political framework was constructed in the New Deal and built up on in the 1960s. Already, it is out of date, unable to deal with the economic and political problems that characterized the stagflation decade. As it did in the 1930s, the nation will have to come up with new ways to deal with some old problems and some new ways of thinking about new problems. A revised framework has to focus on new decision-making arenas and consensus-generating mechanisms that by their internal checks and balances can bring greater impartiality and credibility, to revitalize our core principles and institutions. The question is as much one of "process" as "content."

The new framework will not supplant or ride roughshod over the nation's traditional beliefs and values. A major reliance on private enterprise will continue as the basic means to meet the criterion of efficiency. Our legal and political rights will continue their constraining role in business to ensure the striving for equity and participation goals that are demanded by a democracy. In fact, it is the very need to preserve our most cherished beliefs and values that makes the political challenge of the 1980s so crucial.

Nevertheless, if at the same time the most worthwhile of America's democratic traditions are to be sustained, there will have to be trade-offs among competing beliefs. Some of the country's cherished but antiquated philosophical predilections must be discarded. One of these is the assumption, of which the pioneering innovations described in the last chapter should make us wary—that democratically-arrived-at policies must involve only adversarial relations—for example, business versus labor; or environmentalists, conservationists, and consumer groups confronting managers and workers. Another, a corollary of more recent vintage, is the notion that these adversary groups can turn only to government for arbitration, either in intense lobbying duels in the legislative and executive branches or in pitched fights in an already overburdened judiciary. By contrast, there is another postwar idea to be borrowed from abroad and from our own past: America in the 1980s can implement new forms of business-government cooperation, but with novel checks and balances that guard against boondoggles and windfalls for the rich. Our current antiquated vision of a market economy needs to be updated by another American quality, the willingness to experiment and innovate.

As we have in the past two chapters, we will offer some of our own ideas and proposals, centering on energy, nuclear power, industrial development, and the use of credit and tax policy to curb inflation and to increase equity. They are not blueprints for the future; nor are they panaceas. They are offered in the expectation of stimulating debate.

II

While the intellectual terrain appears barren, the physical terrain approaches that point literally. The global economy faces what Robert Heilbroner has called a set of crucial "cross-over points." Sometime between 1990 and 2000, the combination of environmental constraints, resource scarcities, and pollution will catch up with the global economy. Oil is the most dramatic example. Almost all scientists agree that well before the year 2000 the supply of oil will fail to meet demand. As one study noted, the fifteen major industrial oil-importing nations "have perhaps as few as five years or perhaps as many as 20 in which to accomplish a transition from dependence on oil."

This is true not only of oil. It will be just as true of water in the American West and in many parts of Africa, Asia, and Latin America. The International Task Force of Scientists, directed by Nobel Laureate Wassily Leontief, concluded in a 1977 study for the UN that there will be further cross-over points in food and minerals in the next twenty-five years. "The most pressing problem facing the globe is feeding its 4 billion inhabitants," the report asserted. "The tasks are technically feasible, but are contingent on drastic measures of public policy." Referring to mineral scarcity and pollution, the report said, "The principal limits to sustained economic growth and accelerated development are political, social and institutional in character rather than physical." The report was more pessimistic about the physical limits after the year 2000.

Imminent shortages are not a new phenomenon. Historically, critical junctures have coincided with the Kondratief Cycle of resource shortages that appear to recur every forty to sixty years though somewhat more frequently in this century. As economic historian Walt Rostow has observed, past critical junctures have always been accompanied by wars, often for resources, and dramatic social reform that precede a new economic "takeoff." The same convergence of physical and social forces is occurring now. Thinkers of various political views—Rostow, Daniel Bell, Alvin Toffler—agree. One leading statesman, West Germany's Helmut Schmidt, foresees the danger of resource wars. As he told *Time* in the spring of 1979, "I think that the scarcity of oil and the rising prices for crude, which are a menace to the functioning of our economies, can lead to wars." This gloomy prognosis was echoed a few months later by the president of OPEC, Saeed al Otaiba. Addressing a seminar of industry experts, Otaiba said, "If there is another world war, it will be over petroleum."

That Soviet-American *detente* could unravel in the Persian Gulf was already becoming clear by the 1979 Brezhnev-Carter summit in Vienna. While the two Presidents were trying to regulate the strategic arms race and other vestiges of the Cold War conflict, new threats to the peace were appearing in the struggle for influence in the Middle East with its oil and in Africa with its oil and minerals. The Soviet invasion of Afghanistan confirmed the shift of superpower conflict from such old flashpoints as Berlin to the new ones of the Gulf and southern and western Africa. And while the Western Europeans criticized the United States for overreacting to events around the Gulf, the French and Belgian excursions in Zaire showed that these nations are also ready to resort to force to protect their economic interests.

Perhaps because of the American experience of abundance, this country has had the most difficulty facing the realities of physical limitations. Our energy debate has been characterized by a search for villains—in the oil companies and government—rather than by an adaptation to new limitations. What has flowed from one failure is another—to recognize that a new system of trade-offs must be entered into the political and economic decision-making machinery. The trade-offs up to now have been between equity, efficiency, and participation. The traditional trade-offs will remain, but their labels will be transformed in the new debate over private versus social goods, productive versus nonproductive wealth.

The nation's social infrastructure is being rapidly depleted and is reaching a domestic cross-over point. Our railroads will require an estimated $4.2 billion a year for the next ten years to restore them to the condition they were in in the 1940s. Highways, critical to a nation dependent on truck transportation, are wearing out 50 percent faster than they are being replaced; as of 1975 it was estimated that 42 percent of all paved roads were rated "fair" or "poor." Simply to maintain highways in their 1975 condition will require an estimated $21.8 billion a year until 1990. Seventy-five percent of our nation's 564,000 bridges were built before 1935 and are overdue for replacement. This will require immense sums for financing capital formation. There will be, as well, huge demands for private investment. An exact estimate is impossible, but the total could range from $500 billion to $670 billion every year just to avoid slipping into industrial underdevelopment.

"Choose we must," wrote Columbia University sociologist Amitai Etzioni. For the nation, he believes, will be unable to foot this bill for industrial redevelopment and simultaneously make the expenditure of an additional $150 to $225 billion each year for such quality-of-life projects as pollution control, parks and recreation, and cultural facilities that many are demanding. For Etzioni the new trade-offs involve a fundamental choice between a society that wants "a high power development drive and a rather thin quality of life program for the next decade" or "a quite effective quality of life program with growing underdevelopment." This nation placed growing stress on the "quality" during the sixties, and underdevelopment followed. Etzioni and others who believe that the emphasis will return to "reindustrialization" during the 1980s have overlooked the central point. They feel that the choice of industrialization must be of a particular, and perhaps brutal, kind, and that there must be a choice of growth over quality of life. But by the 1990s the planet's finite ecological and resource constraints and social demands will leave little choice but to adapt to quality-of-life and environmental objectives. By then, what we now consider luxuries, will be necessities: using fewer resources, using less-polluting technologies, and more fairly distributing global wealth. Thus a reindustrialization program in the 1980s must be of a particular and enormously expensive kind: one that has the foresight to recognize the interdependence of present growth with future constraints.

These new trade-offs are complex, and the leaders of the antinuclear Left and those of the cowboy Right have been equally blind to them. The nuclear power debate, for example, cannot be limited to the issue of stop or go. If we go, there are trade-offs in health and safety and the environment. If we stop, there are the trade-offs of more expensive gas and oil, of the dangers of coal, and of figuring out ways to provide electricity to such cities as Chicago, which is now 50 percent dependent on nuclear power.

Between these blind spots of the Left and the Right is the political fragmentation of a crumbling center. The Vietnam War sapped the intellectual vitality of the foreign policy elite and shattered its postwar convictions of military interventionism. Stagflation has sapped the intellectual vitality of the economic policy elite, both the mainstream Democratic fiscalists and the monetarist Republicans, and shattered their convictions of post-Depression Keynesian demand management interventionism. The often wavering policies of the Carter Administration are not only the result of the President's inexperience or lack of philosophical core but reflect more deeply the intellectual stalemate of our sagging center.

The stalemate of politics is not only intellectual. Government, literally, is overloaded as more and more disputes are pushed higher and higher up the ladder for resolution or irresolution. The two political parties, whose basic function is to offer voters philosophical choices in Congress and the Presidency, become increasingly skewed by the competing claims of more and more single-interest groups going to government for satisfaction of their demands. From the second term of the New Deal through the Kennedy Administration, Democratic Presidents had to push their programs, often unsuccessfully, past a coalition of Southern Democrats and conservative Republicans. That coalition has disappeared as moderates have replaced old Southern conservative segregationists. Now Presidents are likely to continue to be throttled in Congress by one-day coalitions responding primarily to the single-issue demands of the moment.

We will be turning repeatedly in this and the next chapter to proposals for creating consensus-building mechanisms in *and* out of government. The parties in Congress and the White House can and should fight over the large issues and the direction of policy. The various institutions and reforms we are suggesting can resolve some disputes. They can create boundaries of consensus where conflict now exists, just as the various labor reform acts of the New Deal created mechanisms for solving labor-management disputes primarily at their "grass roots" source—the large corporation. Disagreements would be taken to the national level only if the mechanisms failed. Similar mechanisms are now needed for energy, the environment, safety, and corporate policy-making.

Such political and institutional changes have been spawned in periods of transformation. The Wagner Act emerged as a centerpiece of the New Deal; banking and antitrust reforms followed the late-nineteenth-century industrialization of this country, and British parliamentary reform followed the first industrial revolution.

But, as we have noted, the initial stage of post-transformation reforms has, in the past, been preceded by a regression to conservatism. The growth of neoconservatism in this country (and other industrial democracies) in the 1970s fits the historical pattern of Hoover's response to the Depression with increasingly conservative programs, and by Roosevelt's wavering before he committed himself to more experimental programs. As John Kenneth Galbraith said in *The Nature of Mass Poverty,* "Diagnosis proceeds from the available remedy." The pendulum eventually swings back. As Bernard Nossiter commented, "A Keynes conceives his general theory when it is evident to every person in the street—if not to fellow economists—that mass unemployment is not a temporary aberration to be cured by cutting wages." But Nossiter, surveying today's mainstream of economic and social thinkers for the Washington *Post,* found that by their own admission, "the cupboard of ideas is bare."

America's history does, however, offer a hopeful alternative. "When existing theory fails," wrote Arthur Schlesinger, Jr., "the older American way was experimentation." That is the path Roosevelt, after wavering, chose. "If it fails, admit it frankly, and try another," Roosevelt said. From the experiments and experiences eventually emerged the new theory that was Keynes's synthesis and which became the foundation for national economic policy. "That is, after all, not a bad way to arrive at theory," wrote Schlesinger, and Keynesian policy did guide the country through some two decades of inflation-free prosperity. Only from new experimentation and a willingness to consider new problems in new ways will come the theories and policies that can turn the 1980s into a growth decade.

III

The breakdown of government in Washington results from a clash of an old policy framework, based on a market economy, with the reality of a post-market economy. New interest groups, new "stakeholders" in the social contract—consumer groups, environmental groups, and health and safety lobbies—turn to Congress and the Executive because the economy has not adjusted to their demands.

As recently as the spring of 1979, a public relations executive from Du Pont told *The Wall Street Journal* that "business has a democratic legitimacy only because it is controlled by the market and does what the market wants." And to the extent that consumers responded to the 1979 gas shortage as they did to the 1973 gas shortage, with a short-run spurt of small-car buying and rejection of gas guzzlers, the executive's statement contains a kernel of truth.

But consumers' control over choices of products and prices, the so-called "consumer sovereignty," is steadily eroding as the trend to concentration and bigness brings greater "market imperfection." And as consumers' choices diminish, the new stakeholders turn to government. "Market imperfections" produce organized consumer political action to replace economic action. As a result, government regulation is replacing imperfect markets as the means by which consumers exercise their sovereignty.

The postwar decades have seen an explosion of econopolitical legislation. Government has redressed the more blatant market failures with an array of environmental, conservation, consumer-protection, health, and safety laws. But persistent stagflation has raised the question whether this postwar process of econopolitics can provide both equity for the new stakeholders and efficiency, growth, and stability for business and the economy generally. By the late 1970s the answer was clearly "no." The process had brought stalemate and paralysis. The conservatives and neoconservatives proposed the old solution of reducing government regulation. The liberals offered few new alternatives and continued to regard government as the agent for preserving the claims of equity.

This old debate between conservative and liberal camps over the extent of government intervention was modified during the stagflation decade by the newer claim of neoconservatives that government had become overloaded. The critique has both a certain validity and appeal; but to conclude from this that the government should play a less activist role is, at the least, naive and, as a policy prescription, anachronistic.

The legitimacy of the government's activist role stems from the dysfunctioning and malfunctioning of our "free market" system. As shown in chapter 2, the concentration of economic power in business, labor, and government has dealt a mortal blow to the free functioning of competitive markets. A less activist role by government thus will not restore a "free" market. But a less activist role could greatly increase human suffering and widen inequalities. The issue is not less or more government but how government overload can be reduced, how government institutions can be made more efficient, and how economic efficiency and equity can be balanced.

The success of the new lobby groups represents "top down" decision making. Their influence in Washington produces results throughout the country and across the entire economy. Missing in the fight by new stakeholders are "bottom up" efforts to achieve their aims at levels lower than Congress, the White House, federal agencies, and the courts.

In this respect, the new groups are a generation behind traditional business and labor interests. Management and labor also wield influence at the top, but for them the New Deal did create mechanisms for "bottom up" solutions to many of their disputes. When the basic rights of unions were legitimized by the Wagner Act, workers could bargain and strike and settle many disputes at the corporate level. Only when they were deadlocked did they take their disputes to the National Labor Relations Board for resolution. Labor's long-held claim that free markets failed to guarantee its rights and share of wealth was recognized in law. But the ingenuity of the national policy reform was that it held government interference to a minimum with "new automatic" self-correcting mechanisms at the grass roots level of the economy, namely, the corporation.

Like labor, the new stakeholders in the environmental, consumer, health, and safety groups have had their rights legitimized in the last two decades. But reform has been only "top down" and now threatens to drown business and society in a sea of regulations and bureaucracy. The ingenuity of the labor reform is so far missing for these groups. There is no mechanism to resolve their disputes with corporations elsewhere than in Washington and other centers of government. But rather than seeking new mechanisms, the various adversaries fight harder within government, taking increasingly dogmatic and uncompromising positions and contributing to the fragmentation and breakdown of the nation's political machinery.

The most effective way to reduce this government overload is to pioneer decentralized econopolitical decision-making, to turn to the grass roots level of the economy. The heart of the grass roots is the corporation, especially the 1,000 or so major corporations publicly owned by shareholders.

The new stakeholders have little access to those corporations now and almost no influence over them except through government. Among contending proposals, it is becoming clear that the quickest, most economically viable and politically credible way to give them that grass roots influence is to open the boards of directors to interest groups and labor alike.

Many big business leaders will deplore the suggestion, but it is hardly a radical departure that threatens private enterprise or the profit motive. Some small corporations already have expanded their boards to include the new stakeholders. Various European countries are experimenting with ways to democratize corporate boards, even though many labor representatives on these boards are still skeptical about what they achieve there. Even so, labor is playing a bigger role in European corporate decision-making, especially in West Germany and Sweden, two of Europe's wealthiest nations.

Grass roots reform also has its basis in both traditional and contemporary American philosophy regarding the corporation as a "legally created individual." As one early legal writer observed, "A corporation was only an artificial personality and therefore did not have a soul or conscience. Lacking a conscience, it had no morals and was *prima facie* dangerous." Adam Smith, a moral philosopher—not an economist by training—recognized the problem by tying his "invisible hand" solution to a competitive marketplace economy of numerous buyers and sellers, each with "perfect information." Smith argued that if these conditions were not met, the problems of concentrated corporate power would be difficult to reconcile with democracy.

Owing to a variety of technological and organizational imperatives, much of America's 1980s economy cannot revert to the classical checks and balances of competitive markets. "Only limited (external) restraints can ever be exerted on senior managers by securities laws, spasms of public indignation, and shareholder suits," notes Columbia law professor Harvey J. Goldschmidt. "In general, each of these provides no check until crisis occurs. Where possible, we should move from after-the-fact palliatives—or draconian measures—to sensible, ongoing cures."

Over the past century the nation has periodically enacted reforms to correct the problems of increasingly weak and failing markets. Today, for reasons of both equity and efficiency, this effort must be matched again with experiments at the soul of the nation's economy. "The strength of our form of political democracy is in its system of checks and balances more than in the rule of the majority," observed Courtney Brown, dean emeritus of the Columbia University Graduate School of Business. "As the modern corporation confronts the progressively more complex problems of what has been called the post-industrial era, it will stand in progressively greater need of the advantages of a system of checks and balances within its own operation."

Yale University professor of economics and political science Charles E. Lindblom ends his widely acclaimed book *Politics and Markets* with this summary of the challenge posed to the existence of the large corporation in a democracy:

> It has been a curious feature of democratic thought that it has not faced up to the private corporation as a peculiar organization in an ostensible democracy. Enormously large, rich in resources, the big corporations, we have seen, command more resources than do most government

> units. They can also, over a broad range, insist that government meet their demands, even if these demands run counter to those of citizens expressed through their polyarchal controls. Moreover, they do not disqualify themselves from playing the partisan role of a citizen—for the corporation is legally a person. And they exercise unusual veto powers. They are on all these counts disproportionately powerful, we have seen. The large private corporation fits oddly into democratic theory and vision. Indeed, it does not fit.

Support for corporate reform is widening. William McChesney Martin, former head of the Federal Reserve, proposes having 50 percent of the New York Stock Exchange's board made up of members of the public. Ralph Nader and other consumer leaders have advocated federal chartering for all large corporations, chartering that would establish specific operating rules and mandate the composition of boards.

Within big business, advocates of internal reform are growing more numerous and more vocal. Some corporations like Texas Instruments, notes business consultant T. H. Hubbard, are bringing in outsider board members, highly competent and well-paid experts to improve entrepreneurship and commercial performance. But others, like First Pennsylvania Corporation, have added blacks, women, and even a student, to "make it clear that the board is not an exclusive club, stocked with friends of John Bunting," said the former chairman, describing his own decision to innovate. Other business leaders, among them H. M. Williams, former chairman of the Securities and Exchange Commission, are going public with their criticisms of corporate governance: "The board, in effect, often insulates management rather than holding it accountable." For Williams (and others) "the core question is whether we can improve the existing process and make it work better or whether we should take steps to modify or replace it." And for many corporate leaders, "replacing it," writes Hubbard, the chairman of THinc Consulting Group International Inc., "might mean the straight-jacket of federal chartering." Voluntary reform, Hubbard advises his clients, is a way to avoid what may become inevitable. "Reform does not invent itself, but must be pioneered by leaders with a certain daring, and a desire to improve on accepted norms of behavior."

For business innovators, voluntary board reform is a way to enhance what they call corporate social responsibility. Its aim is to prevent the abuses of unconstrained corporate power, abuses that have led public interest groups to call for federal chartering. An equally compelling but neglected reason for reform is efficiency. Efficiency, especially from the taxpayer's standpoint, improves if corporate reform can reduce the number of disputes that must be solved by ever larger numbers of bureaucrats and courts. Private efficiency improves when corporations adopt controls designed to work at the source, through compromise rather than overkill, and not in the distant confrontational arenas of Washington.

But perhaps the most compelling reason for corporate board reform, especially for the inclusion of labor representatives, is that it offers a vital key for initiating innovations in government-business cooperation. This kind of cooperation will become increasingly essential as more U.S. industries are pressed to the wall during the adjustment decade of the 1980s. Labor participation on boards of directors has already created a new arena of political consensus in several Western European nations, opening the way for business-government cooperation in structural adjustment programs. The Chrysler case is just the first warning that this country will have to broaden its industrial policy choices beyond bail-outs or bankruptcy. Board reform with labor participation offers one new choice.

In 1976 the United Auto Workers proposed to Chrysler the idea of labor representation on the company board. It was the first time an American union had made such a proposal formally. But the company turned down the idea.

"If you're willing to do it in Britain, why aren't you willing to do it in the United States?" asked Leonard Woodcock, then the union president. He was referring to a Chrysler offer to a union at one of its British plants beset with labor strife.

Douglas Fraser, who made the proposal and who later succeeded Woodcock as the UAW president, said prophetically in 1976 that labor representation on the Chrysler board "would help save it from repeating the kind of blunders" the company had made in trying to obtain labor sacrifices to bolster its sagging finances in the 1974 recession. In 1979 the company appealed again to the union for sacrifice, a temporary wage freeze, but again refused to yield anything in return.

By the end of 1979 the company, the union, and the government in Washington were in a three-way standoff. Facing a $1 billion loss, Chrysler asked the government for help. It asked the union for a temporary wage freeze. The union said the government should give Chrysler a $1 billion cash injection in return for the government's taking over 30 percent of the company's equity. The government turned down the union plan and began lengthy negotiations with the company over possible loan guarantees. Many in Congress indicated hostility to any government rescue effort. As the negotiations and political maneuvering dragged on, Chrysler sank deeper into debt.

"The longer Washington waits," warned *Business Week,* "the more money Chrysler will need."

There were two debates going on. The first and public debate was the blame casting, whether bad management or government regulation was the cause of Chrysler's troubles. Chrysler blamed expensive regulations. The environmentalists said the company was trying to duck its legal obligations for pollution control, safety, and fuel efficiency. But as the company's peril deepened, a second debate began focusing on finding a politically credible way to rescue the company and the thousands of jobs at stake, not only in Detroit but in scores of midwestern towns and cities with factories providing auto supplies.

Some of the businessmen surveyed by *The Wall Street Journal* saw the need for a new Chrysler board. One executive called for "an independent board" to provide fresh analysis of Chrysler's prospects. The businessman was thinking more in terms of bankers and marketing experts, but other groups would have to be added to gain political as well as financial credibility.

Political credibility was paramount among many in Congress. The author joined a group of members of Congress to develop a Chrysler rescue plan. The proposal had two aims: to help the company avert collapse and thereby save jobs, and "to establish a framework of corporate and public checks and balances that protects the public interest."

The proposed rescue plan would work in two phases. First, it would provide an immediate but partial injection of money to keep the company going and to keep anxious creditors at bay. The second phase of government aid would then come only after a broadened and representative board of directors had submitted a development plan to the President and Congress.

Although few in Washington wanted to admit it, the Chrysler case caused concern as well as confusion because many officials realized it was not a fluke. The domestic operations of the Ford Motor Company were heading deeply into the red. Ford has been kept profitable only through foreign earnings; if they sag in a worldwide recession, then the question posed by numerous analysts, "Is Ford next?," becomes a pressing one.

After much last-minute drama, Congress did pass a multibillion dollar "rescue" program for Chrysler. And the corporation took the precedent-setting step of inviting the UAW's Fraser to join its board of directors. But even as the government committed itself to Chrysler loan guarantees, there were many experts in Washington, Detroit and New York convinced that the company would not survive the immense new pressures on the American auto industry.

A weak market has been made weaker by the recession and by competition of gas-efficient imports. At the same time, the automakers face multibillion-dollar investments to meet government safety, environmental, and fuel-efficiency regulations. The smaller the company, the more expensive the unit costs of the investments. General Motors, because of its huge production runs, may be the only U.S. auto company that can afford this expensive retooling of assembly lines. The solution for American Motors was to reach to France's Renault for an infusion of cash and technology in return for giving up a controlling 22.5 percent of the ownership. The result is formation of the first domestic joint venture between American private enterprise and a foreign state-owned firm.

The American auto industry, a central generator of economic growth and jobs, is leading industrial America into the adjustment decade of the 1980s. Structural adjustment programs will have a variety of elements, including government assistance. But one vital element, especially for securing political credibility (and therefore more rapid decision-making) to launch these programs, is broadening participation at the bottom, through corporate board reform.

Whether new self-correcting grass roots mechanisms arise through voluntary or legally mandated reform of the boards of the nation's largest corporations, they will be effective only if they adhere to some basic principles of corporate governance. Board members must have full access to all information available to management, and they must have sufficient staffs or consultants, competitively paid, for the hard, time-consuming work demanded of them by the already existing legal principle of "due diligence" that is supposed to guide the function of board representatives. Unless these criteria are met, board reform will be effective neither for a proper accounting of stockholders' profit motives nor for other stakeholders' social claims.

Most corporate boards in the United States have been expanded already to include blacks and women. While some of the appointments represent tokenism and window dressing, the black and female board members have been able to sensitize corporate managements. Combined with the threat and reality of equal opportunity laws, their influence has pushed the big corporations into giving women and blacks more and better jobs. Women have probably benefited more than blacks because more trained and educated women have been available for hiring and promotion.

These limited successes resemble the New Deal experience of labor and show how new stakeholders must rely on a combination of "top down" and "bottom up" reforms. Before they could compete successfully in business, women had to have their rights mandated by equal employment, equal credit, and other affirmative action laws. Similarly, civil rights laws had to be fought for and enacted before blacks could begin pressing their political and economic claims at the local level.

The "bottom up" approach to economic and political reform has gained acceptance among well-known futurologists, who are often consultants to the largest corporations. Futurologists of varying political persuasions, such as Herman Kahn and Jay Forrester, used to count on technological change to solve the problems of pollution and economic growth, and they looked to national governments and international organizations to rescue the planet from resource and food scarcities. That faith is waning. Edward Cornish, president of the World Future Society, observed, "As we survey the array of institutions that we have in the world today, there does not seem to be any obvious place for the needed leadership to begin to develop, and we may have to face the fact that the present institutions are simply not capable of providing the leadership needed to surmount the growing crisis."

Synthesizing the views of Cornish and other futurologists, American University business professor William E. Halal wrote in an award-winning essay for the Club of Rome, "Many futurists now recognize the need . . . [for] the development of a microscopic, grass roots foundation of social systems for handling these problems. In doing so, the world problematique could not only be addressed from the 'top down' but also from the 'bottom up.' " Halal is one of a small but significant minority of business and social thinkers who maintain that "bottom up" reform must start with reform of the governance of large corporations and the broadening of boards of directors to include effective representation "composed of investors, employees, customers, the public and others in order to facilitate collaborative policy-making." And one of the major reasons for this "is that the principle of market competition is increasingly a fiction in the large industries that are dominated by a few giant corporations, whose assets often exceed those of major world powers."

More than adding a few chairs around the board table is involved in such reforms. As Charles Powers, former Cummins Engines corporate vice-president for social responsibility and Harvard University ethics professor, said, the standard business audit will have to be accompanied by a "social audit." His statement was an explicit recognition that corporations are social as well as business institutions. Powers said that all corporations, whatever their product and management differences, have one thing in common—information systems and decision guidelines that permit measurement not only of profits to shareholders but of social costs and benefits to consumers, environmental costs, and health costs and benefits.

The new and expanded boards would make corporate management read both sets of balance sheets and respond to them. Individual board members, going to an occasional meeting, can have only limited influence. Their presence would have to be bolstered through staff and access to the right information.

"What we need," said Daniel Bell, "is a system of social

accounts which would broaden our concept of costs and benefits, and put economic accounting into a broader framework. The eventual purpose would be to create a 'balance sheet' that would be useful in clarifying policy choices." As Alvin Toffler noted, the social and information technologies are already in place and it is a matter of bridging the corporate policy lags. "We do have the potential for achieving tremendous breakthroughs in democratic decision-making if we make use of the new technologies, both 'hard' and 'soft,' that bear on the problem."

Bringing community representation to corporate boards is not the only proposal for self-correcting grass roots mechanisms. Another is local mediation by agreed-upon arbitrators, already successfully being used to resolve certain environmental and conservation disputes. In 1978 a national nonprofit group, Resolve, was created to promote third-party mediation. Its board includes a former head of the Environmental Protection Agency, a high official of the Sierra Club, an AFL–CIO official representing construction unions, and the president of the U.S. Council of the International Chamber of Commerce. It was founded on the principle that many ecological "disputes could be resolved if the parties would sit down and talk to each other."

As Washington *Post* environmental reporter Margot Hornblower observed, mediation has been successful in settling a growing number of cases, including coal mining, power dams, and water disputes. Yet there are limits. Resolve participants note that "many disputes won't lend themselves to mediation in, for example, the nuclear breeder controversy." In such instances, unlike negotiated compromises on smaller dam or better mine reclamation projects, opposition is based on fundamental differences over the principle of safety.

Whatever the success of grass roots reform, the new stakeholders will have to bring some of their problems to Washington for resolution. And the government machinery, like the corporate machinery, must be reformed to accommodate these demands in a setting other than one of constant confrontation. The results of this are either stalemate or overkill, swings of the policy pendulum from equity goals to efficiency and back again, accompanied by teach-ins, demonstrations, and the sometimes violent forms of social dislocation that can come from mass protests of the frustrated.

Defusing the confrontation will require achieving some consensus on information, the lifeblood not only of government but of all the contending groups trying to influence it.

At present each agency and lobby group has its own information and statistics, its own battery of experts and PhDs, each imputing a certain verity to what is often basically conjecture. So much misinformation has been fed to officials and through them to the public that the basic credibility of government remains in question. The people's doubts about the existence of energy shortages, even as they sit in gas lines, shows how deep and persistent the credibility and information problem has become.

Meg Greenfield asked the basic question in a *Newsweek* column: "What accounts for the collapse of practically everyone's position on everything?

"One obvious answer is that so many of the public questions that concern us turn on technical information that is incomplete or speculative. Another is that we all fail to concede as much in our arguments, converting a hunch or assumption into certainties that are sitting ducks for quick destruction. The moral value and political meaning with which you imbue a fact can hardly be expected to survive when the fact turns out to have been so much bad guesswork."

The built-in confrontation design of almost all Federal Government decision-making processes merely heightens the conflict over information between competing interest groups and between different agencies and departments. Presidential promises to tell the truth and government reorganization plans prove to be empty remedies. The creation of a $9-billion-a-year, 20,000-employee Energy Department ("A Bad Idea Gone Haywire," concluded a Washington *Post* survey of experts and opinion makers) has, if anything, only exacerbated the credibility program on that issue.

In our view, successful government reform requires two components so far missing to promote national-level consensus. The first is better labeling of information; the second is broader participation. In fact, without the latter the former is unlikely to occur. Creating effective functional representation in the array of current advisory councils attached to each government department is one easy step in this direction. Such units as the Council on Environmental Quality and the Council of Consumer Affairs, just as much as corporate boards, need to be broadened to include more than banner wavers for a specific group's interests.

For example, the President created an Export Council in 1979 to give advice on trade policy. He praised its "broad-based membership" and said it would be "able to reflect a national consensus." In reality, of its twenty-seven private-sector members, only one is a consumer representative. Environmentalists are totally unrepresented, and small businessmen have no effective voice. Yet, as we have already noted, the failure to achieve coordinated international environmental standards has been a real barrier to American exports, whose higher costs than those of competing products are one consequence of our more exacting environmental regulations. It is in such bodies as the Export Council and the Consumer and Environmental councils that the issues of equity versus efficiency and the trade-offs between environment and exports should be debated. If representatives of business, labor, and other stakeholders could argue in each of these arenas, consensus recommendations could be promoted where possible and confrontation reduced. Instead, technical disputes get pushed higher up the government ladder as assistant secretaries and Cabinet officers advance the arguments of their department's constituencies to the White House. Officials elected and appointed to make political decisions become mired in technical detail and surrounded by the increasingly loud babble of competing claims based on dubious information.

Such debates in broadly representative councils would be a first step at the national level toward dealing with the credibility and information crisis. Business and environmental representatives, for example, could reach some kind of resolution; they could argue and decide on what are certifiable facts, what information is in dispute, and what information should be clearly labeled as conjecture. Such "forced consensus processes" do not yield a "first-best" solution of perfect information. They would, however, generate a "second-best" coherent presentation of what is certain and uncertain, clearly labeled and packaged from a central source that is credible because of the internal checks and balances of effective representation and participation of adversarial groups.

Presented with even this kind of clarity, the Cabinet officers, the President, and the congressional committees could spend less of their time in perpetual cross-checking of disputed sources and weighing the accuracy and objectivity of "technical information" and thereby gain more time to make the political choices and tradeoffs between equity and efficiency.

Information and its veracity become increasingly important as the links of interdependence grow within the economy and between economies. Through truckers and fertilizer factories, the farmer is linked to the oil producers. A steelworker's job may be at stake because of environmental regulations, and a textile worker's job because of foreign imports. But our machinery for making economic policy and decisions is still based on the vision of a market economy.

While recognizing the imperfections and failures of markets, we have still not created a government machinery that matches the realities of a post-market world and government's growing inability to meet and balance the new and conflicting claims that have sprung from it. The result is stalemate and confrontation amid the demands of a bewildered and angry citizenry for straight answers. Just as the New Deal responded to the market imperfections of the Depression era, government in the post-market economy must innovate and experiment, even grope, toward new policies and the machinery to put these policies in place. The New Deal and its machinery addressed itself to the problems of unemployment, labor rights, rural and regional development, and a more equitable distribution of wealth. To adjust and adapt to the global revolution, government in the post-market era must address itself to energy and resources, the supply economics of industrial development policy and refinements to demand management to deal with inflation, international financial instability, and social programs.

CHAPTER 9

U.S. Energy and Econopolitics

I

DURING THE GAS CRUNCH OF 1979 the national mood was best captured by an account of a California gas-station owner who shut down his pumps and hung out a sign reading: "Temporarily out of phony excuses." Like this resigned station-owner, our country is out of phony excuses for the energy crisis, and phony culprits as well.

For nearly a decade now, we have heard clarion calls for action and declarations of energy independence. What has actually taken place is quite the opposite. We are now more dependent than ever on imports, and a national energy policy is no less elusive than before. Energy is the most vivid example of the government's inability to adjust to the global economic revolution and to the post-market economy. Energy was the first sector in which post-market forces of multinational conglomerates and governments replaced classical competitive markets. Not coincidentally, it has become the political issue that has drawn out the conflicting claims of the most powerful interest groups—consumers, environmentalists, conservationists, organized labor, the energy conglomerates, and the independent producers. Amid their disputes, information has become misinformation, and energy policy-making has been stymied by the loss of credibility and trust in institutions.

To end the paralysis and begin developing an energy policy requires action flowing from a set of principles. The first is encouragement of conservation, but not in ways that are punitive or redolent of austerity. Conservation and economic growth can and should be complementary, not antithetical, as they are so often posed. Second, even with conservation, new sources, and new technologies, we will continue to need oil imports for another decade. That is the one certainty of the 1980s, and it will therefore require a new set of principles and policies to create more stable economic and political relationships with OPEC and other oil-exporting nations. Third, to encourage more production and new technologies our energy programs at home need to be built on three fundamental features—self-financing, participatory and consensus-building management, and development banking. That means the principles of expanded corporate boards need to be applied by or imposed on the oil companies. In government, that means that new energy agencies should not be standard old-line bureaus but quasi-public, quasi-private autonomous organs to function through self-financing and to promote energy programs with development-banking techniques. Fourth, a much clearer link needs to be established between energy policy and economic development policy. The essential element of that link is a national transportation policy that clearly relates the two.

II

Assigning "blame" for the energy crisis is as senseless as designating which among a house of cards was responsible for its collapse. The same "laws of motion" that have been guiding the development of much of our post-market economy, with its huge corporations and government bureaucracies, have guided the energy sector. Together they have created the U.S. dependence on foreign oil. The public blames the multinational energy conglomerates, a suspicion warranted both by their often unscrupulous history and by their mammoth size. Certainly, high prices benefit the companies, and they are indeed enjoying record profits. The multinational oil industry, from the Achnacarry Agreement of 1928 until the early 1970s, was clearly—often flagrantly—in charge of the globe's oil supplies. But now the decision to pump or not to pump most of the free world's oil is made by the governments of the OPEC nations, not by the oil companies. In fact, by the end of this decade, OPEC will be refining and transporting much of its own oil, displacing the Seven Sisters still further.

If the energy crunch was not made by big oil, why not by big government? Senators from oil-producing states are fond of depicting an oafish and naive Federal Government as the source of our energy troubles. Government, for example, ordered 1979 stockpiling of heating oil, which helped cause the 1979 gas lines. The control of crude oil prices has forestalled many conservation investments and held back some limited amounts of domestic oil production. As a 1979 report by the Congressional Budget Office indicated, the decontrol of crude oil (with no windfall profits tax) could lower 1985 imports by more than a million barrels per day. Yet such a reduction would amount to only about 10 percent of the imports projected for that year. Decontrol of crude oil prices reflects an important realization that oil is, indeed, no longer cheap, but decontrol alone will not solve the energy supply problem. For all the complaints about the Energy Department, the real problem is uncertain Presidential and congressional leadership interested more in not upsetting the voters rather than in developing a coherent energy policy.

The environmentalists have become the third phony culprit. They are depicted as no-growth fanatics intent on bringing economic progress to a halt. Yet environmental concerns are proving ever more legitimate. The uncertainties of nuclear waste disposal, buildups of carbon dioxide in the atmosphere which threaten world climate, and the possibility of a real-life "China Syndrome" are realities that require bringing environmental concerns into a consensus on the future of our energy policies. As a 1978 study by economist Lester Lave of Carnegie-Mellon University indicated, federal regulations regarding coal-burning emissions, by reducing deaths and illnesses, have provided real though hard-to-measure economic benefits for the entire economy, far in excess of the costs of implementing them. Environmentalists should be spared the fate of the messenger who brought bad news.

Finally, OPEC emerges as the point of blame for our energy problems. Since the 1973–74 price jolt, OPEC prices have increased dramatically at great pain to us. In the absence of policies that more quickly encourage alternatives or conservation, we keep paying them. For the OPEC nations, the price of oil is not too high.

Rather, it has finally caught up to its true value. And with the higher prices, the underdeveloped nations of OPEC, particularly in the Middle East, have the one-time opportunity of using a non-renewable resource to lift themselves into self-sustaining development. For decades, the price of oil was artificially low as the major companies used their technological and marketing power to monopolize access to low-cost Middle Eastern oil fields and to keep potential competition at bay. We should not forget that until 1973, foreign oil was so cheap that domestic producers demanded and received U.S. Government protection through import quotas. For producing nations, the price of oil sold to the West stayed the same or rose only slightly, while the price of everything purchased from the West—food, machinery, capital—rose steadily. Producing nations saw that the major companies were not drilling the properties leased from them, but merely "shutting in" those prospective fields to keep others away from them. With the companies in control, the producing nations were played off against each other at will, most dramatically during the U.S. embargo of Iranian oil in 1953.

Oil consumption in the U.S. grew exponentially as more people moved to more sprawling suburbs and increasingly relied on bigger gas-guzzling cars to go to work, to shop, and to play. Also by the 1960s, oil had supplanted coal as a heating fuel, while domestic production, with limits on reserves, began its decline. By 1973 the nation suddenly found itself dependent on foreign oil, importing twice what it had five years before. The oil multinationals had established the centralization of oil production in the Middle East. But it was OPEC that took full advantage of this opportunity to secure control of both output and prices.

Are the nations of OPEC, then, to be blamed? In 1973 they followed the old maxim of George Washington Plunkitt, a nineteenth-century Tammany Hall leader, who once said, "I saw my chances, and I took 'em."

III

Unfortunately, phony solutions are as abundant as phony culprits in the energy crisis. First and foremost is the campaign for synthetic fuels or "synfuels," a Washington neologism more telling than intended. The program is really a patchwork of loan arrangements and price guarantees that will cost billions and not produce significant quantities of oil until the 1990s. By that time there could be either technological progress in many different energy sources, both renewable and nonrenewable, or increased efficiency in energy that could make these white-elephant programs pointless or obsolete.

While doing nothing to relieve our appetite for foreign oil in this decade, and perhaps the next, the synfuels program would create a new federal bureaucracy, interlocked with the few conglomerates lucky enough to win federal synthetic fuel contracts. The program would increase concentration and diminish competition by effectively shutting out the losing corporations, big and small, from the energy business of the future. With its lack of credible checks and balances, the program would threaten to magnify the worst abuses and waste of the government-business interlock—the revolving door between a few corporate contract recipients and the donor government agencies.*

Despite the call for wartime-like austerity, the synfuel plans were filled with pork-barrel giveaways and contract procedures typical of the worst aspects of the defense budget and Pentagon procurement practices.

A second "solution" that does not solve can be termed "the electrification of everything." Proponents of either coal or nuclear power prefer their energy source as the alternative to foreign oil. Yet even if we were to conduct an all-out nuclear program, not much oil would be replaced. Half of the oil we use goes into transportation uses that cannot be electrified until more than 150 million U.S. cars, trucks, and other vehicles, plus the U.S. air fleet, are retired and replaced with electric vehicles that are not now eco-

* In the quest to prove "something is being done," to convince voters that there were precedents in American tradition for these actions, the then energy secretary likened the 1979 Administration proposal for an independent synfuels corporation to the Reconstruction Finance Corporation. Yet there was no mention that the RFC was one of the worst examples of the New Deal, that its abolition was due to the absence of internal management safeguards, which allowed favoritism and special access and massive inefficiency. It ended its "bureaucratic life," wrote *New York Times* reporter Judith Miller, "mixed in political scandal and corruption charges."

nomically viable or technologically mature. And while electricity can be used to heat homes, a unit of electric heat already costs the typical household twice as much as oil heat. Improving the efficiency of oil heating in industry, commercial structures, and residences will save more oil and money than attempting to electrify them.

Yet phony solutions like these are continually given credence and are readily accepted. As Senator Dale Bumpers said when the Senate debated synfuels legislation in 1979, "The American people want us to do something even if it is wrong." Bumpers was right—the solutions are wrong. Such misbegotten ideas as President Nixon's "Project Independence" represent a messianic striving for independence in an interdependent world. They deny the realities of the globe's North-South linkages and force the United States into a new isolationism.

The 1980s will be a decade of oil imports. U.S. production, even with decontrol, will steadily decrease, agree industry and government sources alike. A government study projects import levels of 10 million barrels per day in 1985, and 11 million in 1990 (compared with the 1980 level of about 7.5 million) unless prices go up drastically. Neither nuclear power, synfuels, solar energy, nor conservation will eliminate imports in the next ten years—perhaps twenty. This basic fact requires that we develop two energy policies to address two distinct problems in two separate timeframes. First, we must have a foreign economic policy that allows us to survive the economic impact of unavoidable oil imports in the 1980s. Second, we must have a domestic energy policy that allows us by the 1990s to cross over to the post-petroleum era of the year 2000 and beyond. To these two problems we turn.

IV

Understanding the energy problems of the 1980s requires understanding OPEC. The image of OPEC is of an overlord of global oil supplies. But behind the image its members face a myriad of problems. To be sure, OPEC has accomplished its initial goals, which were first presented in a unified fashion in their June 1968 "Declaratory Statement of Petroleum Policy in Member Countries." The Declaratory Statement was a blueprint of things to come. It called for governments of the producing countries to take part in exploration, production, and price-setting. By 1973 these goals were accomplished, and world oil entered the OPEC era.

Yet while the 1973–74 price increases solved OPEC's old problems, they also created new ones. The first was that higher OPEC oil prices were continually eroded, after their initial burst, by higher costs of imports from the Western consuming nations. Dominant among these imports were capital goods and machines, the basic tools of economic development that OPEC sought in return for its oil income. In addition, oil payments were in dollars that continually depreciated against other currencies. So OPEC had to buy German and Japanese imports with more expensive marks and yen while receiving its wealth in dollars of diminishing value.

OPEC's second problem has been the decline in value of many of the assets in which it stored its oil wealth. Much of the initial OPEC surplus went into U.S. Treasury bills and other U.S. paper assets, but depreciation of the dollar and U.S. inflation sharply reduced their worth. By 1977, most of the new OPEC surplus was moving into the Eurocurrency banking system, adding even more fuel to international currency instability. Real estate had also become more attractive. And in the last two years there has been a massive exchange of petrodollars for gold. But these are speculative investments. As one OPEC finance minister told me, "The problem with gold, like real estate, if we continue to emphasize it as a safe haven, is that it will lead to a global depression." In other words, with more money going into gold, the less there is for productive investments that create new jobs and growth.

At the same time, many of the OECD industrial nations, including the United States, imposed new restrictions on the types of assets OPEC could buy in their countries. While the World Bank was willing to use OPEC's money, it was unwilling to give OPEC a proportionate voice in how it would be dispensed. And at home there were problems of absorbing the new wealth without creating a revolution. OPEC nations could only wonder: perhaps the best alternative was to keep their oil in the ground.

OPEC's third problem is paradoxically the source of its power —the refusal of Western nations, even after the 1973–74 price jolts, to slow down their oil consumption. For the OPEC nations, scarcity and demand are twin issues. Throughout the 1970s, there were momentary mirages of oil gluts, and this helped encourage more consumption. They also misled some economists and analysts. Milton Friedman, in a *Newsweek* column in 1974, predicted an imminent drop in prices to "a dime a barrel." Georgetown University's Theodore Moran predicted that significant excess capacity would drive down prices in 1980. The economists were tied to outmoded doctrines of short-run market behavior and did not grasp the fundamental point that scarcity is the foundation of OPEC's post-market power. Neither the economists nor the Western consuming nations have yet to absorb OPEC's central message: oil is scarce, nonrenewable, and will be depleted within the next generation.

OPEC sees itself in a unique bind. It is collecting income, but it cannot translate that income into productive wealth. In a generation the oil will be gone, and all that OPEC may have left will be the barren assets of money, gold, or other nonproductive assets. For many of the otherwise resource-poor OPEC Middle East nations, their one opportunity to generate lasting economic development and diversification will have been squandered. As long as this situation persists, OPEC will restrain production and jack up prices whenever it can. The object is not so much to collect more money, but to hold on to its oil as long as possible. It will opt for assets that it feels cannot be devalued, deflated, or seized, such as gold or "oil in the ground." But by pursuing this course, OPEC creates, in part, the inflation and uncertainty that have left us with an idle global cash pool and worldwide stagflation.

The state of the world oil market poses obvious problems for the consuming nations as well. Foreign oil, by its very nature, is made an uncertain supply through political instability, accident, and outright embargo. Oil's price and availability become paralyzing uncertainties for both government and industry. There is a massive outflow of our national wealth. Petrodollars go unspent and disappear into the already volatile Eurodollar system. Industry is hampered in trying to invent and plan new technologies. We are facing at least another decade of oil imports, but have yet to address these problems.

It is clear, therefore, that neither OPEC nor the oil-consuming nations are well served by the way oil is now bought and sold. For Western countries, oil supplies are a source of paralyzing instability. For OPEC, these supplies are wasting its sole economic endowment. The objective of U.S. oil policy for the 1980s is to find a middle ground—a set of principles for managing oil supplies as well as the world economy that hinges on them. The challenge is to create durable relationships between the producers and the consumers of oil.

The center of a foreign-policy strategy to find this common ground must be built on the economic principle of mutual interest. The proposed global Marshall Plan noted in chapter 6 is a pragmatic program for applying this principle. The goal of the global Marshall Plan is to link the world's idle capital to its most pressing but unfunded tasks. It is a coordination of the world's economic resources in order to create momentum toward long-term growth.

The global Marshall Plan would require a new cooperation between OPEC, industrial, and Third World nations. It would provide political and economic benefits to all three groups. It would bring closer to fruition OPEC's long-term goal of joint development with the OECD, which OPEC first proposed at its Geneva ministerial meeting in June 1979. The global Marshall Plan would also provide OPEC with a means to assist non-oil developing nations. It would create an alternative to keeping oil in the ground—a stake in the growth of the world economy. Importantly, if OPEC's surplus is directed into Third World growth, U.S. exports will rise, and so will growth and employment.

For many important OPEC nations, such as Nigeria, Venezuela, and Iraq, surpluses are not the problem. Each faces its own pressing need for development in the mode it deems appropriate. Unlike the "banker states" of Saudi Arabia and Kuwait, these nations have traditionally run balance-of-payments deficits, spending all their oil income, and then more, on imports. Until recently, these nations produced at what are thought to be maximum rates, usually at 90 percent or more of their capacity. But the 1979 price increases might have changed this situation. As energy economist Everett M. Ehrlich explained:

> The price increases of this past year have been so large so as to be unabsorbable. In 1980, Iraq will probably earn

> three times what it did in 1978. Nigeria's earnings will increase two-and-a-half times over that period. These nations simply can't do anything worthwhile with all those dollars, and many, therefore, will start to restrict production when prices go up. In economists' terms, the supply of oil is becoming "backward bending": the higher the price, the less they'll supply. If we want these nations to continue to maximize production, we're going to have to help them with technology transfers, marketing concessions, and other ways to increase their absorption capacity. The alternative is going to be chaos in the oil market.

The U.S. could also address OPEC nations individually. It would make straight purchases of energy and more actively pursue swaps of foreign oil for American industrial goods, technology, and management services. A direct strategy to cooperate with OPEC wherever possible offers a chance to address simultaneously the interdependent issues of energy and the balance of trade and the strength of the dollar.

One possible vehicle for this strategy would be a quasi-public, quasi-private energy corporation to act as the sole U.S. purchaser of foreign energy. The idea was first proposed by MIT energy economist Morris Adelman and more recently redesigned by Professor Paul Davidson of Rutgers. Numerous bills to create such an agency have been pending in Congress. As a sole bargaining agent, it would prevent OPEC and other producers from playing off the oil companies against one another as they have in the past. It would also provide a stronger incentive to bargain harder than the oil companies, whose profits have risen by an equal or greater rate with every OPEC price hike. Its competitors would be the corresponding sole buying agents from other importing nations. The corporation could also be empowered to arrange the swap deals, as state corporations in other industrial countries have been doing. Ehrlich makes the point this way:

> If we are going to have oil imports, then how will these imports affect the U.S. economy? Under the current arrangement, we have no way to actively diversify our overseas supply sources nor to promote trade for petrodollars. This is because the majors' basic interest is the

> distribution, refining and the marketing of world oil and not its overall social and economic consequences. But a public sector entity could tie social goals, like dollar stabilization, to oil purchases and seek out the new Mexicos and Chinas—nations like the Sudan, Egypt, Pakistan, and Bangladesh.

We described in chapters 5 and 6 the proliferation of energy, technology, and trade deals. France, Japan, and Canada have negotiated swaps with Mexico which give them a guaranteed volume of oil at a set price in exchange for exports of technology, capital goods, and services. Canada, for example, made a ten-year agreement with Mexico for 100,000 barrels daily in exchange for nuclear technology assistance and at least 3 million tons of Canadian coal. This kind of typical post-market deal, valued at $7 billion, also gives Canadian private businesses a piece of the action through management and services contracts awarded by Mexican public enterprises to develop their mining industries. By centralizing the oil-importing and trade-related functions, another efficiency advantage can be seized. Many U.S. independents are now confined to domestic stripper wells and small discoveries. But the financing and marketing that a public-sector entity could offer would allow them to compete for foreign exploration and extraction projects.

By means of this new brand of post-market business-government cooperation, Japan, West Germany, Sweden, and other nations have been able to pay for oil with exports and thereby lower their oil-induced balance-of-trade deficits. This helps to stabilize their currencies. Such cooperation also assures a steadier source of supply. Japan now gets some 20 percent of its oil from post-market deals, and France in 1979 was purchasing one-third of its oil supplies from Saudi Arabia with long-term contract swaps.

Beyond conservation, the objectives of a domestic energy strategy to cope with imports would be to maximize competition and efficiency in the private sector and to minimize government interference and costs in the public sector. The starting point of a domestic strategy, like that of a global strategy, would be to recognize the post-market structures now at work in energy, the first of the world's industries to enter the post-market era. Government would perform as an overseer to prevent abuses, but would not make the vital investment decisions that the present legislation would force upon it. That role would be left as much as possible to private industry, with the role of government limited to autonomous quasi-public and self-financing agencies that would award management contracts and provide development-banking assistance. An energy development bank, which we will describe in more detail later, would operate as do existing development banks in other nations. There would be some start-up government money, but eventually the bank would become self-financing through interest returned on its loans. The energy corporation would also require some start-up money but would become self-sustaining from fees earned from its oil operation and on cost-plus management contracts awarded to private firms.

A U.S. energy corporation would work, as do those of other nations described in chapter 4, by awarding management contracts to private enterprise for large domestic expansion programs. This same energy corporation would also be the sole purchaser of foreign oil and would offer it to American oil companies at public auctions through sealed and competitive bids. Such a post-market "honest broker" role is essential for opening up domestic competition for foreign oil by giving independent U.S. producers a direct crack at the imported supplies, instead of having to purchase them from the majors as they do now.

There would also be a small markup on the auction sales both to pay for administrative costs of the agency and to help finance oil exploration in non-OPEC developing countries. This might stimulate competition between the American independents and the majors by competitively awarding some of the overseas exploration money to the independents.

The corporation could also manage large-scale exploration and exploitation in the continental United States and its territorial waters, thereby replacing the present leasing system, which is so expensive that only the majors can afford to participate. Instead there would be management contracts in the first phase for exploration offshore and on publicly owned land. This is the system that other countries use, and the oil companies have learned to operate under it and still profit from it. A second phase of management contracts would be offered, under the same sealed-bid auction process, for exploitation once energy reserves had been discovered.

The energy extracted, whether coal, oil, or gas, would be public property. Here too the corporation would play "honest broker" and sell this by competitive auction, just as it would imported oil, to private companies for distribution but with limited constraints to account for regional differences. The public auctions would perform the function of a competitive market where there is none now. (Not coincidentally, in his *Wealth of Nations,* Adam Smith likened competitive markets to a public auction. All competitors have the same information about the same product and therefore can compete fairly.)

For years the major oil multinationals had a near monopoly and stranglehold over much of the allocation and distribution of petroleum. In the seventies, executive agencies and, later in the decade, the Energy Department intervened in the crucial allocation function. Neither has done much to assure stable and efficient energy supplies. The public auctions and "honest broker" role of a quasi-public corporation could break this deadlock, and, as Rutgers' Davidson argues, "would eliminate the price surveillance mechanism of the internationals, which is a strong prop holding the OPEC cartel together." In short, it would be a credible means of restoring both supply and demand conditions as a determinant of price and distribution through competitive forces.

Finally, but most important for the short term, there is conservation. An intellectual consensus is developing among independent experts, typified by the Harvard Business School's *Energy Future* report, that there must be a much stronger emphasis on conservation (coupled with an intensified solar conversion program). The coeditors of the report, Robert Stobaugh and Daniel Yergin, estimate that an effective but nonpunitive conservation program could cut a projected late 1980s demand of 51 million barrels a day by as much as 8 million barrels. In other words, conservation could keep imports at present levels.

But as Stobaugh and Yergin pointed out, conservation "has no clear constituency." And it has some strong opponents, the classically well-organized and powerful few against the unorganized many. Most of the major U.S. oil companies, with the exception of Atlantic Richfield, play on fears that conservation will mean cold houses, fewer car trips, and declining living standards. In Europe, where scarcity is more real, some of the state-controlled firms, especially British Petroleum, are actively encouraging conservation. BP officials insist conservation can be achieved without curbing economic growth.

Unfortunately, conservation in this country has often meant frustrated government officials berating gas-hungry citizens and imposing such edicts as unpopular thermostat controls. These methods compound one of the problems in getting political support for conservation noted by the studies of Princeton University scientists L. J. Becker and G. S. Dutt: ". . . to many people, conservation means freezing in the dark." Beyond much-more-fuel-efficient cars, conservation is not a grandiose plan but a collection of many relatively simple and inexpensive programs. For example, better insulation and "fine-tuning" of home furnaces could save the nation up to 1.6 billion barrels of oil a day by 1985, and, they note, "People will not have to sacrifice comfort or convenience to save energy [through such programs]." Yet, in the absence of effective and broad-scale conservation programs, the best inducement to saving remains escalating prices.

With these types of new policy approaches—the global Marshall Plan, bilateral agreements, and a public energy corporation—the United States, once again, will have a chance to obtain "breathing space" for a transition to the inevitable post-petroleum world. But policies that allow us to import oil on "the best available terms" in the short run, do not provide momentum for a massive technological transition to energy sources other than oil in the long term. A separate, but parallel, strategy must be developed to convert the U.S. economy.

V

Ask an economist what will happen when the price of oil skyrockets, and he will tell you that the higher prices will bring about new supplies, reduce demand, and encourage development of substitutes. Ask a realist, and he will tell you that the geology of the United States will not produce significant new amounts of oil, that the opportunities to conserve are many, individual, small, and require cash up front that many households and enterprises may not have, and that alternate fuel sources will take a decade to develop.

In short, the conversion of our economy will require a strong leadership and planning role by the government, and cannot be left to outmoded notions about "market forces."

We are not unfamiliar with the task of making sweeping changes in an economy; we have already discussed the tools used by planners in developing countries to promote development. Energy conversion in the industrialized nations requires a planning strategy like that used to promote development. And like development, conversion happens at many levels. Consider these situations:

- A homeowner would like to upgrade his residence, but lacks the $2,000 necessary to install insulation and storm windows, even though these will create fuel savings that will pay back the initial cost in six or seven years.
- A community seeks to use waste heat from its local power plant in an economic "district heating" plan, similar to those found in Scandinavia. The utility's waste heat is piped into the homes in the community, making use of energy that would otherwise be discharged into the atmosphere or local river.
- A public utility seeks to convert from oil to coal, but its local rate-setting public service commission, justifiably, denies it the right to raise funds to pay for this project by sending its present customers higher bills. Frightened by the strict regulation of utility rates, banks refuse to lend the necessary funds to the utility.
- A construction firm creates a new design for a wind-powered electric generation facility that it seeks to incorporate into a new residential development it is building. Again, however, financing is not available.

Everyone wants to do his part in converting the economy, yet money for these tasks is elusive. Subsidies, either through cash grants and tax credits, do work, but an across-the-board approach invites inefficiency. Tax credits often miss the poor and elderly. Mandated conservation, in either household or industry, proves inefficient and creates random hardship. How, then, can these four hypothetical bottom-up innovations be realized?

The tool of developing countries for promoting major economic changes is development banking. As we have seen, development banking provides a middle ground between doing nothing in the face of risk and using tax monies to spend one's way out of trouble. And development banking, in the long run, eliminates the need for continued government spending.

Yet the ultimate advantage of a development-banking approach to our energy problem is that it allows grass-roots, bottom-up solutions to occur. Consider each of the four innovators just described—the homeowner, the community, the public utility, and the builder. Each is pursuing an activity that amounts to part of the energy solution. Their approaches demonstrate the variety of pioneering tasks necessary to transform the economy: a blend of conservation and new production, a switch to appropriate funds, a return to community-scale projects, a balance between centralized and decentralized energy sources based on the nature of the jobs energy must accomplish.

And the projects vary in risk. The homeowner's improvements are as sound an investment as gold. With the assistance of energy auditors perhaps from the local utilities as some studies suggest, a homeowner can pay back many improvements in several years. It is a sure thing. The electric utility's conversion to coal also will pay for itself in lower fuel costs, but over a slightly longer time period. And the annualized cost of the project can be included in the utility's rate base.

The community-scale project has large fixed costs. Streets must be torn up; connections to private homes and other structures must be made. But once the project is underway, costs are minimal, since the basic energy source is waste heat. This project, then, will also pay for itself, but perhaps over a thirty- or forty-year time horizon.

Finally, the builder's windmill may never pay for itself. Windmills have come a long way from the Depression days, when Bullet Bob Feller's father used one to light a field so his son could pitch baseball at night. But the needs windmills must fill have evolved as well. Fuel prices could rise high enough to make many sources like this one economic, but there is no 100 percent guarantee when and if they will. Yet this type of project does promise environmental benefits that should not go unrealized.

Each of these four projects would face some amount of difficulty in obtaining funds from those sources of capital to which it now has access. But a national energy development bank could profitably fund all four projects by pooling their risk and payback periods. Initial funding for an energy development bank would come from taxes on windfall profits realized through crude-oil decontrol; but, over time, revenues would come from the payback of earlier loans and fresh capital from the sale of bonds and preferred stock. Those instruments could be issued either through the Treasury Department or through private capital markets. Eventually, after repayment of loans, reinvestment would generate profits. These could be used to finance operating costs and the riskier or so-called soft loans, which do not always return a profit. Congress could also occasionally replenish the soft-loan fund. This is the pattern of financing used in existing multilateral and foreign development banks.

Like these banks, a quasi-public U.S. energy development bank would have "hard-loan windows," which would finance projects that pay off their loans at a profit. These would include certain selected synfuel projects and, importantly, large industrial conservation undertakings, such as "cogeneration," which uses the waste heat from current technology to generate additional energy. The bank's "profits" from these hard projects would then be plowed back into its "soft-loan windows" for higher-risk projects —for example, large "seed-financing" for photovoltaic conversion of solar into electric energy, for large fuel cells of utilities during peak power loads, for giant wind turbine electric generators, and, ultimately, for fusion. Development banking, unlike private banking, measures social cost-benefits as well as the chances and rate of private return before making loans. Social cost-benefits are very tangible things, in this instance the amount of imported oil saved or not saved by undertaking a project versus the environmental effect of a coal conversion project or the costs to a region in lost jobs if there is no local energy supply. A private bank's analysis of a loan is simply whether it will be paid off at a profit. A development bank makes loans on the expectation that there will be social as well as private economic returns.

"The art of development banking," as a former official of the Asian Development Bank in Manila said in an interview, "is to make enough from your hard window to help pay for your soft loans to the greatest extent possible." The inflation-riddled American economy, the Treasury, and hard-pressed taxpayers certainly have every incentive to pioneer such self-financing mechanisms rather than paying out a hundred billion dollars in straight gifts to a few corporations ready to invest in synthetic fuel.

The functions of an energy development bank would not embrace technological research and development. For this, a sister quasi-public corporation to work in tandem with the energy development bank could be used. The research and technology corporation would evaluate both small and large innovation proposals in energy production and conservation, but itself would fund only smaller-scale research contracts, with the bank financing the larger and higher-risk ventures. The research corporation's costs would eventually be offset, at least partially, by a share of the royalties from its sponsored innovations that are commercially exploited. The corporation would be managed by a large and representative board of directors as a check against the monopolistic kinds of arrangements that have developed in thirty years of "revolving-door boondoggles," as one former official called similar arrangements between the Pentagon and defense technology firms ("because the same large companies keep revolving in for contracts, with newcomers rarely penetrating since they don't know the cast of characters inside"). Because the corporation would be funding relatively small-scale projects, the potential for boondoggles would be limited. Finally, this system would require that the results of successfully funded R&D be made available through licensing and royalties to other producers to prevent technology monopolies from emerging, as has happened with past federal R&D funding. A U.S. energy research and technology corporation thus becomes a central clearinghouse for current and potential technology alternatives as well as an "outreach system" that encompasses programs for both small- and large-scale innovation.

Finally, an energy conversion program must also address the "side effects" it would create. An important aspect of our long-term energy strategy is the decontrol of energy prices. As we have discussed, it is imperative that our energy prices reflect the reality of scarcity. Yet doing so will have a profound effect on the distribution of income and wealth in the United States. A 1979 Congressional Budget Office study demonstrated that consumers will pay more than $600 billion in higher prices resulting from decontrol for oil that would have been produced even under continued controls. In this decade, allowing this vast sum to be simply transferred to the oil industry, dominated by the majors, will only create more inflation, lower consumer income, and reduce the profits of other industries and reduce economic growth. Energy conversion need not occur at that high a price.

The domestic oil industry cannot spend $600 billion productively on oil and gas exploration in the next decade. The surplus cash will only fuel their conglomeratization and increase global economic concentration. Moreover, other uses for the funds, such as all the projects described above, are just as pressing. As we have discussed, windfall profits taxes become the key link in the conversion strategy by financing the energy conversion fund.

Yet not all the windfall tax revenues should be directed to the energy development bank or to energy research and development. A good portion of the funds should be directed at reducing social security taxes, increasing social security payments, and otherwise putting income back into the hands of U.S. households. Otherwise, decontrol will create a bonanza for a few firms, at the expense of those of us least able to bear the burden.

Some of the tax money could go into developing and implementing a national transportation policy that links energy and economic development (with gas taxes, for example, a transportation development bank could be created). Our economic and energy policy makers, for the most part, have failed to see the vital role that transportation plays in their choices. They even have failed to see that much of our present oil dependence flowed from deliberate transportation policies, but policies unfortunately reflecting the single-minded drive of giant corporations for profits. If big corporations aided by government can plan us into a mess, then government aided by innovative companies can help plan us out of the same mess.

The exhortations and sermons of government leaders to save gas ignore the historical role of government and industry in promoting the public's oil addiction. A house and a yard became the American dream. But it was the lobbies of private industry and government's response to them, not Jane Doe in the gas lines, who built the superhighways, who let the cities crumble, who provided the cheap loans for suburban housing—all helping to create this energy-consuming way of life.

It was manipulation by the oil companies that helped create "an America spaced out on oil," wrote Carl Solberg, a former *Newsweek* editor, in his book *Oil Power*. If Californians are so wedded to their automobiles and freeways that a near civil war erupts when the gas runs out, that is largely the result of manipulations by the oil companies. From Anthony Sampson's chronicles of the *Seven Sisters* to John Blair's meticulous *Control of Oil*, we see that the cases are legion, and we live every day with the consequences. Bradford Snell of the U.S. Senate Subcommittee on Antitrust methodically documented the postwar destruction of public transportation systems in twenty-eight cities by a combination of giant corporations. Most prominent were the Los Angeles and San Francisco public trolley systems, among the most efficient in the nation. In Los Angeles, General Motors, Standard Oil of California, and Firestone took over the trolley company in 1944 and stripped up hundreds of miles of track and electric transmission lines. Put in its place were General Motors buses burning Standard of California fuel and rolling on Firestone tires. To no one's surprise, Los Angeles residents abandoned this inefficient and dirty form of bus transport for their private cars. The same free-enterprise strategy was successfully pursued in scores of other American cities. In San Francisco, GM teamed up with Esso (now Exxon) and Goodyear Tire and junked that city's efficient trolley system, replacing it with buses. Thirty years later, San Francisco and U.S. taxpayers paid more than $4 billion to replace that system with a still-struggling subway network. When the costly rapid-transit system was inaugurated, the city's mayor denounced the companies for deliberately destroying in the 1940s an efficient mass transit that, in the name of energy conservation, they were now applauding in newspaper ads in the 1970s.

There is a real question whether building a new BART or a Washington, D.C., subway system may actually consume more energy than it will eventually save. And multibillion-dollar costs for their construction are prohibitive. But where systems already exist, such as New York and other older cities, a commitment to making them safe and comfortable would rebound in great economic gains. In New York, rebuilding and adequately policing the subway system would be the single greatest economic development measure the city could undertake. Thousands of disillusioned suburbanites and weary commuters and small and medium-sized, job-creating companies could be induced back to the city—to still-pleasant neighborhoods with good, solid housing in the outer boroughs now threatened with deterioration—if they could only be guaranteed a safe subway ride to work. Similarly, the city is losing corporations to the suburbs and other regions because of the terrible state of the commuter trains.

But in most parts of the country, such mass transportation is not really the answer. What need to be explored are imaginative new methods of moving people about which take into account the convenience of driving around in one's own car. We have already seen how higher gas prices make people look for other ways to travel. But that will be temporary unless new transportation systems are developed. For starters, these include trains that run on time and more-fuel-efficient autos, both within the easy reach of technology but seemingly beyond our political ability to achieve.

Transportation has always been a fundamental factor in economic development. Now it is all the more so in determining our energy choices. It is time that it stopped being treated as an afterthought.

Since the 1979 debacle at Three Mile Island, it is clear that there will be no more "business as usual" for the nuclear power industry and the government agencies that simultaneously regulate and protect it. Always controversial, nuclear power has now become the ultimate symbol of stalemate, an energy source going nowhere. And because it is wrapped up in such intense emotions, nuclear power should be spun off from other energy programs and subject to an entirely different group of regulators and promoters.

Perhaps because their energy dependence is greater, the French and West German governments, even after Three Mile Island, remain committed to going ahead with full-scale nuclear power development—although their voters are becoming less enthusiastic about that commitment. Chancellor Schmidt said Europe must rely on nuclear power or face the alternative of risking energy wars. But his coalition is threatened by a growing "Green Movement" of antinuclear and environmental activists. How long-lasting the determination of Schmidt and French President Giscard d'Estaing will be is an open question. Antinuclear forces toppled a government in Sweden, and protests have been growing elsewhere in Europe and Japan.

In the United States, the nuclear power issue has generated not only intense emotion but a welter of conflicting information and passionate advocates on both sides who bandy their "facts" in endless debate. Of all the energy issues, and especially since Three Mile Island, the nuclear is most afflicted with credibility problems. Nuclear proponents said Three Mile Island could never happen, and it did. Nuclear opponents talk even of closing down existing plants without mentioning the trade-offs in costs, the environmental and health and safety risks of alternative sources, such as coal, or where to find power for cities, like Chicago, now dependent on nuclear fuel. There are referenda in different states, and very recently there have been antinuclear demonstrations reminiscent of the 1960s in size and fervor.

All the potential problems involving nuclear power—from waste to accidents—and all the problems involved in stopping or dismantling the program make nuclear reliance an issue that cannot be handled in the conventional manner by government. The cozy relationship between the Nuclear Regulatory Commission (an offspring of the old Atomic Energy Commission) and the regulated industry suffered its own form of meltdown with Three Mile Island. Neither the government regulators nor the companies will regain their credibility any time soon.

Therefore, a new nuclear agency, a quasi-public corporation instead of yet another government department, needs to be created and separated from the other energy corporations. A board of directors including nuclear proponents as well as opponents, scientists as well as environmentalists, big and small business, and regional representatives, is absolutely essential to begin developing a consensus, if any is indeed possible, on both future development and information. Private industry participation, should production continue, will have to be through management contracts rather than through mere licensing and haphazard regulation.

A new framework needs to be created for nuclear policy. In the 1960s, decisions to pursue commercial development of nuclear power were made by a few companies in combination with the Atomic Energy Commission, which subsidized part of the risk. Few, but not many, in Congress knew about the potential risks, and neither the industry nor the AEC made any effort to reveal them. Competitive market forces were hardly existent in this relationship between a few major corporations and a secretive government agency.

In the present atmosphere, it seems unlikely that any new fission reactors of the present generation will be approved for construction in the next few years. Presumably, however, technology will improve, and at that point a quasi-public nuclear corporation could decide whether to award a management contract. Within this new framework, start-up money would come from federal appropriations and longer-term funds from loan guarantees from the corporation. A quasi-public nuclear corporation would also receive funds from royalties on commercially successful applications of its research projects. But it is essential, from our point of view, to keep the nuclear debate separate from the political debate that will determine other energy production and uses in the years immediately ahead. And as the *Washington Post*'s William Greider observed about the current process by which decisions on nuclear power are made, "It seems a rather crude way for a nation to make its fundamental choices, bruising one another until necessity yields a decision."

CHAPTER 10

Road from Inflation: America's Reindustrialization

I

ENERGY IS ONLY ONE of the two great conversions in production that face the post-market global economy during the 1980s. The second challenge to the supply side, especially in the United States, is the structural adjustment of industry, its adaptation to the dramatic shifts in investment, trade, and competitiveness wrought by the postwar global economic revolution. When Helmut Schmidt was asked in June 1979, "What are the greatest problems facing the world's economy?" he listed three. After inflation and energy, the third was the growing economic power of the Third World, which "has led to the necessity for a rather wide-ranging restructuring of industrial capacities and professional capabilities in the developed world. This process is not going fast enough," said Schmidt of the inability of the industrial nations to adapt and modernize their industry.

Although existing statutes make no reference to it, the United States does have a wide-sweeping national industrial development policy. Government pursues an industrial policy throughout the country, but no federal agency has been given a mandate to conduct it. Daily from the Congress and the Executive, pulsating down to the grass roots level of production, are requirements, incentives, disincentives, and restrictions that structure the organization of capital and labor and the performance of technology.

From the Occupational Safety and Health Administration

(OSHA) and the Justice Department's Antitrust Division to the regional and industry loan-guarantee programs of Commerce and to the Department of Defense and the Environmental Protection Agency, this *de facto* industrial policy steers the supply side of America's economy. Each of the policy activities originates out of legitimate concerns of contending stakeholders in the U.S. economy. But the synergism—the sum total of the effects of all these disparate policies—is not really known. This failure to devise and experiment with mechanisms to replace the fragmented approach to supply economics is another signal national policy-lag.

This chapter explores the ideas and mechanisms for creating an explicit industrial development policy framework that integrates both supply and demand economics. Our purpose is not to impinge further on private enterprise but rather to seek to revitalize its capacity to meet the adjustment and conversion challenge of the 1980s. The major political issues of industrial development on the supply side are corporate power, antitrust, and small business; remedies for declining productivity, including the humanization and reorganization of work, technological innovation, and regulatory policies; structural adjustment and adaptation to overcome problems in international trade and regional imbalances; and, on the demand side, new tax and credit policies. They are political issues because each involves equity and efficiency trade-offs. And they are political because they challenge the stalemate of the status quo.

National planning was crucial to rebuilding war-torn Europe and Japan. It is a threat neither to private enterprise nor to democracy. As we saw in chapter 7, Germany has at least established the criteria and some of the mechanisms for industrial development policy. The Common Market has implemented a basic early-warning system and funding mechanisms for anticipatory adjustment policies. France has downplayed its tradition of indicative planning but nevertheless continues active business-government collaboration in strategic sectors. And Japan has explicit guidance mechanisms through its ministries of planning, finance, and industry and trade. None of these can serve as "the model" for a U.S. industrial policy framework, but separately and together they bear a central message for a post-market globally interdependent economy in a modern democracy: the need for public-private collaboration to pursue economic development.

A 1980s industrial development program must have the same political objectives as the energy programs and global industrial programs we have described earlier. First, it should promote growth as much as possible through semi-autonomous and quasi-public institutions and agencies that become self-financing. Second, that growth should give economies and governments the breathing space to cope with the inflation, financial instability, and social dislocations created in the postwar decades of the global economic revolution.

The object of industrial development policy is to help crack the supply-side vicious circle of the economy—sagging investor confidence and investment, which contribute to declining productivity growth that brings even lower investment, which further diminishes productivity and is a basis of faltering trade competitiveness, an unstable dollar and inflation itself.

We look with both envy and fear at the ability of our industrial partners to adapt often more quickly than we to rapidly changing global economic conditions. Simultaneously, we waste precious time and resources in the name of protecting free enterprise when that is not what is at stake. The real question is how to overcome the adjustment crisis that can no longer be handled through the workings of classical competitive markets simply because to a large extent they are no longer with us. The crucial issue has moved beyond the question of whether we have planning or whether we do not. Planning already exists. The question is, What kind of planning are we going to have and who is going to control it?

The major institutions shaping the economy are engaged intensely in planning: big business, big labor, and the large Executive agencies of government. Yet a difference between the private and public sectors is that business has coherent management tools for coordinating the individual activities of its sub-units and the profit criteria to measure its private efficiency, while government does not. The multinational conglomerate is a fitting example of management coordination over far-flung and widely diverse subsidiaries engaged in a multitude of activities. This managerial imperative, planning, is recognized for large private sector bureaucracies. But the word has drawn hysterical reaction since the New Deal, when some thinkers raised the idea that economic planning might be a useful tool for government. Referring to that negative reaction, Senator Jacob Javits once remarked, "What puzzles me is why it is good for AT&T and not good for the USA."

Conservatives hail hierarchy in the corporation but not in the government, and liberals are now fearful of suggesting any new departures in government. Both are guilty of timidity in their failure to seek a middle way—experimenting in government-business collaboration but collaboration subject to new yardsticks for measuring public-sector efficiency and to internal checks and balances and safeguards against abuses of information and other forms of power.

Our national industrial policy, such as it is, emerges from the independent and uncoordinated decisions of the Executive branch, Congress, and, with increasing frequency, the courts. "For good or ill," notes Walt W. Rostow, "governments are so inextricably enmeshed in the sectors on which both full employment and structural adjustment depend that the necessary alterations in the pattern of investment will not occur without conscious government policy."

This remark expresses a developing consensus on the need for planning, a consensus that has vaulted over the old objections and includes such diverse adherents as Leonard Woodcock, former head of the United Auto Workers, various members of the Joint Economic Committee of Congress, the Committee for Economic Development, and corporate leaders like Thornton Bradshaw of Atlantic Richfield and Henry Schact of Cummins Engines.

II

Yet as broad as the consensus is on the need for planning and industrial development policy, little has come from it. One reason is that the advocates of planning have wanted to put the planning agency or mechanism within the Executive branch of government and to have it function as yet another line agency. They have not been able to devise a new set of checks and balances on such an agency, to restrain its power, and to give it credibility with all the various and conflicting economic and political interests it would serve. Without these checks, such an agency would become subject to the same pressures of the political-business cycle that now thwart demand management. But the way out of this political trap is to create a planning mechanism set apart from such agencies as the President's Economic Advisers and the Congress with its specific constituencies and their pressing daily demands.

One proposal came from Dr. Albert T. Sommers, chief economist of the Conference Board, which represents the leaders of many large corporations.

> An independent economic commission, isolated as much as possible from politics and free of the short-term concerns that occupy the Council of Economic Advisers, is an inevitable future development in the making of economic policy, and in recommending changes in policy equipment. Most of our international competitors are equipped with such a body.

In other words, the task of an autonomous and quasi-public body, rather than a line agency of government, would be to make recommendations, offer forecasts and information, and suggest priority "targets" for industrial development. Its deliberations would suggest the existence or absence of a consensus. The final decision on adopting the targets—and making political choices involved in trade-offs—still would be left to the President and Congress.

Both in structure and in function, an autonomous and quasi-public national industrial development board would be a different creature from the planning agency that many groups have asked Congress to establish. Structurally, its essential elements would make it credible where others are not. Like the energy agencies discussed earlier, it would include a broad-based and consensus-generating management or board of directors. It would try to draw areas of compromise and agreement from diverse economic, social, and regional representatives. When consensus is not possible, it would have to tell Congress, the President, and the nation why, and what the costs of that disunity entail.

Functionally, the board would be advisory—i.e., it would not make planning decisions but would make evaluations and recommendations. It would have three major tasks.

The first would be to determine an agenda of national industrial development priorities for the 1980s, including a review of all federal programs affecting development. The board would suggest which sectors of the economy needed restructuring, which were healthy, and which were beyond saving. It would recommend to the President and Congress which industries had priority for restructuring and whether new or revised programs should be put into place. In short, it would make recommendations on equity versus efficiency trade-offs in industrial development with the final political choices left to Congress and the President.

America's first and only systematic structural adjustment program, the shoe case profiled in chapter 7, was almost killed by contradictory and overlapping federal bureaucracies. Numerous bureaucratic fiefdoms involved in adjustment assistance vented their jealousies. As a result, this collaborative business-labor-government pioneering was stalled in its tracks. But for eighteen months the shoe assistance program saved American taxpayers the unemployment benefits that would have gone to workers who had lost their jobs. American consumers also saved because they avoided paying the extra costs of higher tariffs and quotas on foreign-made shoes.

The review and evaluation of existing federal programs by the national industrial development board would be a step toward a permanent and politically credible mechanism to identify overlap and excessive bureaucratic costs. Moreover, as the record of planning shows—from Jean Monnet's postwar office in France to the ministries of the Third World—the work of the board can be done with small and compact staffs, not large and cumbersome new bureaucracies.

The second task would be the monitoring of global economic changes, to provide an early warning to policy makers and to the vast majority of companies which cannot afford such sophisticated information systems. Thus the board would develop the "anticipatory policy" design for structural adjustment that in the coming years will be necessary for affected industries. The board would monitor changes in global plant capacity, consumption, raw material prices, protectionist barriers, and the movement and development of industry. Along with its monitoring, which could be done in conjunction with international agencies noted in chapter 6, the board would offer recommendations for anticipated structural adjustments.

Chrysler is but the tip of America's industrial iceberg. Without planned readjustment programs based on credible early-warning information, we face many more politically wrenching and highly costly bail-out schemes for adapting to the structural adjustments of the eighties.

The third function of the board would be the development and application of social cost-benefit analysis. Its purpose here would be to measure and report to the President and Congress on the tangible social costs and tangible benefits of any supply-side decision regarding regulations, subsidies, investments, and the like. And its measurements, it should be emphasized, would go beyond the efforts to gauge "regulatory budget costs" now so much in vogue in Washington.

At present, the costs of enforcing regulations are measured in terms of government budget dollars spent. But even the secretary of commerce acknowledged that "would not be the complete answer" to the regulatory question. Regulatory budget costs are but a small part of a more important question: How much are regulations benefiting people and the overall economy? The benefits, hard to measure, are safer workplaces, cleaner air, better land use, the payoffs in reduced accident insurance and medical costs, and lowered costs of water-erosion-prevention programs. The costs of such regulations are lowered productivity, forgone exports and increased imports, lost jobs, and diminished investment and capital formation. But besides environmental, health, and safety regulations, there are other supply policies that have been resistant to social cost-benefit measurement. In the seventies these included antitrust and government subsidies for R&D, defense, and education. In the 1980s they will increasingly include the financing of structural adjustment programs for ailing industries.

The techniques of social cost-benefit analysis are well known and long-used in other industrial and Third World nations. Yet their application in the U.S. involves a basically political problem. The catch is the choice of what should be counted as costs and benefits. In the case of environmental controls, business and, increasingly, labor will tend to emphasize the direct costs of meeting standards while the environmental lobbies and regulators turn their emphasis to the quality-of-life benefits. What one downplays, the other overkills. As a result, it is becoming increasingly difficult for government agencies and legislative committees to develop politically credible "economic impact" statements.* The requirements for such statements are being increasingly ignored or sidestepped.

A national industrial development board should play an important role in providing information needed to make development policy choices. Essential to a cost-benefit analysis is credible information. A board with internal checks and balances and adversarial representation among its directors and staff has the potential to provide this kind of information. It clearly would be an experiment, not a foolproof way to obtain absolutely impartial information. But "facts" that are in dispute would be labeled as such, and the whole approach certainly would be an improvement over the present one in which development decisions are made on the basis of sketchy and often controversial information.

It is frustrating in a so-called scientific age with the advent of the necessary software technologies and information systems, as Alvin Toffler and others have emphasized, that reliable social accounting is unavailable because of a failure in institutional political innovation. A significant number of politicians, regulators, and corporate executives interviewed for this book made a common point, summarized by one as follows: "Not just government agencies have client biases. Too many universities have become captives of certain funding sources and even the philanthropic foundations have their political biases, some more blatant than others. The quest for reliable and impartial analyses in economics is thwarted at all turns by political roadblocks."

III

Industrial conversion, no matter how it is achieved, will be expensive. Mobilizing capital will be difficult, especially given the many existing blockages to capital formation. The combination of fundamental post-market constraints and the enormous costs of structural conversion and adjustment will require, as in energy, the

* A number of congressional staff members and regulators interviewed, for example, complained bitterly that they spent most of their time searching for private consulting companies to perform cost-benefit estimates impartially because so many of them had private corporations as their biggest clients "and had consciously or unconsciously adapted their choices of definitions and methods," in the words of one OSHA regulator.

approach of a national industrial development bank to draw out the capital and to help finance investments. Like a quasi-public energy bank, it should have a broadly representative board of directors to assure regional equity and to tackle the different claims of business, labor, environmentalists, and other stakeholders on the projects funded. (This is similar, for example, to agencies in Norway.) Based on priorities recommended by the industrial development advisory board, it would finance loans pegged to a national development agenda. Initial funding would come from Congress, but like other development banks it would become self-sustaining through the sale of bonds and the return on its "hard window" loans. Beyond industrial conversion projects, it could finance programs in work humanization, productivity, and technological innovation. A certain proportion of loans would go to small and medium businesses.

An industrial development program, financed in part through a development bank, would operate on two levels. On the one hand, it would promote and finance so-called "demonstration" projects. On the other, it would participate in the programs for industrial adjustment and conversion.

Among the demonstration projects that could be financed are employee acquisitions of subsidiaries of conglomerates. For various reasons, corporations occasionally want to spin off a subsidiary, and they have been doing it with increasing frequency in the last few years. There are tax incentives already to help these employee acquisitions, but the real need is for loans during the start-up period to bridge the relatively high costs of creating new marketing, distribution, and advertising networks.

Similarly, in shoes and now in apparel, companies are trying to make the adjustment to new competition, and this requires new technology and new forms of marketing. The problem is obtaining venture capital loans for the first five to ten years of the adjustment period. Also, as we have mentioned before, small and medium companies are frequently the source of innovation and new technology, especially in energy-saving and environmental protection. But they often hit a financing crunch right after developing a successful prototype and need new money to market their product widely. All too often at such turning points, these innovative companies are swallowed up by conglomerates, and the entrepreneurial innovation is frequently lost in the larger corporate bureaucracy. New sources of financing would preserve the entrepreneurial drive and offer a new brake on conglomerate acquisitions. In the instances in which development bank loans went to new technology, the bank could receive a portion of royalties as part of its return. Experiments in work reorganization in small firms have produced productivity gains as impressive as similar experiments by the conglomerates. Companies making such experiments frequently need an injection of cash to help them through the transition period.

The structural adjustment programs offered so far in the steel industry, and described in chapter 3, are but one example of the problems of pork-barreling when trying to work through traditional government agencies. A development banking approach, using credible social cost-benefit estimates, offers choices not available under the current econopolitics of standard government assistance programs.

Steel is as much a post-market sector as oil. Globally it is characterized by foreign state-owned enterprises and explicit business-government cooperation. Domestically, the sector's dualism is accentuated by the policy lag of a Washington private-public interlock that favors the big conglomerates and neglects the smaller firms. For instance, for the medium-term of five to eight years, many smaller firms could become competitive with the introduction of existing electric-powered furnaces that convert scrap steel. The companies would be able to sell effectively in regional markets and, because of much lower transportation costs, compete against foreign imports. These firms have not been able to raise private money. The present government aid programs, limited to a total of $500 million in loan guarantees and subsidies, have been going to the larger firms. This money has not been tied into any comprehensive restructuring program and instead has gone in trickles to the largest and loudest pleaders to preserve often inefficient companies and jobs. Under a development banking approach, the bank could offer small companies the loans for the purchase of the new technology and set them on their competitive feet.

The long-term (ten years and more) adjustment problem is more complicated. The next generation of technology furnaces that would enable U.S. firms to compete against the overseas giants is available. But in the present uncertainty, banks are reluctant to make the loans, and the available government money is insufficient. And long-term adjustment in the United States would have to be accompanied, as it has been in Europe, Japan, and the Third World, by a "rationalization" of the industry. In Europe this has been given the pejorative label of "cartelization." But what it means is that some companies may have to merge and some enter joint ventures for new projects. Any long-term program will require a degree of cooperation among existing companies, a dividing of the available and shrinking markets. We can learn from both the successes and failures of overseas experiments. One lesson is to tie the development and conversion loans of big steel companies to strict conditions, such as competitive pricing and restrictions on company investments in nonrelated industries. Existing government agencies, such as the Commerce Department, are not equipped by themselves to carry out this combination of aid and industry restructuring. A quasi-public national development bank would be a far more efficient and equitable way to provide the massive funding for major technology and related infrastructure innovations.

Finally, the work of a national development bank can be complemented by regional development banks. This frequently happens in the Third World. Regional development banks have already been proposed for areas of this country, and the recently established urban development bank is a step in the right direction. The experience of the Third World is that the two layers of banking lead to efficiency with the exchange of information and expertise and the ability to move many decisions to more local levels. With such a variety of activity, the benefits of the "demonstration effect" also come into play. As we saw in the Third World, banks learn from each other's experiences.

IV

Conventional tax, spending, and regulatory policies must also have a development component. The name for this is *targeting*. It has long been a principle of the development policies of other nations. Targeting is used to cut the supply-side vicious circles that help perpetuate stagflation. Sectors such as small business, which have special problems, need special remedies. Sectors experiencing global shortages, such as minerals (discussed in chapter 6), will require special stimulation. Similarly, those experiencing global gluts, such as steel, will have to undergo significant structural adjustments to meet stiffening international competition, particularly from the Third World. Steel and other industries employing large-scale technology will be treated very differently from labor-intensive textile and apparel industries, which are also undergoing adjustments to meet rapid shifts in the global division of labor. Targeting was devised by Nobel Laureate Jan Tinbergen from his work in developing nations in the 1950s. It is beginning to come into vogue in U.S. energy planning. But because it clashes with the American policy predilection for simple "black or white" across-the-board solutions, it has yet to be applied systematically to industrial development where it is equally needed.

With targeting absent from existing tax and credit policies, there is a missing link between micro supply programs and the macro policies of aggregate demand management. The only exception is Treasury's ability to set different depreciation allowances for certain industries. But even here the most important options to target, like large versus small firms, new versus standard technologies, are not available. As we described in chapters 2 and 3, the U.S. has many characteristics of a dual economy similar to dual economies in many Third World nations. The nation's 1,000 or so largest conglomerates in manufacturing and resource sectors control about three-fourths of total assets; more than 11 million small and medium enterprises compete for the remaining assets and sales.

But small business groups are the Washington latecomers in the rise of politically organized single-issue groups. Until recently big business and big labor have been the two major power groups shaping tax and credit policy, and their influence is still predominant. This one-sided influence led to a policy perversity as stagflation deepened in the 1970s. Small business accounted for more than 92 percent of all new jobs created in the private sector even though it held a miniscule percentage of total investment assets. The labor-intensive nature of small business ventures meant that a dollar's worth of new investment by them created far more jobs than the same investment by a big firm. Nevertheless, the credit and austerity programs designed to combat inflation in the 1970s hit small business first and hardest and accelerated the absorption of small firms by big firms. At the same time, the tax cuts designed to create more private-sector employment favored the conglomerates, which were actually adding less than 8 percent of all new jobs.

"In short, the firms that can and do generate the most jobs are the most difficult to reach through conventional policy initiatives," were the findings of an M.I.T. research program conducted by David L. Birch. "It is no wonder that efforts to stem the tide of job decline have been so frustrating—and largely unsuccessful," he added. "The easier strategy of working with larger, 'known' corporations whose behavior is better understood will not be, and has not been, very productive."

Only in late 1978 did Congress legislate a graduated corporate income tax and reduced capital gains, the two policies most needed to help small firms. The graduation of the taxes was at the lower end of the scale, with staggered rates on corporate income from $25,000 through $100,000, and still treating a corporation earning $250,000 profit at the same rate as General Motors or Exxon with billion dollar earnings. But even weaker than this step was the decision to make the capital gains cut an across-the-board rather than a targeted measure. This gave investors no incentive to look at small business and left them with the opportunity to put their savings into the better-known and less-risky investments of conglomerate stocks. What was really needed, as the House Committee on Small Business suggested, was "a targeting of preferential treatment of capital gains specifically for investments in small business."

As Congress once again confronted a recession threat in 1980, there were new calls for stimulus measures such as faster depreciation allowances. But again, the suggestions were across the board, reflecting the lobbying weight of the bigger corporations. Small businesses gain less from such measures because they do not have the large capital items to depreciate. As we detail in the next section, a targeting policy based on the Tinbergen Rule would offer instead measures respectively targeted at large and small businesses with the ultimate objective of creating more employment and output from both. As M.I.T.'s Birch summarized, "What we need, and have lacked, is the ability to target our incentives to those who can make good use of them without wasting taxpayer monies on those who cannot."

The targeting of restructuring programs for an entire industry is more ambitious and would have to begin with a few selected cases in obvious need of help. One early candidate for supply-side planning, through targeted tax and credit policies, is the defense industry. Since government already totally controls demand, research and development, finance, and many aspects of its management, it could use the industry as a demonstration project and in a politically acceptable manner. As Jacques Gansler asserts in his forthcoming *The Defense Industry,* such restructuring could improve productivity and result in more defense for less money. Innovations in defense could be passed on to the civilian side of the economy as they already have in such important areas as semiconductors, computers, and jet engines.

Perhaps the biggest challenge to an effective targeting policy arises in the area of government regulation. Ironically, many of the new regulations of the 1960s and 1970s were aimed at correcting the market imperfections and failures generated by the big conglomerates of the economy. But they were largely applied across the board to every business, with the result that the crushing load of paperwork and red tape has landed hardest on the smallest. According to the Commission on Federal Paperwork, small business spends $15 billion a year just filling out federal forms and coping with red tape.

As John Quarles, a former official in the Environmental Protection Administration, remarked, "The current system of single-purpose reviews, each conducted separately and according to its own timetable, is not the best solution."

An independent industrial development board, as earlier noted, would review all federal programs to assess their effect on industrial policy. A board could similarly recommend approaches for targeted regulation. These could include different standards in some industries between large and small firms and temporary escape clauses for firms threatened by an upsurge in imports.

The Chrysler case of 1979 illustrates the problems of imposing across-the-board regulation on an already weak firm that is also trying simultaneously to meet stiffening foreign and domestic competition. To be sure, part of Chrysler's problems stemmed from bad management decisions in the past. But the adroitly managed American Motors, after a successful comeback in the mid-1970s, was forced to resort to a joint venture with Renault for cash and technology to meet new fuel and safety regulations. Even Ford was experiencing difficulties, suffering a cash squeeze, as we noted in chapter 8. Only the giant, General Motors, seemed able to cope. The problem was a failure to target the new regulatory standards in a way that took account of the cost differences between large and small firms. (GM's unit costs are roughly one-half those of smaller automakers!) But to make such distinctions is politically sensitive and technically difficult. Both Congress, when it legislated the new standards, and the Department of Transportation, when it implemented them, could have benefited from a politically and technically credible industrial advisory board in making such distinctions.

As Quarles noted, "the combined effect [of all the new regulations] may be to transfer ultimate control over the basic questions of when, where and what types of industrial development will occur in various regions of the country from private corporations to public agencies."

The question raised by Quarles and other liberal critics is not so much one of how big a government, but what kind of government. If government is making decisions that so directly affect industrial development, then development should be a vital element of policy—not an incidental by-product. Targeting regulatory policy adds a vital option in dealing with the trade-offs involved in unavoidable regulatory decisions that will shape the nation's development in the decade ahead.

V

Corporate power is another major supply-side issue that must be included in a national industrial development policy. In the critical juncture of the 1980s, the power of big business will be a major political theme, just as it was at the turn of the century and during the Depression. Antitrust has been one tool—of limited effectiveness—in dealing with corporate power. But in the 1980s, as corporate power has been transformed to new dimensions, antitrust will have to take new approaches that concentrate more on spurring efficiency and curbing abuses and less on trying to recreate idealized and outdated notions of marketplace competition.

If nothing else, America's competitive position in an interdependent world economy must force a new approach to antitrust. As heretical as it sounds, bigness in some kinds of business activity may have to be encouraged rather than discouraged. So too might certain amounts of collaboration and information-sharing within strictly enforced limits. While many mergers do not enhance efficiency, some conglomerate acquisitions could promote economic viability and competitiveness in international markets. As in tax and regulatory policy, the American predilection for across-the-board rules is no longer working effectively in antitrust.

Since the first antitrust laws were passed in 1890, U.S. antitrust policy has been a catch-up endeavor, always lagging behind the ability of corporations to find loopholes in existing laws and to increase concentration. By the early 1960s the antitrust laws had been strengthened to prevent sizable horizontal mergers (between two companies in the same industry) and vertical mergers (a corporation buying out one of its buyers or suppliers). Since then, almost 70 percent of corporate mergers have been "conglomerate," the buying up of companies in unrelated fields.

Now there is a new push for antitrust legislation aimed squarely at conglomerates and an equally intense fight by them to stop it. The enforcement of existing antitrust laws has become bogged down in court and regulatory agency battles, some lasting as long as twenty years or more, to break up such giants as IBM and AT&T. The AT&T case has consumed more than $100 million just in legal fees without answering the basic question of what is to be achieved by breaking up the world's most efficient telephone system.

Striking out against the "robber barons" is the tradition of American antitrust policy. But in a globally interdependent post-market economy dominated by the combination of conglomerates, state-owned enterprises, and government, new guidelines for antitrust reform need to be developed. The traditional fight against monopolistic behavior can go on but with different approaches to complement old ones.

The new approach to antitrust needs to be grounded in the somewhat esoteric-sounding "General Theory of Second Best." The theory was pioneered in 1954 by Robert Lipsey and K. J. Lancaster and used in conjunction with the industrial organization and trade policy for the economic development of the European Common Market. The economic theory has a political parallel in the tradition of American pragmatism found in *The Federalist Papers*. "If men were angels," observed James Madison, "no government would be necessary." It is a view of democracy being governed through somewhat less than ideal checks and balances as it deals with the basic imperfections of human conduct. Similarly, Lipsey and Lancaster's second-best theory is the basis for developing economic policy criteria in a situation in which the first-best ideal of Adam Smith's perfect competition of free markets has been displaced by an economy characterized by conglomerate, unions, and government concentration.

The second-best theory is beyond dispute among all economists regardless of their political leanings, but the policy implications in antitrust have not been grasped by many in the U.S. government. The policy lag was reflected in the response of an assistant attorney general who was asked in 1978 if job preservation or loss of foreign trade competitiveness should be considered in antitrust. His response was "no" because consideration of these factors would "involve regulating the economy, rather than letting competition do the regulating." Competition is doing increasingly less regulating in a post-market economy. A traditional antitrust policy based on classical marketplace theories and aimed solely at increasing classical competition will no longer guarantee the results that competition has traditionally yielded—efficiency, productivity, and competitive pricing. It may or may not, depending on the individual case, but the actual results can be determined only by social cost-benefit measures.

A second-best approach toward concentration which meets the demands for economic growth has increasingly characterized the policies of Japan and the European Common Market. One policy criterion is "optimal firm size." What our economic rivals have done is permit and often encourage the merger of firms in certain sectors to achieve the size necessary to produce products that can compete with imports and gain new export markets. This does not always mean giant conglomerates, but in durable goods and high-technology industries the firm size is usually large. Financial leverage is needed to sustain worldwide marketing organizations and efficient production and even to sustain temporary losses for the sake of gaining long-term viability, say, in the global arena of automotive competition.

The benefits and problems in this approach are also reflected in the efforts of the European Community to "rationalize" its steel industry in the face of new global competition. The European steel program, known as the Davignon Plan, has been criticized as a backdoor effort to revive cartels. It is more complicated than that. Its goal is "optimal firm size" to create steel companies that can compete on world markets. This requires a certain amount of cooperation and collaboration among the steel industries of the Common Market nations. Some plants will have to be shut down. There is some collaboration in determining market shares and the apportioning of aid to help some plants modernize. It is clearly a second-best alternative, not pure first-best competition, but neither is it our present third-best situation of rising unemployment in a markedly uncompetitive and inefficient industry that must rely increasingly on tariff protection to hold its domestic markets. If the United States is to transcend this third-best choice in steel and other industries, it will have to begin thinking about second-best approaches, despite their imperfections.

The multinational character of many U.S. industries is another consideration that forces the application of "second-best" analysis. It is one question to bar an attempted merger but quite another to follow the routine practice of breaking up a corporation long after the fact. Spinning off parts of existing conglomerates must entail the question of what happens to the foreign subsidiaries of the newly created satellite. Could General Motors' Opel-Werke subsidiary, for example, still effectively compete with other German automobile manufacturers such as Daimler-Benz and Volkswagen if Opel became part of a forced divestiture that spun off Chevrolet as a separate corporation? The modern global economy creates new kinds of questions, and demands new sorts of answers in the application of antitrust measures.

One revision of antitrust law should concentrate on simplifying the procedures for resolving antitrust actions. As FTC Commissioner Robert Pitofsky said, some of these cases are taking so long to resolve that "they become self-defeating." Thanks to a variety of laws and court opinions, companies can delay antitrust actions into a seeming eternity. An antitrust case against eight major oil companies has gone on for eight years and is still in pretrial motions. Procedure has clearly supplanted substance, and unless the procedural logjam is broken, any new laws will only further clog the courts and enrich the lawyers.

A second essential reform is to take much of what now comes under antitrust out of the already overburdened federal court system. As an *Economist* study of U.S. antitrust practices observed, "In other countries it would be unthinkable to make the courts rather than the legislature the arena for god-like acts of industrial reorganization." The American courts wholeheartedly agree that they are not the proper instruments to determine optimal size and competitiveness. As the Supreme Court said in one opinion, "ultimate reckoning of economic debits and credits involves value judgments beyond the limits of judicial competence." These are decisions that should be made by the economic agencies of government and, as we have suggested, with the advice of an independent industrial development board. In other words, Congress must modify antitrust laws to include social cost-benefit criteria in determining the efficiency of mergers. That is a politically thankless but economically necessary task.

There also needs to be a harmonization of antitrust laws among the industrial nations. It does little good to break up American companies, for instance IBM, if overseas competitors are allowed to operate under different rules. Besides dealing with "second-best" efficiency criteria that accept bigness if necessary, antitrust policy must also develop new approaches to curb abuses of corporate power. These include price gouging, price fixing, false advertising, collusion, and heavy cross-subsidization of a subsidiary to drive its competitors out of business. Such abuses are subject now to fines and, for some violations, prison sentences. But for the multibillion dollar conglomerates the fines are ludicrously small, and the prison sentences often reduced or suspended.

The need to make the punishment fit the crime is illustrated in the cowboy economics saga of General Motors and its collusive oil and rubber partners to destroy the rapid electric rail systems of twenty-eight major cities, discussed earlier. The ringleader of the enterprise, the treasurer of GM, was finally convicted of collusion and received a $5,000 fine and a six-month prison sentence, subsequently reduced. Yet the companies made millions from the collusion.

Finally, as a device to curb corporate abuses, antitrust will work more effectively if coupled with proposals for internal corporate reform covered in chapter 8. In several European countries, for instance, government decisions allowing companies to reach optimal plant size have been coupled with laws requiring broader representation on corporate boards of directors. Efficiency and equity decisions and trade-offs can be made just as easily in tandem as in the isolation of adversary proceedings held only in distant Washington.

VI

The problem of demand management in the stagflation decade is not that it has been able to do too little but that it has been asked to do too much. Demand management has been called upon to do all sorts of things that its founder Keynes never anticipated. To make demand management work in the future will require that it be used far more selectively and sparingly and as a complement to and not as a substitute for supply management.

Making demand management work in the future will also require new mechanisms to promote consensus. In an atmosphere of constant confrontation among competing interests, the demand management tools of tax, budget, and credit policies become blunted and increasingly ineffective. In the post-market economy, as more groups press their claims on government to balance market imperfections, consensus has become more elusive and demand management more difficult. Demand management tools can succeed only when the groups in society reach minimum consensus on the trade-offs between their conflicting claims on the social contract.

Achieving the consensus that helps make demand management work is beyond the realm of economic managers. This is the political challenge of the 1980s. How much a country can change its political habits to adjust to new economic realities is an open question. But it is no coincidence that the nations that have been the most willing to experiment with consensus-seeking devices—such as West Germany, Austria, Sweden, and Japan—also happen to be among the most prosperous and the most successful in carrying out demand management policies. They have, however, also been the most successful in adapting coordinated supply economics to demand management tools. Those societies whose economic policies are forged in confrontation—and that includes in varying degrees the United States, Britain, and Italy—are the most prone to the swings of stagflation and have had the least success in developing supply-side policy tools.

Even so, the foreign models offer only limited guidance for revising American demand management policies. Our proposals rest on two basic assumptions. The first is that demand management should be doing less, not more. Neither the fiscal policies espoused by liberals nor the monetary policies advanced by conservatives are capable on their own of fulfilling the multitude of objectives now facing our economy, from creating jobs to controlling inflation to allocating budget dollars. The second is that no economic policy will work effectively unless the competing claims of the old and new interest groups are channeled into the democratic process and a balance is created between conflict and consensus.

A refinement of demand management requires more selective use of all three of its now overworked tools—taxing, spending, and credit. More elements of tax policy, now generally applied across the board to stimulate or moderate demand, need to be reassigned to the supply side in the form of targeted tax cuts to promote job creation and production. Budget policy should be limited to guiding and controlling federal expenditures. As a device to control demand it has become increasingly less effective because budgets only go up, never down. Monetary and credit policy should be freed to counteract inflation and to stabilize the dollar. In its present multipurpose role, monetary policy is sometimes used on the one hand to stimulate domestic demand, even if the lowering of interest rates puts pressure on the dollar.

Demand management is sagging because the pressures of the political business cycle are imposing too many demands for quick fixes. Political and economic managers, in the words of the 1979

Joint Economic Committee report, are "too tempted by short run benefits." Stagflation deepens and confidence is undermined by the reliance on spending and across-the-board tax cuts to lift the economy out of recessions before an election and by the reliance on fiscal austerity and monetary policy to hold down the ensuing post-election bouts of inflation.

More of the same policies are likely to produce more of the same problems. Therefore, we are suggesting a series of refinements to demand management, proposals that clearly fall under the label of *second best*. They are offered as an alternative to the utopian first-best suggestions of liberal fiscalists and conservative monetarists respectively. Up to now these have produced a political standoff and the status quo third-best result of stagflation. We offer second-best suggestions, because without them we run the risk of falling into a fourth-best situation: deeper stagflation and the assumption by government of more centralized powers to break the stalemate.

As Washington once again pursues the quick fix of demand management remedies, there is clearly a growing awareness of the need for supply management. *The Wall Street Journal* columnist Richard F. Janssen pointed to a disintegration of the "postwar consensus of liberals and conservatives," a drift away from demand management and a new awareness that "the cause [of inflation] isn't just 'too much money' but maybe 'too few goods' *as well.*"

Unfortunately, this new appreciation of supply economics is already becoming faddish and overdrawn and is falling into the same trap of across-the-board solutions. The potential is for supply policy overkill, which would only perpetuate the paralysis induced by demand policy overkill. For example, Congressman Jack Kemp views supply policy as a means for dealing with "unnecessary overregulation and excessively high tax rates." To Treasury Secretary Miller, supply economics means accelerated depreciation for business. Even many liberals and moderates, according to columnist Janssen, seek a new emphasis on "faster business write-offs to spur more factory construction and removal of many semi-paralyzing rules."

This simplistic view of supply management offers an intellectually acceptable way for big business to raid the treasury and to break the back of regulators. And it has already begun to create a backlash. To some consumer, labor, and environmental groups, supply economics looks like old-fashioned conservative economics in fancy new clothes. Yet both the support *and* opposition to this kind of supply economics are misplaced.

The problem with this all-or-nothing approach to supply economics is that it rests on the same faulty premise as currently hobbles demand management—the presumed existence of a competitive marketplace. If it is impossible to adjust demand adequately, the voguish wisdom goes, then try to adjust supply policies. Then the laws of supply and demand working through competitive marketplaces will restore the nation to noninflationary growth. A supply economics policy based on that rationale will take us along the same route that we suffered under demand management: a decade of stagflation.

The point of a refined demand management policy coupled with a new supply policy is to get away from the all-or-nothing, across-the-board approach to economic problem solving. Supply policy, to work politically and as an economic management tool, will have to take account of important differences among sectors of the economy. Its purpose is to break the logjams, the gluts, and the scarcities. It should be seen as a complement to, not a substitute for, demand management.

The centerpiece of revised demand management policies is the establishment of national growth targets, geared to what the nation can afford in a range of trade-offs between limits on inflation, limits on balance-of-payments deficits, limits on available resources, and limits on the amount of permanent environmental damage we can inflict on the country's health and on its air and water supplies. This principle was accepted in the Humphrey-Hawkins bill. But its establishment of employment targets unrealistic in the present inflation era reduced its credibility after passage to almost zero. Growth targets have to be realistic targets, the product of more consensus than exists now.

Our proposed national industrial development advisory board offers a forum for business and labor and other groups in which to try to achieve at least limited consensus on five-year targets for growth, inflation, productivity, energy use, trade balances, and investment. (The final decisions are up to the President, his economic advisors, and Congress.) However, only when realistic targets are set, with the idea that they will be maintained, will there appear the stability and confidence necessary to lure savings out of their present havens and overcome the shortfalls in capital formation. Now, for example, big money is in hiding partly because of uncertainty over questions of energy and regulation, but also because investors do not know from one day to the next whether an administration is going to go for price and wage controls, a bigger stimulus program, or continued guidelines and budget austerity.

A consensus-achieving mechanism is a vital part of a growth targets policy because that policy must include an incomes policy if it is to be successful in holding down inflation. And an incomes policy, whether of voluntary wage and price guidelines or mandatory controls (or incentive schemes like the late Arthur Okun's "tax-based income policy" [T.I.P.]), will work only when both labor and business agree to it. As long as they refuse to, the outlook is for more of the confusion that has marked every attempt at incomes policy since the 1971 price and wage freeze.

The first response to any suggestion for an incomes policy is that it will not work. Its failure to work in the last decade has been a principal cause of our present political and economic stalemate. But its not having worked in the past does not mean that it cannot work at all.

The success of West Germany and Austria in holding their inflation rates below 3 percent through much of the 1970s is not an accident. Nor is it explained by simplistic views on balanced budgets: their relative deficits average no lower than ours. But what is different are their variety of consensus-seeking arenas in which government, business, and labor can debate and argue over the consequences of various policy proposals. Business and labor are given a chance to look at the government's large-scale national models, to see the likely consequences on prices, profits, and wages stemming from the government's proposed growth targets. Conversely, through the use of the same models, business and labor can project the likely consequences of pressing their ultimate wishes and demands. Although it is not legally binding, this arrangement has the force of what Walter Heller calls a "concerted action that strikes a bargain reached between business, labor, and government." This consensus has occasionally broken down.

Some critics incorrectly say, on the other hand, that its general success is primarily the result of servile labor unions. Yet the objective of the consensus is not a complete harmony of interests, which is neither likely nor desirable, but greater understanding and enlarged areas of agreement. The Nobel Laureate Wassily Leontief offered this appraisal of the economic success of West Germany and Austria:

> While an effective combination of fiscal and monetary policies is indispensable for effective management of a modern economy, their success is predicated not only on tacit mutual understanding, but institutionalized day by day cooperation between business and labor.

Our experience with incomes policy, as well as Britain's, has not been a happy one, and this is one reason why almost all politicians now oppose it. And, of course, we did not suffer the traumatic kind of inflation that Germany had in the 1920s. Those memories and the ghastly consequences are still a major force behind the anti-inflation policy consensus in government and the private sector. Even so, vast majorities of those responding to every public opinion poll in this country say they favor controls. Of course, responses to polls are hypothetical answers to hypothetical questions. The respondents tend to assume there will be a degree of fairness in the reality of controls which often becomes a personal unfairness against them. Achieving consensus on an incomes policy largely comes down to creating mechanisms that split the sacrifices and create the reality as well as the impression that the limits are equitably imposed on prices as well as wages.

Even in wartime conditions, in World War II and the Korean conflict, wage and price controls drew criticism for being cumbersome and unfair. Efforts at peacetime controls have done little but create controversy. The principal one is labor's somewhat valid contention that it is easier to control wages in relatively few union contracts than to control the prices of millions of items in millions of transactions. "Jawboning" worked in the Kennedy and early Johnson administrations, a period of high consensus, high productivity, cheap resources, and economic expansion; but it collapsed in the first heat of Vietnam War inflation. The surprise Nixon wage and price freeze of 1971 achieved immediate success, partly through its shock value. But gradually it was undermined, largely from within, and it was abandoned so abruptly in 1973 that prices went through the roof. As Jack Duvall, a price controller in the Nixon Administration, wrote, even controls were not absent from that Administration's pattern of corruption:

> The disaster of wage and price controls in the Nixon regime was not intrinsic to the concept of controls; it was the product in large measure of the abuse of privilege and the disuse of integrity that were all too prevalent in that administration.

The economist Robert Nathan made a different point, saying that putting Nixon's free-market dogmatists in charge of an incomes policy was like putting a madam in charge of a convent.

Another major problem with controls, compared with voluntary guidelines, is that they take a large staff to administer effectively. With large bureaucracies, and a hefty dose of patriotism, controls worked reasonably fairly and effectively in World War II. The global economy is now far more complex and correspondingly more difficult to administer, especially in peacetime. Indeed a precondition to any form of incomes policy, be it controls or incentive schemes, is the achievement of a consensus-building process. Should mandatory controls have to be imposed in an inflationary emergency, they ought to be implemented with standby machinery designed in advance by labor and business with government. For only then would they enjoy the credibility needed to assure political acceptance.

The 1971–73 experience with controls has made them anathema to politicians, labor, and business. Yet, even so, the other tools of demand management quite likely will not work in the absence of an incomes policy. This view is held not just by John Kenneth Galbraith and other liberals but by monetarists and post-Keynesians as well.

Philip Cagan, a monetarist, told the Joint Economic Committee in 1979:

> What disturbs me is that I doubt whether [a policy of monetary restraint on aggregate demand] can be carried through unless there is a clear political consensus behind

> it which makes it credible that the policy will be maintained until inflation is subdued. . . . I do not yet see such a consensus.

Post-Keynesian economist Alfred Eichner offered this prescription for consensus:

> There must be some means of arranging for a dialogue to take place among the various private interest groups which have to lend their support to an incomes policy, together with key public officials. . . . These choices require that a bargain be struck at the top among all the affected interest groups, with that bargain then ratified, as part of a "social contract" through the subsequent actions of public officials.

Thereafter, the principles of targeting could be applied to aspects of demand management, including tax, credit, and budget policy. Further, beyond targeting for national growth, we will have to establish goals for key sectors in industry—basic industries, such as steel, which have important multiplier effects throughout the economy, and specific labor-intensive industries, such as textiles and electrical appliances, which are under assault by imports and require structural adjustment. With a combination of national and industrial targets thus established, Congress and the President could then create tax and budget policies and the Federal Reserve monetary policies that would themselves pursue targets and not merely aggregate goals as they do now.

Tax policy has been used since 1963 to provide across-the-board aggregate demand stimulus or contraction to the economy. Much of this leverage must be removed from demand objectives and linked to supply goals by "targeting" tax policies that match different taxes with the different problems of various sectors. Targeting, however, is compatible with achieving variable levels of aggregate tax revenues.

To get maximum employment gains per dollars of tax incentive, policy should be targeted to provide the most suitable forms of breaks and incentives to smaller businesses, which create more new jobs than big business. Investment in smaller companies should be given higher capital gains reductions, and the present progressive but narrow graduation of corporate income taxes should be expanded. Accelerated depreciation allowances and investment tax credits, now offered across the board, should similarly be targeted to conglomerate businesses, but only to those investing in new plant and machinery, not to those acquiring this equipment through mergers and acquisitions, which do not expand supply capacity. What tax allowances are granted for mergers should be permitted only when a clear case can be made that they will improve productivity. In short, productive investments of corporations should be induced by carrots with none or very few offered for acquisitions.

A similar targeting concept could be applied to foreign tax credits for multinationals, except for the energy conglomerates, where such credits should be eliminated. Political consensus to eliminate all foreign tax credits for nonenergy multinationals may be unachievable and, in certain cases, economically undesirable, if our industrial partners insist on maintaining theirs. Nevertheless, the 1980s is clearly the decade for refurbishing America's plants, technologies, and machinery, to make them competitive with others. The carrot here is a tax incentive for domestic plant- and equipment-building which is clearly more generous than that for foreign activities. This is not tax isolationism. A global view requires global targeting as well.

There remains the question of targeting to take account of structural adjustment. This will be difficult, for there are limits to the degree of detail that can be written into general tax legislation. The difficulty will be all the greater if there are no mechanisms like the national industrial development bank and the advisory board to guide policy and investments. But assuming congressional innovativeness to experiment with such mechanisms, what then could be done? An obvious and relatively simple tax tool is to afford extra and temporary tax benefits to industries with special structural adjustment problems and to those experiencing global gluts. This tool, however, should be used only if we first seek to reduce protectionist levels currently worsening the stagflation syndrome.*

* The dispute over creating a new trade agency in the Federal Government illustrates the problems of balancing the overlapping and conflicting demands of adjustment and protectionism. The agencies directly involved, the Special Trade Representative, the Treasury and Commerce departments, were viewed by labor

When politicians ignore targeting and opt for the quick demand fix to stop rising unemployment, there is an unfortunate and unnecessary consequence. Across-the-board income tax reductions put dollars in the hands of consumers and stimulate demand. But in the stagflation decade, to recall chapter 2, investment has failed to expand supply sufficiently to meet rising demand. Investor uncertainty about more inflation is confirmed as administered prices and wages rise in the conglomerate and unionized sectors. These set precedents for less-concentrated sectors, including the need to raise legal minimum wages. The insufficient investment then thwarts expansion and other sectors of shortages adding to the inflationary fires. The vicious circle of the quick fix stimulation creates a tremendous cost: it worsens the fundamental causes of inflation. Linking targeting to demand management would accomplish at least an equal amount of economic stimulation but would also hold out the prospect of attacking some of inflation's fundamental causes. "Fine-tuned" incentives respectively aimed at small and big investors might have a chance at overcoming their crisis in confidence that blocks capital formation.

Beyond tax targeting, there remain the problems of controlling expenditures and refining budget tools, and this part of demand management will be even more difficult. It is quite clear that at present the only pressure on budgets is upward. Our various proposals for "bottom up," grass roots reform to replace regulation and our proposals for self-sustaining development programs are aimed at holding down budgetary outlays. The self-financing experiments, if they prove successful in energy and industrial development, could be expanded to water resource management and railroads and urban mass transit, all programs now consuming ever larger budget outlays.

As budget and tax policy has increasingly failed to combat stagflation, and in some ways has contributed to it, there has been a tendency to rely more on monetary policy, with the result of

---

and protection-seeking industries as too free trade and too aligned with big business. The Tariff Commission was distrusted by free trade advocates. Bureaucratic rivalries proliferate. New and more representative advisory boards at the existing agencies and perhaps a subunit of a national industrial development advisory board need to be created to come up with recommendations for tax targeting for structural adjustment.

either too much credit or too little. With more effective and supply-oriented tax and budget programs, monetary policy could and should be allowed to resume its classical role as a device for combatting inflation and short-run bouts of dollar instability. The pure monetarist hope of pegging monetary growth to the growth of real output in the economy may never be achievable, but there are steps that can move monetary policy in this direction and in a politically acceptable way.

But such steps must be preceded by certain reforms. First, as we have already suggested in chapters 2 and 3, the Federal Reserve and other central banks need to enact reserve requirements and reporting regulations governing the now uncontrolled branch activities of U.S. banks operating in Eurocurrency markets. As Yale economist Robert Triffin noted in a *Foreign Affairs* article, "the explosion of private banks' foreign lending . . . can hardly be explained other than as an attempt to evade domestic taxes or regulation." Triffin, like others, has called for a coordinated, international effort to bring this market under control. Until such controls are in place, the Federal Reserve will be trying to manage monetary policy while billions of dollars float between countries in complete disregard of any nation's monetary and credit policies to combat inflation.

A second prerequisite to sound monetary reform is the stimulation of savings. In an era of continuing inflation, only a deep recession can stop the middle class from letting its level of savings hit record lows. The Gray Panthers, a lobby for the elderly, wore yellow buttons to a congressional hearing in the summer of 1979 that read: "Savings May Be Hazardous to Your Health," reflecting the fact that it cost more to save than to buy on credit. This undermining of the savings ethic, which has its basis in the Bible as well as economic convention, was summed up in an article in the popular magazine *Money*. According to *Money,* a couple was better off buying a stereo with a credit card than saving the $300 and buying it a year later. In fact, between several price increases and tax deductions for interest payments, "they'll have saved $15," noted the editors, "and they can disco all year in front of those big speakers."

Savings became a bad investment in the 1970s because the interest on savings accounts came nowhere close to matching inflation rates. As a way to encourage middle-class savers, Congress, Treasury, and the Fed are offering marginal tax incentives and higher-yield savings instruments, such as certificates of deposit, at lower denominations than the current $10,000. An even more direct approach would be to permit banks and thrift institutions to index savings-account interest rates to the rate of inflation. Government officials fear any expansion of indexing as a step toward Third World economic practices. Yet the indexing of savings accounts would offer the middle class what the rich now enjoy through their accountants' and attorneys' use of other financial devices. Had these instruments not been available to the rich and sophisticated savers, the price of gold would have gone much higher—and fixed investment much lower—than it did.

Indexing savings-account interest is an example of monetary policy targeting: directing income away from consumer demand as the economy overheats. But it uses a carrot, rather than an austerity stick, to fulfill credit and monetary policy objectives. It gives monetary managers flexibility, allowing them to avoid last-ditch, across-the-board credit bludgeons that can send a stagflation economy into a tailspin, as in 1980.

At the same time, this targeting tool eliminates the sort of overexpansion in the housing and domestic automotive industries that makes them the chief scapegoats of current policy approaches. As excess buying occurs, prospective buyers become more leery, since they pay a double penalty—extra-high credit costs and extra-high interest income they would forgo by not saving.

Third and finally, a stronger commitment to national development banking, both domestically and internationally, would offer hope of getting the Fed out of the business of tinkering with interest rates solely in order to draw hidden capital into productive investment. An emphasis on development banking would stimulate the Fed's proper role as a "credit mobilizer" while leaving the Fed free to pursue long-range monetary policies.

It took from the onset of the Depression until 1946 for Congress and the Executive to recognize and enshrine into policy the basic tenets of demand management. It took another twenty years, until the late 1960s, for the glitter of demand management policies in a period of great global growth to dim. The ensuing decade of stagflation subsequently showed the limitations of both conservative and liberal versions of the conventional wisdom of demand management.

In confronting a global economic revolution and the dynamics of a post-market economy, we will still need to manage aggregate demand. But the overriding focus of demand management will be on short-run corrections to fight inflation; such management will rely largely on revised monetary and credit tools. The lesson of the stagflation decade is that we can no longer afford the economic simplicity and political temptations that, under the rationale of "managing" demand, have made tax and budget policies into something that Keynes, their pioneer, never intended.

REFERENCE AND EXPLANATORY NOTES

Chapter 1: Global Revolution

7 Postwar global transformation and its turning point, first developed and statistically identified in Ronald E. Müller, "Global Corporations and Structural Transformation: The Need for Social Planning," a paper prepared for the panel on "Alternative Perspectives on Planning and Competition," Allied Social Sciences annual meetings, Dec. 21, 1974, San Francisco, and published in *Journal of Economic Issues,* June 1975.

9 Quotation by German general found in Barbara Tuchman, *The Guns of August,* New York: Macmillan, 1962, p. 335.

9 Financial, industrial, and trade statistics marking the start of the turning point between 1965 and 1968 are in Richard J. Barnet and Ronald E. Müller, *Global Reach: The Power of the Multinational Corporations,* New York: Simon & Schuster, 1974, pp. 233–34, 270, 432–33, 449.

9 Transformation thesis: a most recent statement is given in Ronald E. Müller, "National Economic Growth and Stabilization Policy in the Age of Multinational Corporations: The Challenge of Our Post-Market Economy," commissioned and published by the Joint Economic Committee of the U.S. Congress in vol. 12, *Economic Growth in the International Context,* of the series *U.S. Economic Growth from 1976 to 1986: Prospects, Problems and Patterns,* Washington, D.C.: GPO, May 23, 1977, pp. 35–77.

0 Structural "transformation," or, alternatively, "revolution," conceptually draws from the historical work of Joseph Schumpeter and Alexander Gerschenkron. For a similar view of the postwar transformation, see Celso Furtado, "Post-National Capitalism," in the LARU studies (Latin American Research Unit), monograph, *The Internationalization of Capital,* Ontario, vol. 2, no. 1, Oct. 1977, pp. 1–25. For Gerschenkron see his *Economic Backwardness in Historical Perspective: A Book of Essays,* Cambridge, Mass.: Harvard University Press, 1962. For laws of motion and the similarity to Marx, see Joseph Schumpeter, *Capitalism, Socialism and Democracy,* New York: Harper, 1942.

p. 21 "Post-market" and the concept of a post-market global economy was first developed in Ronald E. Müller, "National Instability and Global Corporations: Must They Grow Together?," *Business and Society Review,* fall/winter, Nov. 1974.

p. 22 During the turning point and critical juncture of transformation, a significant cause of U.S. and global economic instability comes from the policy lag in government and in the intellectual lag in revising theoretical and operational forecasting models on which policy depends. This is a major hypothesis shaping the framework of this book. A detailed analysis is in (coauthored with David H. Moore) *Stagflation in the OECD Nations: Global and Domestic Causes and National Policy Alternatives,* monograph prepared for the OECD Development Centre, Paris: July 20, 1978; and in Müller, "National Economic Growth . . . ," *op. cit.*

p. 22 Survey of futurists taken from *Are You Ready for the 80s,* San Francisco: Foundation for National Progress, 1980.

p. 22 Recessions of 1970 and 1974–75, and the U.S. precedent of simultaneous inflation, see Arthur M. Okun, "An Efficient Strategy to Combat Inflation," *The Brookings Bulletin,* vol. 16, no. 4, spring 1979, pp. 1–2.

p. 23 Financial and industrial concentration in the U.S. private sector, statistical sources and methods given in Müller, "National Economic Growth . . . ," *op. cit.;* and in Barnet and Müller, *op. cit.,* text and reference note pages, ch. 9, 10.

p. 23 Circular or cumulative concentration process for corporations and banks whereby domestic concentration spurs global expansion, in turn increasing domestic concentration, is verified for industrial sectors by C. Fred Bergsten, Thomas Horst, and Theodore H. Moran, *American Multinationals and American Interests,* Washington, D.C.: The Brookings Institution, 1978, ch. 7.

p. 23 For higher estimates of the extent of concentration of international trade and finance in the world economy, see Charles Albert Michalet, *Les Firmes Multinationales et la Nouvelle Division Internationale du Travail,* Geneva: International Labour Office, 1975.

p. 23 For multinational banks, the concentration hypothesis and findings are based on Frank Mastrapasqua, "U.S. Bank Expansion via Foreign Branching: Monetary Policy Implications," *The Bulletin* of the New York University Graduate School of Business and Administration, Institute of Finance, nos. 87, 88, Jan. 1973; and George Budzeika, "Lending to Business by New York City Banks," *The Bulletin,* nos. 76, 77, Sept. 1971.

p. 24 Size of Eurocurrency pool was over $1.1 trillion in 1979 and will grow to $1.5 trillion in 1980 as estimated by the Chase Manhattan Bank, N.A., New York. "Chase International Finance," Feb. 4, 1980.

24 Peter F. Drucker on pension fund data, from his *The Unseen Revolution: How Pension Fund Socialism Came to America,* New York: Harper & Row, 1976.

24 On "pension-fund power" see Jeffrey Kaye, "Union Map Investment Guidelines," Washington *Post,* Mar. 9, 1980, p. G-1, particularly on the impact of Jeremy Rifkin and Randy Barber, *The North Will Rise Again,* 1978.

24 Kenneth E. Boulding, *The Economy of Love and Fear: A Preface to Grants Economics,* Belmont, Cal.: Wadsworth Publishing Co., 1973.

25 State-owned and state-controlled enterprises, data for, from *Economist,* "The State in the Market," Dec. 30, 1978, pp. 37–58; and Hugh D. Menzies, "U.S. Companies in Unequal Combat," *Fortune,* Apr. 9, 1979, pp. 102–10.

25 Stephen Hymer, "The Multinational Corporation and the Law of Uneven Development," Jagdish Bhagwati, ed., *Economics and World Order: From the 1970's to the 1990's,* London: Macmillan, 1972, pp. 113–40.

26 "Our old rules of thumb no longer work," statement of Lyle Gramley, former member, Council of Economic Advisers, quoted in Juan Cameron, "I Don't Trust Any Economist Today," *Fortune,* Sept. 11, 1978.

26 Arthur Burns quoted from his commencement address to Albion College, Mich., Dec. 20, 1975.

26 Michael Blumenthal's remarks quoted in Cameron, *op. cit.*

27 "Revolution of rising entitlements," from Daniel Bell, "The Future World Disorder," *Foreign Policy,* no. 27, summer 1977; see also Bell's *The Cultural Contradictions of Capitalism,* New York: Basic Books, 1976.

27 Robert Lekachman observed that the concept of "entitlements" can be attributed to Daniel Yankelovich. See also Daniel Bell, *The Coming of Post-Industrial Society: A Venture in Social Forecasting,* New York: Basic Books, 1973.

28 "Politics not catching up with economic . . ." from Joseph Kraft, Washington *Post,* Mar. 23, 1978.

28 Nathan Glazer quoted in Washington *Post,* May 20, 1979, p. B1.

28 "Practical men . . . ," from John Maynard Keynes, *The General Theory of Employment, Interest and Money,* London: Macmillan, 1936, p. 383.

29 For an analytical breakdown of the similarities and differences between monetarists and fiscalists demand management theory, as well as a fundamental critique, see Helmut Arndt, *Irrwege der Politischen Oekonomie,* Munich: Beck Verlag, 1979.

29 On monetarists and fiscalists and their sharing of the Keynesian vision of aggregate demand management policies in a market economy: although they hold certain theoretical differences, these are overshadowed by what they agree on, and by the fact that when making or advising on

policy decisions they both rely on demand management policies. It was in this sense that Milton Friedman, many years ago, noted that to one degree or another, "we are all Keynesians now." The monetarist and fiscalist debate is about two different sets of demand management policies. It is not about the need for a different policy paradigm. The basis of their two different versions of demand management policy are: the monetarists contend that the demand for money is relatively interest-inelastic, while fiscalists believe it interest-elastic. In addition, monetarists view investment demand as relatively interest-elastic, whereas fiscalists believe it inelastic. From these differences flow their well-known preferences in the actual use of demand management policy. Fiscalists believe that fiscal stimulus is more effective than monetary policy, while monetarists hold the opposite. But whatever particular policy lever they prefer, both sides employ an "across-the-board" use of policy tools. This stems from what they theoretically have in common. These commonalities include 1) a comparative static equilibrium framework; 2) a high level of aggregation and homogeneity across different markets; 3) a belief in traditional four-market aggregation (product market, money market, bond market, and labor market); 4) a reluctance to incorporate administered pricing in their tools and models; and finally, 5) an admission of the uniqueness of the labor market from all others in the economy. For details, see Robin Hahnel and Ronald Müller, "Development Economics in Relation to Conventional and Non-conventional Economic Theory," app. B, in Müller and Moore, *op. cit.*

p. 29 Myron Sharpe quote taken from James P. Gannon, "The Idea Shortage," *The Wall Street Journal,* Apr. 9, 1975, p. 1.

p. 29 Walt W. Rostow quote taken from an interview with him by Leonard Silk, *The New York Times,* May 21, 1978, p. F1, in conjunction with Rostow's two recent books, *The World Economy: History and Prospects,* Austin: University of Texas Press, 1978; and *Getting from Here to There,* New York: McGraw-Hill, 1978.

p. 29 Peter Drucker quote about "the impact of societal transformation . . . ," taken from his "Aftermath of a Go-Go Decade," *The Wall Street Journal,* Mar. 25, 1975, p. 18.

p. 30 Henry Kissinger on "the political evolution . . . ," taken from his speech to the Ministerial Council of the Organization for Economic Cooperation and Development (OECD), May 28, 1975, as excerpted in *The New York Times,* June 8, 1975.

p. 30 Adlai Stevenson on "a fundamental shift in the world economic and political order," address delivered to Chicago Bar Association, June 26, 1975.

p. 31 Figures on declining U.S. share of world economy from R. W. Johnson, "Face It, America, Your Era Is Over," Washington *Post,* May 8, 1980, p. D-4.

31 Frank Church on end of "the American Era," quoted from his address to Brigham Young University, Provo, Utah, Dec. 12, 1978.

33 "Cross-over points," from Robert L. Heilbroner, *Beyond Boom and Crash,* New York: Norton, 1978, ch. 9. For the oil "cross-over point" Heilbroner relies on Andrew Flower, "World Oil Production," *Scientific American,* Mar. 1978. Heilbroner defines the oil cross-over as "the day . . . when it is the pull of demand and not the prop of a cartel agreement, that sets the price of oil" (p. 81).

33 Ecological and natural resource constraints, see Wassily Leontief *et al., The Future of the World Economy: A United Nations Study,* New York: U.N., 1977.

33 On strategic metals, see *Business Week,* "Now the Squeeze on Metals," July 2, 1979, pp. 46–51; and *World Development Letter,* Agency for International Development, vol. 2, no. 15, Aug. 13, 1979.

36 On 1980s capital expenditure requirements for infrastructure, see Amitai Etzioni, "Choose We Must," *The Individual and the Future of Organizations,* fall 1979, by the Publishing Services Division, College of Business Administration, Georgia State University.

36 For capital investment figures, see reference notes to ch. 3, below.

36 "Vicious circle," of low productivity growth and low investment is a concept that runs throughout development economics literature. *Cf.* Gunnar Myrdal, particularly his *Rich Lands and Poor,* New York: Harper, 1958, and his *Against the Stream: Critical Essays on Economics,* New York: Pantheon Books, 1973; and Ragner Nurske, *Problems of Capital Formation in Underdeveloped Countries,* New York: Oxford University Press, 1967.

36 A "global cash pool" vs. investor reluctance for new productive investments is statistically derived and technically developed in David H. Moore and Ronald E. Müller, *Estimating the Effect of a Global Stimulation Program on U.S. Export Sales, Employment and Income* (Phase I), report of Analytic Sciences Corp. for the U.S. Department of Labor, Washington, D.C., June 1979. The term *cash pool* is simplified here for purposes of a wider reading audience. Technically, it refers to liquid and near-liquid assets. On the debate whether medium-term assets, in Euromarkets, for example, through Bank intermediation lead to productive investment—which we believe a mute point—see chapter 6 and its reference notes. In short, our basic premise is that globally there has existed since the mid-1970s a situation of *ex ante* "excess" or "underutilized" savings relative to *ex ante* productive investment.

37 Global Marshall Plan for the Third World: first complete proposal was prepared by Ronald E. Müller for Venezuelan President Carlos Andres Perez in June of 1977. Since then the author and others have developed additional proposals for both industrial nations and other Third World countries. For complete reference notes, see ch. 6. The first U.S. recorded public mention of taking a Marshall Plan approach to the Third World was made by Richard M. Brennan, director of International Affairs of Union Carbide Corp., to the Conference Board, New York, Jan. 19, 1977.

p. 42 "Latin Americanization of the United States," first fully developed in Ronald E. Müller, "Global Corporations . . . ," *op. cit.;* and in Barnet and Müller, *op. cit.*, ch. 9.

p. 43 Development economics concepts of vicious circles, structural bottlenecks, and Myrdal's "cumulative causation" are similar to those of two other nonconventional schools of thought critical of mainstream monetarist and fiscalist macro-economic models. These include the "neo-Keynesians" such as Axel Leijonhufvud, *On Keynesian Economics and the Economics of Keynes,* New York: Oxford University Press, 1968; R. W. Clower, "A Reconsideration of the Micro Foundations of Monetary Theory," *Western Economic Journal,* 1967; and the so-called "neo-Ricardian School," represented by such writers as Joan Robinson and Pierre Straffa (see his *The Production of Commodities by Means of Commodities,* London: CUP). For a representative illustration of development economics used as policy paradigm for industrialized nations, *cf.* Marcelo Diamond, "Towards a Change in the Economics Paradigm Through the Experiences of Developing Countries," Center for Latin American Development Studies, Boston University, *Discussion Paper Series,* no. 24, Feb. 1977. This and other work is summarized in Hahnel and Müller, *op. cit.*

p. 44 Need for supply-side policy emphasis from Senator Lloyd Bentsen, "Chairman's Introduction, *The 1979 Joint Economic Report,* Joint Economic Committee of the U.S. Congress, Washington, D.C.: GPO, Mar. 15, 1979, p. 4.

p. 44 Robert Nathan quoted from Hobart Rowan, "Slowdown to Growth," Washington *Post,* June 7, 1979, p. A17.

Chapter 2: The Politics and Economics of Stagflation

p. 48 Figures on OECD unemployment are taken from *Outlook*, Paris: OECD, Dec. 1978 and Dec. 1979; OECD inflation, *ibid*; GNP data from the economic report of the President, Washington, D.C.: GPO, 1978 and 1979.

p. 49 The contribution of OPEC oil price hikes to increasing inflation are from Lawrence Klein's Wharton modeling project, which was the highest estimate at roughly one-third (telephone interview with Prof. Girard Adams at Wharton on July 23, 1979). Wharton found that an annual inflation rate of 3 percent was directly and indirectly attributable to OPEC price hikes between 1973 and 1979. For 1970–78, Data

Resources, Inc., estimated one percent (interview with William Cunningham of DRI) was attributable to oil price increases, which affects the U.S. "core rate" of 5.4 percent. Dr. H. A. Merklein puts the OPEC cumulative effect at no more than 0.53 percent (*World Oil,* May 1979, pp. 67–71) for the period of 1973 to the end of 1979. The effect on increasing the unemployment rate, he concludes, "is, for all practical purposes, unnoticeable."

50 The historical distillation of comparative transformations and growth spurts in England, France, and Germany is developed from Alexander Gerschenkron's *Economic Backwardness in Historical Perspective: A Book of Essays,* Cambridge, Mass.: Harvard University Press, 1962. For the U.S. see Ronald E. Müller, "Global Corporations and Structural Transformation: The Need for Social Planning," *Journal of Economic Issues,* June 1975.

51 Charles Kindleberger, *The World in Depression, 1929–1939,* Berkeley and Los Angeles: University of California Press, 1973, p. 21.

n. Roosevelt and his shuffling is from Robert Lekachman, *The Age of Keynes,* New York: Random House, 1973, pp. 114, 124. See also Arthur Schlesinger, *The Age of Roosevelt,* vol. 2, "The Coming of the New Deal," Boston: Houghton Mifflin, 1956.

53 On concentrated power and the market price system, see Walter Adams, *The Economics of Monopoly,* 4th ed., Englewood Cliffs, N.J.: Prentice-Hall, 1974.

55 Pension fund obligations on the federal level, from Peter F. Drucker, *The Unseen Revolution,* New York: Harper & Row, 1976.

56 President Carter on special interest budget pressures, from the Washington *Post,* Feb. 24, 1979, p. A20.

57 Edward R. Tufte, *Political Control of the Economy,* Princeton, N.J.: Princeton University Press, 1968, pp. 153–54. All quotes and statistics concerning the political business-cycle in the Johnson and Nixon years are taken from this source. It is the first work to synthesize what is an all-too-meager area of research, and first to establish a quantitative basis for developing political variables as part of macro-economic analysis.

58 Richard M. Nixon, *Six Crises,* Garden City, N.Y.: Doubleday, 1962, p. 309.

58 Edward R. Tufte, *op. cit.,* p. 24.

58 *Ibid.,* ch. 2.

59 *Ibid.,* pp. 67–69.

59 Role of political business cycles in the 1973–74 downturn in OECD countries, from "Towards Full Employment and Price Stability," a report to the OECD by a group of independent experts directed by Paul McCracken, OECD, France, June 1977, p. 51.

60 Edward R. Tufte, *op. cit.,* p. 69.

p. 60 Statistics on shares of U.S. GNP and trade of small and big businesses from Ronald E. Müller, "National Economic Growth and Stabilization Policy in the Age of Multinational Corporations: The Challenge of Our Post-Market Economy," commissioned and published by the Joint Economic Committee of the U.S. Congress in vol. 12, *Economic Growth in the International Context,* of the series *U.S. Economic Growth from 1976 to 1986: Prospects, Problems and Patterns,* Washington, D.C.: GPO, May 23, 1977, pp. 35–79. See also Richard J. Barnet and Ronald E. Müller, *Global Reach: The Power of the Multinational Corporations,* New York: Simon & Schuster, 1974, ch. 9. Also see the Report of the Subcommittee on Antitrust, Consumers and Employment of the Committee on Small Business, U.S. House of Representatives, *The Future of Small Business in America,* Washington, D.C.: GPO, 1978.

p. 60 A. A. Berle, Jr., and Gardner C. Means, *The Modern Corporation and Private Property,* New York: Commerce Clearing House, 1932.

p. 60 For George Stigler's views on the price behavior of firms, see his *Pricing in the American Economy,* New York: Norton, 1970.

p. 60 J. Fred Weston's findings and results on competition among multinationals can be found in Carl Madden, ed., *The Multinational Corporation,* New York: National Chamber Foundation, 1976.

p. 61 Alfred S. Eichner, *The Megacorp and Oligopoly,* Cambridge, Mass.: Cambridge University Press, 1976, p. 38.

p. 62 Statistics on United States auto company pricing in the 1973–74 recession from David L. Cowles, "The Pricing Behavior of U.S. Auto Firms in the 1970's," graduate research paper, The American University, Department of Economics, Washington, D.C., fall 1976. Also see Howard Wachtel and Peter D. Adelsheim, "The Inflationary Impact of Unemployment: Price Markup During Post-War Recession," Joint Economic Committee, Washington, D.C.: GPO, Nov. 1976, pp. 21–23, 31.

p. 62 Raymond Vernon on worldwide pricing of tractors, quoted from Raymond Vernon, *Storm over the Multinationals,* Cambridge, Mass.: Harvard University Press, 1977, p. 82.

p. 63 Kenneth Boulding, *The Economy of Love and Fear,* Belmont, Cal.: Wadsworth Publishing Co., 1973, p. 47.

p. 63 Wachtel and Adelsheim, *op. cit.* For a review of other studies and an alternative theory of oligopoly-conglomerate pricing, see Müller, "National Economic Growth . . . ," *op. cit.,* pp. 70–74.

p. 63 Corwin Edwards and the example of Clorox, quoted from Ralph Nader and Mark Green, *The New York Times,* Apr. 17, 1979, p. A19; Miller Brewing Co. example from *Economist,* Jan. 6, 1979, p. 44.

p. 63 Figures on the spread of administered pricing in U.S. economy derived from Wachtel and Adelsheim, *op. cit.*

p. 64 Low job-creation rate of big corporations from study by David L. Birch for the Securities and Exchange Commission, *The SEC and Small Business,* Washington, D.C.: GPO, 1979.

64 The practice of transfer pricing and cross-subsidization by U.S. firms and the method to measure their extent, from Barnet and Müller, *op. cit.,* text and reference notes, ch. 10; and updated in Müller, "National Economic Growth . . . ," *op. cit.*

64 Charles Albert Michalet's estimate that 45 percent of world trade accounted for by interfirm trade, from his *Les Firmes Multinationales et la Nouvelle Division Internationale du Travail,* Geneva: International Labour Office, 1975, p. 32.

67 Fritz Machlup on "The Mystery Story," from "Euro-dollar Creation: A Mystery Story," *Reprints in International Finance,* Princeton University, no. 16, Dec. 1970.

67 The Eurocurrency banking system and "stateless money," quoted from *Business Week,* Apr. 21, 1978, p. 76.

68 Former Federal Reserve Chairman Miller on Eurodollar leakages affecting U.S. monetary policy, from *The Wall Street Journal,* Feb. 5, 1979.

68 Dr. Hans Mast on the Eurodollar market, quoted in Larry Kramer, "The Money Brokers: Global Systems Hyperventilating," Washington *Post,* Apr. 22, 1979, p. G1. Growth in Eurobanking measured by assets and net liabilities taken from *Business Week, op. cit.;* in gross terms this book relies on the estimate of over $1.3 trillion in 1980; see notes to ch. 1.

69 *The Wall Street Journal,* Feb. 5, 1979, p. 7.

69 *Ibid.*

69 "Press down harder" on smaller lenders to affect U.S. monetary policy, quoted from *The Wall Street Journal,* Feb. 5, 1979, p. 7.

69 Concentration of corporate debt of U.S. multinational corporations by U.S. multinational banks, see Barnet and Müller, *op. cit.*

69 George Budzeika, quoted from "Lending to Business by New York City Banks," *The Bulletin,* New York University Graduate School of Business Administration, Institute of Finance, nos. 76–77, Sept. 1971.

70 Guido Carli on role of Eurodollars, quoted from his, "Why Banks Are Unpopular," the Per Jacobson Foundation, Special Monograph, June 12, 1976.

70 *The Wall Street Journal* article on effects of tight monetary policy on small banks, Apr. 4, 1979, p. 1.

71 Commercial paper market estimate from *The Wall Street Journal,* Mar. 6, 1979, p. 41.

71 *Business Week*, Apr. 23, 1979, pp. 82–88.

72 Arthur Burns quoted from Commencement Address, Albion College, Michigan, Dec. 20, 1975.

p. 72 Former Federal Reserve Chairman Miller, quoted from *The Wall Street Journal,* Mar. 6, 1979.

p. 72 "Latin Americanization" of the United States, see Barnet and Müller, *op. cit.,* ch. 9.

p. 72 Robert T. Averitt, *The Dual Economy: The Dynamics of American Industrial Structure,* New York: Norton, 1968.

p. 74 *Business Week,* Jan. 29, 1979, p. 84.

p. 74 Art Pine, quoted from Washington *Post,* Aug. 12, 1979, p. E1.

*p. 74*fn. Robert Lekachman on bankruptcy of economics profession, quoted from Washington *Post* "Book World," July 6, 1976.

p. 75 Michael Rowan, from personal interview with author.

p. 76 Richard J. Levine on Stewart Alsop and economic policy at "The Center," from *The Wall Street Journal,* Apr. 30, 1979, p. 1.

Chapter 3: Vicious Circles

p. 77 Data on capital formation rate from the Department of Commerce, Bureau of Economic Analysis; and from "The 1979 Economic Report of the President," Washington, D.C.: GPO, 1979.

p. 78 OECD Report on global downturn in capital assessment from "The Reporter," Paris: OECD, June 1979.

p. 78 Joint Economic Committee recommendation that 12 percent of gross national product be committed to new fixed investment, from "Report of the Joint Economic Committee on the Economic Report of the President, 1979," Washington, D.C.: GPO, 1979, p. 133.

p. 79 Marshall Loeb, quoted in *Time* magazine editorial, Apr. 2, 1979, pp. 48–49.

p. 79 Declining rate of return on new capital investment for the United States, taken from "The 1979 Economic Report of the President," *op. cit.,* p. 128; for OECD countries, see "Towards Full Employment and Price Stability," a report to the OECD by a group of independent experts directed by Paul McCracken, OECD, France, June 1977, pp. 162–63.

p. 79 President Jimmy Carter, *The New York Times,* Apr. 5, 1979.

p. 80 Federal Trade Commission study on percentage of new investment taken by conglomerate acquisition from Federal Trade Commission, "Economic Report on Corporate Mergers," Washington, D.C.: GPO, 1969.

p. 80 Figures on amount of OPEC petrodollar surplus committed to fixed investments, taken from graduate research paper for the Department of Economics, American University, Washington, D.C., "The Impact of OPEC Financial Surplus on Capital Formation, A Global Assessment," by Roberto Bacquerizo, Ileana Porges and M. H. Pournik, fall 1977. See also *The New York Times,* June 15, 1978, p. D1, and the Washington *Post,* June 5, 1979, p. A2.

Walt W. Rostow, in *Getting from Here to There*, New York: McGraw-Hill, 1978; see ch. 1, 2.

Data on decline in U.S. productivity from "The 1979 Economic Report of the President," *op. cit.*

OECD nations' decline in productivity see the "Economic Outlook," Paris: OECD, Dec. 1978 and Dec. 1979.

Frederick Knickerbocker, *Oligopolistic Reaction and Multinational Enterprise*, Boston: Basic Books, 1973.

Edward F. Renshaw, *The End of Progress*, N. Scituate, Mass.: Duxbury Press, 1976.

Michael Boretsky, "Trends in U.S. Productivity: A Political Economist's Views," *The American Scientist*, Jan.–Feb. 1975, pp. 70–82.

Example of MNC transfer of technology to the Third World in the electronics industry taken from Richard J. Barnet and Ronald E. Müller, *Global Reach: The Power of the Multinational Corporations*, New York: Simon & Schuster, 1974, pp. 304–8.

Louis Sultanoff, *The American Management Association Forum*, Feb. 1979, pp. 29–30.

Evidence of greater research and development results from small vs. big firms, taken from the hearings before the Subcommittee on Antitrust, Consumers and Employment, and Senate Select Subcommittee on Small Business on "Small Business and Innovation," Aug. 10, 1978, Washington, D.C.: GPO, 1978. Statistics compiled by this subcommittee show that small businesses receive less than 3.5 percent of all federal research and development dollars. However, a Commerce Department study in 1966 showed that small businesses accounted for more than half of all scientific and technological developments since the beginning of this century. A similar study concluded that the same trend applied to the period between 1953 and 1973. Other studies presented during these hearings show that between 1953 and 1973 small firms produced about four times as many innovations per research and development dollar as medium-sized firms, and about twenty-four times as many as the largest firms.

Michael Evans and Edward Denison, studies on factors responsible for decline in U.S. productivity, taken from their Joint Economic Committee testimony, June 13, 1978. Copies obtained from committee files.

Robert Kahn, *The American Management Association Review*, Apr. 1979, p. 17.

Business loss due to shoplifting and employee pilferage from U.S. Chamber of Commerce studies supplied by the Economics Bureau of the national office in Washington, D.C., Sept. 1979.

Herbert Stein, on changes in worker attitudes, Washington *Post*, Apr. 5, 1979, p. A7.

p. 86 James O'Toole, *ibid.*

p. 87 Colin Clark, on the rise of service industries, *The Conditions of Economic Progress,* London: Macmillan, 3rd ed., 1957.

p. 87 The rise of the service sector in the U.S. economy and data on service employment, see Daniel Bell, *The Coming of Post-Industrial Society: A Venture in Social Forecasting,* New York: Basic Books, 1973. Pollster Louis Harris quoted from Washington *Post,* Apr. 5, 1979, p. A7.

p. 87 "The 1979 Economic Report of the President," *op. cit.,* p. 68.

p. 89 *Economist,* on the world chemical industry, Apr. 7, 1979, p. 49.

p. 90 Unemployment of shoe workers in Europe and the United States owing to imports from Third World countries, taken from "Europe," no. 2384, Feb. 9, 1978, p. 8, and "Department of Commerce News," Mar. 1, 1978, p. 5.

p. 90 OECD report, "governments will not watch . . . ," from Jacques Gansler, *The Defense Industry,* Cambridge, Mass.: M.I.T. Press; forthcoming.

p. 91 Sir Roy Denman, quoted from *The New York Times,* Apr. 13, 1979, p. D3.

p. 91 Lord Thomas Balogh, with P. Balacs, "Facts and Fancy in International Economic Relations," *World Development,* Mar.–Apr. 1973.

p. 92 Robert Samuelson, "Steel Industry a State Ward," Washington *Post,* Apr. 3, 1979, p. D7.

p. 93 Indicators on rising U.S. export dependence, from Secretary of Agriculture Bob Bergland, quoted in Hobart Rowan, "Tackling the World Trade Problem," Washington *Post,* June 23, 1977.

p. 94 C. Michael Aho, "Will the United States Lose Its Comparative Advantage in Manufacturing?," *Collegiate Forum,* winter 1979, p. 3. Aho reached a similar conclusion in a more recent econometric analysis done with Richard Carney, to be published in *Weltwirtschaftliches Archiv* and entitled "Is the United States Losing Its Comparative Advantage in Manufacturing?: An Empirical Analysis of the Structure of Manufactures Trade, 1964–1976." Aho is the director of the Office of Foreign Economic Research, U.S. Department of Labor, and is responsible for conducting analyses of the impact of trade on U.S. employment and earnings. The estimates on the number of jobs related to exports are taken from his "The Impact of Changes in Manufacturing Trade on Sectoral Employment Patterns—Progress Report" in *The Employment Effects of International Trade,* National Commission on Employment Policy, Washington, D.C., 1979.

p. 95 U.S. export loss due to Foreign Corrupt Practices Act and human rights policies, given to author anonymously from results of an internal government investigation.

p. 97 Robert Triffin, *Foreign Affairs,* winter 1978/79, pp. 269 *et seq.*

p. 97 Report to the Swedish Foreign Ministry and the Swedish International Development Agency (SIDA), "Protocol for the Meeting of Like

Minded Nations on Massive Resource Transfers," Stockholm, Oct. 18, 1978, p. 2.

98 Bank of England official quoted by Hobart Rowan, "World Bank, IMF Strike Note of Anxiety," Washington *Post,* Oct. 6, 1979, p. A4.

98 "The Great Crash of '79," by Karen W. Avenson, *The New York Times,* Oct. 14, 1979, p. F1.

99 Paul Volker quoted from *The New York Times,* Oct. 18, 1979, p. A1.

99 George Will, Washington *Post,* Apr. 1, 1979, p. B7.

01 Senator Edward Kennedy, quoted from Washington *Post,* Nov. 20, 1978, p. A-19.

Chapter 4: Third World Pioneering

06 Jean-Jacques Servan-Schreiber, *The American Challenge,* New York: Avon, 1969.

06 Japanese and European multinationals challenging American corporations; a wealth of literature exists, but see Lawrence Franko, *The European Multinationals: A Renewed Challenge to American and British Big Business,* Stamford, Conn.: Greylock, 1976; William L. Givens and William V. Rapp, "What It Takes to Meet the Japanese Challenge," *Fortune,* June 18, 1979, pp. 104–20; Yoshi Tsurumi, *The Japanese Are Coming: A Multinational Interaction of Firms and Politics,* Cambridge, Mass.: Ballinger, 1976.

06 The increasing bargaining power and less-lopsided relations of Third World host countries over foreign multinationals was first set forth in Richard J. Barnet and Ronald E. Müller, *Global Reach: The Power of the Multinational Corporations,* New York: Simon & Schuster, 1974, in ch. 8, "The Power of the Poor: Prospects for a Post-colonial World." The example of Chile and quotations are from *The New York Times,* Oct. 4, 1979, p. A7. The example of Morocco is taken from Dan Morgan's 6-part series in Washington *Post,* the issue of Mar. 8, 1979, pp. A-1, A-25.

08 John Kenneth Galbraith, quoted in *Money,* New York: Bantam, 1976, p. 368.

12 Interviews with Pérez Alfonso, conducted by author, Caracas, May 1977.

13 Anthony Sampson, *The Seven Sisters,* New York: Viking Press, 1975.

13 Raymond Vernon, *Storm over the Multinationals,* Cambridge, Mass.: Harvard University Press, 1977.

15 Peter P. Gabriel, "Management of Public Interests by the Multinational Corporations," *The Journal of World Trade Law,* vol. 2, no. 1, Jan.–Feb. 1977, p. 28.

16 Data on the rise of Japanese and German foreign bank affiliates taken from statistics compiled by the transnational banking project of the United

Nations Centre on Transnational Corporations, 1978–79; see Robert Devlin, *Transnational Banks and Their Penetration of the External Finance of the Third World: The Experience of Peru, 1965–1976*, New York: United Nations, Dec. 31, 1979; P. A. Wellons, *Borrowing by Developing on the Euro-Currency Market*, Paris: OECD, 1977; P. A. Wellons and Pankaj Ghemawat, *Trans-national Banks from the United States*, New York: UNCTC, Nov., 1978; and Ronald E. Müller and Philip A. Wellons, *The Strategy of Trans-national Banks and Developing Nations*, Report of the United Nations Center on Transnational Corporations, New York, forthcoming 1980.

p. 118 Thomas W. Waelde, "Lifting the Veil from Transnational Mineral Contracts: A Review of Recent Literature," from *Natural Resources Forum*, no. 1, 1977, p. 277.

p. 120 Example of Befiex in Brazil taken from Ronald E. Müller and David H. Moore, *Three Case Studies of Third World Bargaining Power and the Promotion, Control and Structuring of Multinational Corporations: Brazil, Mexico, and Colombia*, New York: United Nations Centre on Transnational Corporations (UNCTC), Jan. 1978.

p. 120 Information on Ford Motor Company in Brazil taken from "Ford's One Billion Dollar Southern Strategy," *World Business Weekly*, Mar. 3, 1980, p. 9.

p. 124 Jack Baranson, *Foreign Policy*, no. 25, winter 1976–77, p. 184.

p. 125 *Ibid.*, p. 184.

p. 125 Mauricio Maria y Compos, from personal interview with author, Nov. 1978.

p. 126 Nathaniel Leff, *The Journal of Economic Literature*, vol. 17, no. 2, June 1979.

p. 126 David A. Heenan and Warren J. Keegan, "The Rise of Third World Multinationals," *Harvard Business Review*, Jan.–Feb. 1979, pp. 101–9.

p. 127 *Ibid.*, p. 105.

p. 127 *Ibid.*, pp. 101–2.

p. 128 Recent MNC overkill, see Dan Morgan, *Merchants of Grain*, New York: Viking, 1979, and 6-part series on rubber multinationals, from Mar. 4, 1979, to Apr. 10, 1979, in Washington *Post*.

p. 129 Baranson, *op. cit.*, p. 185.

p. 129 "European Community Report," Brussels: EEC, no. 453, Oct. 15, 1977.

Chapter 5: Global Schisms

p. 133 Miguel S. Wionczek, from personal conversation with author. See also his *The NIEO: A Diagnosis of the Past Failures and the Prospects for the Future*, report to the meeting on "Progress in the Establishment of a New International Economic Order: Obstacles and Opportunities," Mexico City, Jan. 1979.

3 On the inadequacy of income distribution in Brazil, see literature references in Richard J. Barnet and Ronald E. Müller, *Global Reach: The Power of the Multinational Corporations,* New York: Simon & Schuster, 1974, pp. 149, 181–82; in general, see *World Development Report,* 1978, Washington, D.C.: The World Bank, Aug. 1978.

5 On the imposition of trade restrictions and the spread of protectionism among industrial nations, see Bahram Nowzad, "The Resurgence of Protectionism," *Finance & Development,* Sept. 1978, pp. 14–19; and Bela Balassa, "World Trade and the International Economy: Trends, Prospects and Policies," *World Bank Staff Working Paper No. 282,* May 1978.

5 On the inflation effects of tariffs on Third World imports for the United States, see William R. Cline, Noboru Kawanabe, T. O. M. Kronsjo, and Thomas Williams, "Trade Negotiations in the Tokyo Round," Washington, D.C.: The Brookings Institution, 1978.

5 For a discussion of newly industrializing country textile exports and their effect on the EEC, see the European Parliament, *Working Documents,* Dec. 13, 1977, no. 438–77, pp. 22–23.

6 Example of Taiwan and effect of shoe exports on the EEC, see *European Report,* Brussels: EEC, no. 453, Oct. 15, 1977, p. 5.

6 *The Wall Street Journal* on newly industrializing country exports, Mar. 19, 1979, p. 21.

7 On Export-Import Bank help to Taiwan leading eventually to steel "dumping" charges, see Elizabeth Sullivan, "The Interdependent," monthly publication of the UN Association, New York, vol. 6, no. 3, Mar. 1979, p. 8.

7 "Protectionism masked by growth . . . ," see Commission of the European Communities, "Report on Some Structural Aspects of Growth," COM 78, no. 255, Brussels: Final, June 22, 1978, p. 1.

8 On EEC Multifiber Agreement leading to flooding of U.S. market, see *European Report, op. cit.,* pp. 24–25.

8 V. D. Ooms and Arnold Packer, "The International Economy and the Federal Budget," Senate Budget Committee, Dec. 1976.

9 Third World debt burdens, see Ronald E. Müller, David H. Moore, and Robert B. Cohen, "LDC Debt and U.S. and World Economic Stagnation: Overcoming Contradictions in Global Interdependence," prepared for the Experts' Meeting on Alternative Solutions to the External Debt Problem of the LCDs (Mexico City, Oct. 27–29, 1977); a revised version is published in Miguel S. Wionczek, ed. *LDC External Debt and the World Economy,* Mexico: College of Mexico, 1978, pp. 231–67.

9 On problems of multinational bank lending practices and other issues with the Third World, see Karin Lissakers, in the report, "International Debt, the Banks and U.S. Foreign Policy," U.S. Senate Sub-committee on Foreign Economic Policy, Washington, D.C.: GPO, 1979; Richard

Weinert, "Why the Banks Did It," *Foreign Policy* Spring 1978, pp. 143–48; and *Business Week,* "The Petro-Crash," Nov. 19, 1979, pp. 176 ff. On impacts to Eurobanking arising out of the Iranian asset freeze by the U.S., see, e.g., the various articles in *Euromoney,* January 1980. An excellent overview for the general reader can be found in L. J. Davis, "Bankers Casino: Gambling in the $900 Billion Euromarket," *Harper's,* Feb. 1980.

p. 140 Richard F. Janssen quoted from *The Wall Street Journal,* Oct. 8, 1979, p. 1.

p. 140 On the potential dilemma between Third World debt owed to multinational banks and force-feeding inflation, see "OPEC: The Cartel's Deadly New Sting," *Business Week,* Apr. 9, 1979, pp. 97–98.

p. 141 "From the gold of Peru . . . ," quotation by I. S. Abdulla, "Development Dialogue," a publication of the Dag Hammarskjöld Foundation, New York, Jan. 1979, pp. 12–13.

p. 143 On decline of ODA funds from developed countries, see *World Development Report, op. cit.,* Table 12, pp. 98–99.

p. 143 Manuel Pérez Guerrero on the uncertainties of the NIEO, from interview with author, New York, June 16, 1978.

p. 143 Collapse of the North-South dialogue is given comprehensive treatment by Roger D. Hansen, *Beyond the North-South Stalemate,* New York: McGraw-Hill, 1979 (1980s Project Council on Foreign Relations), esp. ch. 2, 3; quote is from p. 293.

p. 143 UN Association quotation, "frustrating experience for both sides . . . ," from "The Interdependent," *op. cit.,* p. 6.

p. 144 EEC report on "new international division of labor . . . ," from "Report on Some Structural Aspects of Growth," *op. cit.,* p. 1.

p. 144 Accelerating fragmentation internationally is a theme in Geoffrey Barraclough, "Waiting for the New Order," and "The Struggle for the Third World," *New York Review of Books,* Oct. 26 and Nov. 9, 1978. Also see Constantine Vaitsos, "From a Colonial Past to Asymmetrical Interdependences: The Role of Europe in North-South Relations," paper for General Conference of the European Association of Development Research and Training Institutes, Milan, Sept. 1978.

p. 144 On long-term swap agreements with Mexico for oil, in the case of France, see the *Petroleum Intelligence Weekly,* Dec. 11, 18, 1978; Minister Giraud quoted from *ibid.,* Dec. 18, 1978, p. 1; for the case of Japan see *Latin America Economic Report,* vol. VI, no. 42, Oct. 27, 1978, p. 1.

p. 146 *Far Eastern Economic Review,* Feb. 23, 1979; see also issue of Oct. 20, 1978, pp. 56ff., and issue of Feb. 23, 1979, p. 37 *et seq.*

p. 147 Robert McNamara on GNP growth of Third World nations from increased exports, "Address to the Board of Governors," Washington, D.C.: The World Bank, September 25, 1978.

47 Statistics on resource dependencies of OECD nations, from Martin M. McLaughlin and the staff of the Overseas Development Council, *The United States and World Development: Agenda 1979,* New York: Praeger, 1979.

48 ASEAN car manufacturing discussion, from *The ASEAN Business Quarterly,* 3rd Quarter, 1978, pp. 36–41.

48 EEC Report on "Fierce competition," from "Report on Some Structural Aspects of Growth," *op. cit.,* p. 9.

53 Wilhelm Dilthey, *Pattern and Meaning in History,* New York: Harper, 1962.

Chapter 6: Toward a New Order: The Next Frontier

57 Third World statistics, Martin M. McLaughlin and the staff of the Overseas Development Council, *The United States and World Development: Agenda for Action, 1979,* New York: Praeger, 1979.

58 David Hausego, *Financial Times,* Nov. 14, 1978, p. 14.

60 World military lending, Overseas Development Council, *op. cit.*

61 "Simple Keynesianism" refers to a correct criticism made by John P. Lewis in *Development Cooperation* (Paris: OECD, Nov. 1979) that massive transfer policies, including the Marshall Plan and other similar proposals, are "most commonly understood" as "too simplistically Keynesian." The author's proposal agrees and takes into account what Lewis contends is "the core of present growth problems . . . that complex which economists lump together as 'supply-side' issues. . . ." See, in particular, pp. 26–27.

61 Ronald E. Müller and David H. Moore, "A Description and Preliminary Evaluation of Global Stimulation Proposals," in UNIDO, *Industry 2000—New Perspectives: Collected Background Papers,* vol. I, United Nations Industrial Development Organization, I D/CONF. 4/3, Vienna 1980. In these references a detailed argument is made why these funds are underutilized savings and why short- and medium-term Eurocurrency loans are not felt to represent a fixed investment, capital formation financing.

61 Third World Investment Needs, *World Bank Annual Report,* 1978, Washington, D.C., pp. 17–22; and K. Takeuchi, G. E. Thiebach, and J. Hilmy, "Investment Requirements in the Non-Fuel Mineral Sector in the Developing Countries," *Natural Resources Forum,* World Bank, 1977, p. 11.

62 Helmut Schmidt quoted from address to the International Institute for Strategic Studies, London, Oct. 28, 1977, p. 6.

62 Bruno Kreisky from his speech to the Colloquium on the Attitude of Trade

Unions in Developed Countries Toward the New International Order, Vienna, Oct. 23–24, 1978, p. 12.

p. 163 Carlos Andres Pérez, quoted from personal inverview with author, May 1977, Caracas.

p. 164 Michael D. Barnes quoted from *The Congressional Record,* Jan. 15, 1979, pt. 2, p. B55.

p. 164 Detailed presentations of global Marshall Plans (various proposals and options) and the rationale for these plans are described fully in a report prepared for the Swedish International Development Authority by R. Müller and D. Moore, "An Analysis and Evaluation of Current 'Global Stimulation' Proposals in the Context of the Present Juncture of OECD Economies," The Analytic Sciences Corporation, Washington, D.C., Dec. 1978. See also Ronald E. Müller and Everett M. Ehrlich, "Needed: A Global Marshall Plan," Washington *Post,* "Outlook," Jan. 7, 1979. Japanese Minister of Finance quoted in *Financial Times,* Jan. 15, 1980, p. 19.

p. 164 Japanese Marshall Plan described in Masaki Nakajima, "A Proposition for the 'Global Infrastructure Fund,' " Mitsubishi Research Institute, Tokyo, Aug. 1978.

p. 166 "Charitable inclinations," personal interview with author, Dec. 1978.

p. 166 Technical expertise dependency, interview, Jan. 1979, Washington, D.C.

p. 166 Paul Baran, *The Political Economy of Growth,* New York: Monthly Review Press, 1960, p. 12.

p. 166 Development aid figures from "Development Aid: Another Year of Disappointing Results," *The OECD Observer,* Paris, July 1978, p. 19.

p. 166 Malaysian governor to World Bank board quoted from *World Bank Summary Proceedings,* 1978, Washington, D.C., p. 55.

p. 172 William Lane quoted in Washington *Post,* May 6, 1979.

p. 172 Exxon's resistance to the World Bank's energy program is described in the Washington *Post,* May 6, 1979, p. A4.

p. 172 John Blair, *The Control of Oil,* New York: Vintage Books, 1978, p. 40. Quote is from interview with author, Nov. 1977.

p. 173 See "Spirit and techniques of first Marshall Plan," Commonwealth Secretary General proposal for a Third World plan, quoted by Reginald Dale, "Call for New 'Marshall Plan,' " *Financial Times,* June 24, 1979.

p. 173 The absorption problem, the World Bank's view, and expansion of World Bank quotas, from personal interviews conducted in Bangkok, Kenya, and Washington, D.C., Oct. and Nov. 1978, respectively.

p. 174 Bank lending to developing countries, P. Nagy, "The Richer Developing Countries May Be Poor Risks," *Euromoney,* Oct. 1978, p. 145.

p. 174 Debt service ratios from P. Nagy, *op. cit.*

p. 174 Address by David Rockefeller, Feb. 1980.

p. 174 Alan Greenspan as quoted in Robert Solomon, "A Perspective on the

Debt of Developing Countries," *Brookings Papers on Economic Activity,* no. 2, 1977, p. 503.

75 See *Rich and Poor Nations,* the report of the Brandt Commission, 1980.

75 IMF official, quoted from personal interview, Nov. 1978, Washington, D.C.

75 Solon L. Barraclough, "Social Development and the International Development Strategy," Geneva, UNRISD, 1979, p. 7.

75 James Bass, quoted from personal interview, Washington, D.C., June 1979.

75 On Turkey, *The Wall Street Journal.* Apr. 24, 1979, p. 1.

77 On the size of OPEC's cumulative and current surplus, *Financial Times,* June 29, 1979, p. 26.

78 Rand study, Arthur Smithies, "The Economic Potential of the Arab Countries," Santa Monica, Cal.: The Rand Corp., Nov. 1978.

78 Dr. Odeh Aburdene quoted from *Financial Times,* "A Pension Fund for the Oil States," May 2, 1979, p. 1.

78 On the recent UNCTAD meetings, *Financial Times,* May 8, 1979, p. 18.

79 UN Study, see David H. Moore and Ronald E. Müller, "Estimating the Effects of a Global Stimulation Program on U.S. Export Sales," *op. cit.*

79 Treasury Department study on impact of development assistance, Washington *Post,* May 14, 1979.

79 Figures on Mexico and Brazil and OECD statement on U.S. exports and Third World demand from R. Müller and D. Moore, "A Description and Preliminary Evaluation of Proposals for Global Stimulation," prepared by Analytic Sciences Corp. for United Nations Industrial Development Organization, Vienna, Mar. 15, 1979.

80 Detailed study of the impact of global stimulation program on U.S. industry, from D. Moore and R. Müller, *Estimating the Effect of a Global Stimulation Program on U.S. Export Sales,* vol. 2, prepared by Analytic Sciences Corp. for the U.S. Department of Labor, Washington, D.C.: Oct. 1, 1979.

81 Marina v. N. Whitman, quoted from her "Coordination and Management of the International Economy: A Search for Organizing Principles," in W. Fellner, ed., *Contemporary Economic Problems,* Washington, D.C.: American Enterprise Institute, 1977, p. 293.

83 Benjamin Cohen, *Organizing the World's Money,* New York: Basic Books, 1978, p. 54.

84 *Ibid.,* p. 54.

84 For a discussion of the dollar's past and future role in the international system, see also Robert Triffin, "The International Role and Fate of the Dollar," *Foreign Affairs,* winter 1978/79, pp. 268–69.

84 Hobart Rowan on relative valuation of the dollar from Washington *Post,* May 20, 1979, p. G6.

p. 184 Frank Weil's congressional testimony on U.S. trade deficit quoted from Washington *Post,* June 2, 1979.

p. 185 *Euromoney* on the decline of the dollar, editorial, Nov. 1978, p. 5.

p. 185 IMF survey of central banks and A.W. Clausen's quote are from "How Central Banks Are Ditching the Dollar," *Euromoney,* Oct. 1978, p. 31.

p. 186 Sir Richard King and Eduardo Mayobre, quoted from personal interviews, Washington, D.C., Sept. 1978 and Sept. 1977, respectively.

p. 188 Charles Kindleberger quoted from his *The World in Depression, 1929–39,* Berkeley: University of California Press, 1973, p. 12.

p. 189 Constantine Vaitsos, from his "From a Colonial Past to Asymmetrical Interdependences: The Role of Europe in North-South Relations," paper presented to the General Conference of the European Association of Development Research and Training Institutes, Milan, Sept. 1978.

p. 190 Protectionism quote of experts group, from *The European Economic Community and Changes in the International Division of Labor* (report of an expert group on the reciprocal implications of the internal and external policies of the Community), Commission of the European Communities, Directorate-General for Development, Brussels, Jan. 1979, p. 90.

p. 190 Robert McNamara quote on protectionism against developing countries, address to UNCTAD meetings, Manila, May 10, 1979, p. 16ff.

p. 190 On Third World distrust of existing organizations, quotes from personal interviews, Washington, D.C., Nov. 1979.

p. 191 James Sterba on the 1979 UNCTAD meetings and the new international economic order, *The New York Times,* May 13, 1978.

p. 191 Ferdinand Marcos, address to UNCTAD meetings, Manila, May 10, 1979.

p. 192 On technical expertise of the World Bank, numerous personal interviews with Third World officials conducted during field research for this book between 1975 and 1979.

p. 192 Quotation from personal interviews by author with Third World officials during field research for this book between 1975 and 1979.

p. 192 Teresa Hayter, *Aid as Imperialism,* London: Penguin Books, 1969.

p. 194 Henry Kissinger as quoted in State Department speech, Nov. 1975.

Chapter 7: Pioneering at Home

p. 197 Daniel Bell, quoted from Washington *Post,* May 20, 1979, p. B1.

p. 197 Marriner S. Eccles, quoted from Joseph S. Davis, *The World Between the Wars, 1919–1939: An Economist's View,* Baltimore: Johns Hopkins University Press, 1975, p. 350.

p. 197 Alvin Hansen, testimony before Temporary National Economic Committee, 76th Cong. VII–IX, pp. 3497–557.

197 On President Carter's lack of a "central philosophy," see James Fallows, "The Passionless Presidency," *Atlantic Monthly,* May 1979.

198 Bernard Nossiter; Nathan Glazer; and Robert Lekachman, quoted from Washington *Post,* May 20, 1979, p. B1.

199 Robert Heilbroner, quoted from his *Worldly Philosophers,* 4th ed., New York: Simon & Schuster, 1972, p. 315.

199 Alfred S. Eichner, testimony before the Joint Economic Committee, Special Committee on Economic Change, May 9, 1979. Copy obtained from committee files.

200 George J. Stigler, quoted from Edwin Mansfield, ed. *Monopoly Power and Economic Performance,* 3rd ed., New York: W. W. Norton & Co., 1974, p. 12.

200 Milton Friedman, quoted from Allen Heslop, ed., *Business-Government Relations,* New York: New York University Press, 1976, p. 12.

200 Arthur Okun, testimony before the Joint Economic Committee, Special Committee on Economic Change, Apr. 30, 1979. Copy obtained from committee files.

201 Post-Keynesian economics is best represented through the *Journal of Post-Keynesian Economics,* Paul Davidson and Sidney Weintraub, eds.; as well as *Challenge,* Myron Sharpe, ed. Neo-Keynesians are cited in reference notes to ch. 1, above. An excellent introduction can be found in Alfred S. Eichner, *A Guide to Post-Keynesian Economics,* White Plains, N.Y.: M. E. Sharpe, 1979.

201 Heilbroner, *op. cit.,* p. 320.

203 Russell W. Peterson, quoted from *The New York Times,* Jan. 17, 1979, p. A23.

204 Albert Waterston, *Development Planning: Lessons of Experience,* Baltimore: Johns Hopkins University Press, 1969.

205 Daniel Yankelovich, cited from *The Wall Street Journal,* Oct. 2, 1978, p. 26.

205 Survey by Opinion Research Corporation taken from the *Harvard Business Review,* Jan–Feb. 1979, pp. 117–25.

206 Jerome Rosow, on the reluctance of corporations to publicize work humanization successes, see *Business Week,* July 24, 1978, p. 146.

206 Glenn Watts (CWA president), *The I.U.D. Quarterly,* "Viewpoint," vol. 8, no. 3, 3rd quarter, 1979, p. 8.

206 Helen Dewar on the 1979 Communications Workers of America demonstration, see Washington *Post,* Apr. 29, 1979.

206 On the Bolivar project and the work of Michael Maccoby, see his *The Gamesmen: The New Corporate Leaders,* New York: Simon & Schuster, 1976, pp. 240–41; more recently, his "The Bolivar Project—Productivity and Human Development," *Behavioral Sciences Quarterly,* June 1978; and with his two leading associates at Bolivar, Margaret

Duckles and Robert Duckles, "The Process of Change at Bolivar," *Journal of Applied Behavioral Sciences,* vol. 13, no. 3, summer 1977.

p. 209 Success of GM Tarrytown plant humanization project, see *International Labor Review,* July 1977, p. 53 *et seq.*

p. 210 Attempts to avoid unionization through work improvement projects, particularly until the mid-1970s, *cf.* I. Berg, M. Freedman and M. Freeman, *Managers and Work Reform: A Limited Engagement,* New York: The Free Press. They cite one study that 80 percent of 150 humanization projects were attempts to deter unionization. For a critical review of Berg *et al.,* see Charles F. Sabel in *Challenge,* July–Aug. 1979, pp. 64–66.

p. 210 William Winpisinger (IAM president), quoted in *The I.U.D. Quarterly,* "Viewpoint," *op. cit.,* pp. 21–24.

p. 211 Irving Bluestone (UAW vice-president), quoted from "Human Dignity Is What It's All About," *The I.U.D. Quarterly, op. cit.*

p. 212 Edwin S. (Ted) Mills, *Harvard Business Review,* Nov. 1978, pp. 43–52.

p. 212 Harry Pollak, *The I.U.D. Quarterly,* "Viewpoint," *op. cit.,* p. 28.

p. 213 Pollak, *op. cit.,* pp. 25–29.

p. 213 Bluestone, *op. cit.*

p. 213 On productivity increases for the Bolivar project see Edward R. Lawlor and Lee Ozley, "Winning Union-Management Cooperation on Quality of Worklife Projects," *Management Review,* Mar. 1979, p. 23. See also Barry A. Macey, "The Bolivar Quality of Working Life Experiment: 1972–77," paper presented to the Academy of Management, Aug. 1977. Maccoby has achieved similar gains by his program in a high-fidelity speaker plant in Scotland; see Mary Weir, "Case Study of Tannoy Products, Ltd.," Final Report to the European Foundation for the Improvement of Living and Working Conditions, Glasgow, Nov. 1978.

p. 214 Opinion Research Corporation, *op. cit.*

p. 214 University of Michigan Survey Research Center, quoted from Graham L. Staines, *Challenge,* May–June 1979, p. 39.

p. 214 *Work in America,* Report of a Special Task Force to the Secretary of H.E.W., Cambridge, Mass.: The M.I.T. Press, Jan. 1973, p. 112.

p. 215 Edwin S. Mills, "There has never been an instance . . . ," *Business Week,* July 24, 1978, p. 146.

p. 216 Business Roundtable study on cost of regulations taken from Washington *Post,* Mar. 15, 1979.

p. 216 Examples of saccharin, benzene, taken from *Newsweek,* Mar. 15, 1979, pp. 79–81.

p. 217 The Delaney Amendment and problems of regulatory flexibility, see the "1979 Economic Report of the President," Jan. 1979, Washington, D.C.: GPO, pp. 85–91.

8 Details on Cummins Industries suggestions for the Clean Air Act amendments, from interviews with the author; see also Robert Kahn, *Footprints on the Planet: A Search for an Environmental Ethic,* New York: Universe Books, 1978, ch. 10.

9 On AMAX examples, see Robert Kahn, *op. cit.,* ch. 6; and Robert Kahn for *Management Review,* The American Management Association, Apr. 1979, pp. 18–19.

0 Statistic of $200 per engine from personal interviews with author. Additional costs to U.S. automakers to meet mandated regulations, see *The New York Times Magazine,* June 10, 1979, p. 106.

2 Alfred C. Neal, on business-government relations, quoted from Neil H. Jacoby, ed., *The Business-Government Relationship,* Pacific Palisades, Cal.: Goodyear Publishing, 1975, p. 104.

3 Statistics on involvement in German economy by the German state, see *Economist,* Dec. 31, 1978, pp. 41–42.

4 Statistics on U.S. shoe industry from U.S. Commerce Department "News," Mar. 1, 1978.

5 On the early pessimism about the possibilities for structural adjustment of the U.S. shoe industry, see Washington *Post,* June 30, 1977, p. D1.

5 For a description of the Commerce Department shoe restructuring plan, see "The Department of Commerce News," G78-26, Mar. 1, 1978.

5 Sidney Harman, from interview with author.

6 On success of Commerce Department shoe restructuring program see "Department of Commerce News," Apr. 26, 1979, ITA 79-79; and "Business America," a Department of Commerce publication, Dec. 4, 1978, pp. 12–13. The success of the participating firms has come amid problems of soaring leather-hide prices in the U.S., in part because of hide exports to Third World shoe producers, who "can absorb the rising costs of hides and still export (back) to the U.S. at prices that undercut (average) domestic producers." *Newsweek,* Aug. 6, 1979 (parentheses ours).

6 Sidney Harman, "I am not saying . . . ," from personal interview with author.

7 MITI and example of business-government cooperation in coal in Japan, taken from Yoski Tsurumi, *The Japanese Are Coming,* Cambridge, Mass.: Ballinger, 1976, pp. 12–13.

7 Joint Economic Committee endorsement of supply economics from "Report of the Joint Economic Committee on the Economic Report of the President, 1979," Washington, D.C.: GPO, 1979, p. 2.

8 Sidney Harman, "We need to coordinate our trade problems . . . ," from interview with author.

8 Michael Blumenthal, quoted in Jacoby, *op. cit.,* pp. 95–96.

9 Keizai Doyukai, quoted by Neal, *op. cit.,* p. 99.

p. 229 Joseph Schumpeter, *Capitalism, Socialism and Democracy,* New York: Harper and Row, 1942.

Chapter 8: Quest for a New Vision: The 1980s

p. 231 Data on voter participation by Americans in national elections from the Commission for the Study of the American Electorate.

p. 232 Meg Greenfield, quoted from *Newsweek,* May 21, 1979, p. 104.

p. 235 Robert Heilbroner, on "cross-over points," from his *Beyond Boom and Crash,* New York: Norton, 1978, ch. 9.

p. 235 Study on "cross-over" of five to twenty years of time left for transition from oil, from Dr. Andrew R. Flower, *Scientific American,* vol. 283, no. 3, Mar. 1978, pp. 42–49.

p. 235 Water cross-over in the American West, *cf.,* U.S. Water Resources Council, *The Nation's Water Resources: Second National Water Assessment,* Washington, D.C., GPO, 1978. One noteworthy conclusion: ". . . without renewed dedication to [water conservation and environmental protection] . . . our technological society will seriously deplete and foul the water to the extent that it threatens the very survival of the United States" (p. 49).

p. 235 Wassily Leontief, and the International Task Force of Scientists, *The Future of the World Economy,* New York: UN, 1977.

p. 235 Walt W. Rostow, *The World Economy: History and Prospect,* Austin: University of Texas Press, 1978.

p. 236 Chancellor Helmut Schmidt, quoted in *Time* magazine, June 11, 1979, pp. 39–40.

p. 237 Amitai Etzioni, and figures on capital expenditure needs for U.S. infrastructure, from "Choose We Must," *The Individual and the Future of Organizations,* vol. 9, Atlanta: Georgia State University, College of Business Administration, Publishing Services Division, 1979.

p. 237 *Ibid.*

p. 239 John Kenneth Galbraith, *The Nature of Mass Poverty,* Cambridge, Mass.: Harvard University Press, 1979.

p. 239 Bernard D. Nossiter, Washington *Post,* May 20, 1979, p. B-1.

p. 239 Arthur Schlesinger, Jr., quoted from *The Wall Street Journal,* June 5, 1979, p. 22.

p. 239 Franklin D. Roosevelt, quoted by Schlesinger, *op. cit.*

p. 239 Arthur Schlesinger, Jr., *ibid.*

p. 240 "Business has a democratic legitimacy . . . ," Marvin Olasky, "Manager's Journal," *The Wall Street Journal,* June 4, 1979.

p. 243 Harvey J. Goldschmidt, hearings before the Senate Committee on Commerce, "Corporate Rights and Responsibilities," Washington, D.C.: GPO, 1976, p. 245.

43 Dean Courtney Brown, "The strength of our form . . . ," quoted by Goldschmidt, *op. cit.*, p. 244.

43 Charles E. Lindblom, *Politics and Markets,* New York: Grossman, 1973.

44 Proposals of William McChesney Martin for public representation on the New York Stock Exchange from his "The Securities Market: A Report and Recommendations," prepared for the board of the New York Stock Exchange, Aug. 5, 1971, p. 7.

44 Ralph Nader and Mark Green, on proposal for federal chartering corporations, *Corporate Power in America,* New York: Grossman, 1973, pt. 2.

44 T. H. Hubbard, quoted from *The New York Times,* June 24, 1979, p. F14.

44 H. M. Williams, on insulated corporate boards, from *The New York Times,* June 24, 1979, p. F14.

44 Hubbard, *op. cit.,* p. F14. For a more sanguine view of the voluntary response by corporations to social accountability, see Neil W. Chamberlain, *The Limits of Corporate Responsibility,* New York: Basic Books, 1974.

45 On the problems of Chrysler and the attempts by the UAW to secure board positions, see *The New York Times,* Jan. 4, 1976, p. A7; May 14, 1976, p. D-1; and May 13, 1976, p. A51.

46 *Business Week,* Aug. 20, 1979, p. 110.

46 *The Wall Street Journal,* Sept. 17, 1979, p. 1.

48 Edward Cornish, "As we survey . . . ," quoted in William Halal, below.

49 William E. Halal, on the need for grass roots mechanisms, award-winning essay presented to the 1977 Alternatives to Growth Conference; to appear in Dennis Meadows and Marian McCollum, eds., *Alternatives to Growth II,* Cambridge, Mass.: Ballinger Publishing Co., 1978.

49 Charles Powers, on the need for a "social audit," from interview with author. See also his *Corporate Social Responsibility and Social Ethics,* New York: Praeger, 1975, ch. 2.

49 Daniel Bell, on the need for a system of social accounts, see *The Coming of Post-Industrial Society: A Venture in Social Forecasting,* New York: Basic Books, 1973, p. 326.

50 Alvin Toffler, on existing decision technology, from "The Strategy of Social Futurism," *The Futurists,* New York: Random House, 1972, p. 124.

50 Resolve, on mediation of environmental disputes, see Washington *Post,* Jan. 13, 1978, p. A7.

50 Margot Hornblower, from Washington *Post,* Jan. 13, 1978, p. A7.

51 Greenfield, *op. cit.*

51 Washington *Post* survey of experts on the Department of Energy, *Washington Post Magazine,* June 20, 1979.

52 President Jimmy Carter, on the Export Council, press release, May 24,

1979. See also, "Notes from the Joint Economic Committee," vol. 4, no. 20, Dec. 2, 1978, pp. 1–9.

Chapter 9: U.S. Energy and Econopolitics

p. 256 OPEC movement to become oil refiner, see the OPEC Annual Report, Vienna, 1978.

p. 256 Congressional Budget Office report on effect of oil price decontrol from *Windfall Profit Tax: A Comparative Analysis of Two Bills,* Washington, D.C.: GPO, November 1979.

p. 256 Lester Lave, Washington *Post,* Aug. 21, 1978.

*p. 258*fn. Judith Miller, on the Reconstruction Finance Corporation, *The New York Times,* July 27, 1979, p. F1.

p. 259 Senator Dale Bumpers, "The American people are ready . . . ," comment confirmed by Thomas Walsch of Senator Bumpers' office, Aug. 25, 1979.

p. 259 Figures on 1985 and 1990 imports of crude oil from "The World Oil Markets in the 1980's," Washington, D.C.: Congressional Budget Office, May 1980.

p. 260 OPEC minister quoted from interview with author, Washington, D.C., Dec. 1979.

p. 261 Milton Friedman quoted in *Newsweek,* Mar. 4, 1974.

p. 261 Theodore H. Moran, *Oil Prices and the Future of OPEC,* Washington, D.C.: Resources for the Future, Research Paper R-8, 1978.

p. 262 Everitt M. Ehrlich, from personal interview with the author, Washington, D.C., July 26, 1979.

p. 263 Morris Adelman and Paul Davidson, "Plans for Oil Import Purchasing," *Challenge,* July/August, 1979, p. 45.

p. 263 Everitt M. Ehrlich, *op. cit.*

p. 264 Canada/Mexico "Oil Swaps," see *The Oil Daily,* Jan. 17, 1979.

p. 264 Figures on Japan and French "Oil Swaps," from *Petroleum Economist,* July 1979, and *The Petroleum Intelligence Weekly,* Dec. 18, 1978.

p. 266 Adam Smith, *The Wealth of Nations,* on "Auctions," see, e.g., bk. 1, ch. 7.

p. 266 Paul Davidson, *op. cit.*

p. 266 Robert Stobaugh and Daniel Yergin, *Energy Future,* TV Report of the Energy Project at the Harvard Business School, New York: Random House, 1979.

p. 266 *Ibid.*

p. 267 L. J. Becker and G. S. Dutt, Washington *Post,* July 24, 1979.

p. 267 *Ibid.*

p. 270 Asian Development Bank official, from interview with author, Bangkok, Thailand, Jan. 1978.

72 Congressional Budget Office study, *Windfall Profit Tax: A Comparison of Two Bills, op. cit.*

73 Carl Solberg, *Oil Power,* New York: Mason and Charter, 1976, p. 249.

73 Anthony Sampson, *The Seven Sisters: The Great Oil Companies and the World They Made,* New York: Viking Press, 1975.

73 John M. Blair, *Control of Oil,* New York: Pantheon Books, 1976.

73 Bradford Snell on the Los Angeles and San Francisco public transportation systems, see report, "American Ground Transportation," to the Senate Sub-committee on Anti-Trust and Monopoly of the Committee on the Judiciary, 93rd Cong., 2nd Sess., 1974.

73 *Ibid.*

73 *Ibid.*

76 William Greider, "It Seems a Rather Crude Way . . . ," Washington *Post,* July 22, 1979, p. D2.

Chapter 10: Road from Inflation: America's Reindustrialization

77 Helmut Schmidt, interview in *Time* magazine, June 11, 1979, pp. 39–40.

80 Senator Jacob Javits, "What puzzles me . . . ," from Notes from the Joint Economic Committee, vol. 5, no. 14, June 26, 1979, p. 1.

80 Walt W. Rostow, "For good or ill . . . ," from his *The World Economy: History and Prospects,* Austin: University of Texas Press, 1978, p. 632.

81 Dr. Albert T. Sommers, from his opening remarks to the Joint Economic Committee Special Study on Economic Change, May 7, 1979.

88 For the "Tinbergen Rule," the most refined statement of its use in an industrial economy is found in Robert A. Mundell, "The Appropriate Use of Monetary and Fiscal Policy for Internal and External Stability," *I.M.F. Staff Papers,* Washington, D.C., 1962. Unfortunately, Mundell's seminal work has now been outdated by the postwar structural transformation of the economy. With the dominance of "dualism" and global interdependence, the policy objective is how to increase investment of small businesses vs. concentrated firms, of national industries vs. those dominated by multinational structures. Industries with acute structural adjustment problems may not respond to policy incentives or anti-inflation tools as may those without such problems. Mundell's "principle of effective market classification," derived from Tinbergen's work and meaning that markets could be simply classified into those of the domestic vs. foreign sector, should now be supplemented by the policy principle of "effective structural classification." See Ronald E. Müller, "National Economic Growth and Stabilization Policy in the Age of Multinational Corporations: The Challenge of Our Post-Market Economy," commissioned and published by the Joint Economic Committee of the U.S. Congress in vol. 12, *Economic Growth in the International*

Context, of the series *U.S. Economic Growth from 1976 to 1986: Prospects, Problems and Patterns,* Washington, D.C.: GPO, May 23, 1977, pp. 35–77.

p. 288 Small businesses responsible for most new job creations, see David L. Birch, "The Job Generation Process," report of the M.I.T. program on Neighborhood and Regional Change, Cambridge, Mass., 1979.

p. 289 "Targeting," taxes to small businesses, see Recommendation No. 7, "The Future of Small Businesses in America," Report of the Subcommittee on Antitrust, Consumers, and Employment of the Committee on Small Business, U.S. House of Representatives, Washington, D.C.: GPO, 1978, p. 40.

p. 290 Commission on Federal Paperwork figures for cost to small businesses, "Commission Draft," dated July 20, 1977, p. 22.

p. 290 John Quarles, "Federal Regulation of New Industrial Plants," *The Environmental Reporter,* monograph no. 28, vol. 10, no. 1, May 4, 1979.

p. 292 Seventy percent of all mergers conglomerate in nature, the *Economist,* Jan. 6, 1979, p. 43.

p. 292 Excessive length of time to try antitrust cases, see *The Wall Street Journal,* May 17, 1979; also, *Economist, op. cit.*

p. 293 "The General Theory of Second Best," by Robert G. Lipsey and K. J. Lancaster, *Review of Economics and Statistics,* vol. 24, 1956, pp. 11–32. The theory, first developed for customs union application, has subsequently been extended by other writers to antitrust and other fields. For its application in this book, we have derived its antitrust policy message from the overall principle of second-best theory: in an economy where multiple market distortions co-exist—oligopoly across different sectors, tariffs, subsidies, etc.—then the correction of one or more of these distortions, but not all, along the lines proposed by neoclassical theory of perfect competition, will not necessarily bring the economy closer to Paretoptimality. Thus for antitrust policy, increasing the number of firms in one industry while allowing other distortions in the economy to remain, will not necessarily bring about greater competitive pricing and higher social efficiency of production. It may or it may not. It depends on the individual case. See Ronald E. Müller, "National Economic Growth and Stabilization Policy in the Age of Multinational Corporations: The Challenge of Our Post-Market Economy," in the Joint Economic Committee of the U.S. Congress, *Economic Growth in the International Context,* vol. 12 of *U.S. Economic Growth from 1976 to 1986: Prospects, Problems and Patterns,* Washington, D.C.: GPO, May 23, 1977, pp. 67–68.

p. 293 "If men were angels . . . ," *The Federalist Papers,* James Madison, no. 51.

p. 294 Robert F. Pitofsky (FTC chairman), from *The Wall Street Journal,* May 17, 1979.

295 *Economist,* Jan. 6, 1979, p. 46.

295 Supreme Court decision referred to in *Economist, op. cit.*

295 General Motors and the destruction of mass transit systems, see Bradford Snell, "American Ground Transportation," report to the Senate Subcommittee on Antitrust and Monopoly of the Committee on the Judiciary, 93rd Cong., 2nd Sess., 1974.

297 The Joint Economic Committee Report, see "Notes from the Joint Economic Committee," vol. 5, no. 12, June 11, 1979, p. 1.

298 Richard F. Janssen, "Postwar consensus of . . . ," *The Wall Street Journal,* June 14, 1979, p. 1.

298 Congressman Jack Kemp, Washington *Post,* June 15, 1979.

300 T.I.P. plans, Arthur Okun and George L. Perry eds., "Innovative Policies to Slow Inflation," Washington, D.C.: Brookings Institution, 1978, vol. 2.

300 On the success of Austria and Germany, see testimony of Wassily Leontief before the Joint Economic Committee, Special Committee on Economic Change, May 19, 1979.

300 Walter Heller, on the need for business-government-labor cooperation, "The Realities of Inflation," *The Wall Street Journal,* Jan. 19, 1979, p. 10.

301 Leontief, *op. cit.*

302 Jack Duvall, on wage and price controls under the Nixon Administration; see Washington *Post,* Apr. 22, 1979, p. C5.

302 Philip Cagan, statement before the Joint Economic Committee . . . , *op. cit.,* May 7, 1979.

303 Alfred Eichner, Joint Economic Committee . . . , *op. cit.,* May 9, 1979.

306 Robert Triffin, "The International Role and Fate of the Dollar," *Foreign Affairs,* winter, 1978–79, p. 285.

306 On the Gray Panthers and the advantages of installment buying, see *Money,* June 1979, pp. 39–40.

INDEX